EVOLVING CONSTITUTIONAL RIGHTS

PERSPECTIVES
ON CRIME AND JUSTICE

Joseph A. Schafer,
Series Editor

EVOLVING CONSTITUTIONAL RIGHTS

The Roberts Court and Criminal Justice

Christopher E. Smith

Michael A. McCall

Madhavi M. McCall

Southern Illinois University Press

Carbondale

Southern Illinois University Press
siupress.com

First printed July 2025.

Publication of this book has been underwritten by the
Elmer H. Johnson and Carol Holmes Johnson
criminology fund.

Jacket and cover illustration: Supreme Court building shot in
black and white (colorized). *Dilloncruz72 at Adobe Stock.*

ISBN 978-0-8093-3974-7 (cloth)
ISBN 978-0-8093-3973-0 (paperback)
ISBN 978-0-8093-3975-4 (ebook)

Printed on recycled paper ♻

SIU
Southern Illinois University System

For my wife, Charlotte
—CES

For my mother, Shirley, and siblings, Sherry,
Mark, and Ronda, and their families
—MAM

For my parents, Hasmukh and Nalini, and
brother, Manish, and his family
—MMM

CONTENTS

TABLES

EVOLVING CONSTITUTIONAL RIGHTS

INTRODUCTION

The US Supreme Court plays a central role in shaping law and public policy in the United States. Through interpretations of statutes and the Constitution, the court's nine justices define protected legal rights for individuals. Their decisions also determine limits on the authority of governmental decision-makers and institutions. The Supreme Court's interpretations can change over time through the appointment of new justices who bring differing perspectives into the court's decision-making processes. Interpretations of statutes and the Constitution also develop and change as new issues arise in society. In the twenty-first century, the Supreme Court entered an era of significant controversy and change. There was a decade of extraordinary stability from 1994 through mid-2005 in which the same nine justices served together on the court. Over the subsequent two decades, eight of those nine justices departed through retirement or death. The replacement justices, whose appointments moved the court's composition in a conservative direction, have faced issues reflecting changes in society as the American polity has become increasingly polarized.

By the third decade of the twenty-first century, the Supreme Court placed itself in the center of controversies affecting a wide array of policy issues. Not only did the court hand down decisions that dramatically changed existing law concerning such matters as voting rights, affirmative action, and abortion,[1] but individual justices generated questions about their ethics and impartiality by accepting valuable gifts and refusing to recuse themselves in cases that posed apparent conflicts of interest.[2] These controversies occurred with Chief Justice John Roberts, a 2005 appointee of President George W. Bush, at the court's helm. Thus, snapshot generalizations of the court invariably invoked Roberts's name. For example, US Senator Sheldon Whitehouse (D-RI) described the court as taking a partisan political turn away from its proper role as a legal institution in his article "A Right-Wing Rout: The Roberts Court's Partisan Opinions."[3] A

1

prominent legal scholar declared, "The Roberts Court is not just ideologically conservative, but often seems to be partisanly so."⁴ Although frequently presented by both journalists and scholars, these generalizations tend to focus on specific controversies rather than on systematic examinations of the court's actions. Thus, questions remain about whether such general-izations are accurate and valid for a comprehensive understanding of the role and impact of the Roberts Court.

Since the middle of the twentieth century, criminal justice issues have consumed a notable portion of the justices' time and attention, often constituting more than one-third of the Supreme Court's cases each year. In the twenty-first century, these cases raised issues reflecting new tech-nological developments, such as the extent of police officers' authority to search the contents of individuals' personal cell phones. The court's cases also drew the justices into revisiting long-standing controversies decided in prior cases, such as the contexts in which police officers can search vehicles without a warrant and the permissibility of imposing lifetime imprisonment on juveniles convicted of serious offenses. The justices of the Roberts Court era addressed issues that profoundly affect the con-stitutional rights and ultimate fates of people drawn into contact with criminal justice officials. The justices are certain to continue to do so in the future, especially after the conservative turn in the court's composition led to greater assertiveness in reconsidering precedents established in prior Supreme Court eras. Are the previously cited snapshot generalizations applicable to the Roberts Court's decisions and impacts on criminal justice? This book seeks to provide a nuanced and complete examination of that question through systematic examination of the high court's decisions in this policy area.

Traditional legal analyses of the Supreme Court's decisions focus on the interpretive approaches and legal reasoning expressed in the justices' written opinions. Such analyses typically seek to identify weaknesses and inconsistencies in the reasoning presented in judicial decisions. In the chapters that follow, the examination of the court's criminal justice–related decisions employs the tools of traditional legal analyses. Yet, legal analysis can miss patterns and inconsistencies in justices' decisions. Thus, the book's evaluation of these decisions also utilizes a social science perspective by providing empirical measures to track and compare the votes of individual justices during the Roberts Court era. In addition, the policy implications and human consequences of the court's decisions are discussed.

The Roberts Court Era: Historical Context

For most of American history, the rights described in the Bill of Rights applied only against the federal government. The familiar list of rights in the first eight amendments to the US Constitution, such as the First Amendment protection of free speech and the Fourth Amendment prohibition on unreasonable searches and seizures, provided limitations on laws enacted by Congress and actions by federal government officials, such as US marshals. The Bill of Rights did not initially provide protections for individuals against the actions of state and local governments. This principle was established by the Supreme Court's decision in *Barron v. Baltimore* (1833). When the Fourteenth Amendment was ratified in 1868, the Constitution suddenly had its first provision saying "no State shall" deny certain rights to individuals. The rights described in the Fourteenth Amendment, such as the rights to "due process of law" and "equal protection of the laws," required interpretation by judges to gain specific meaning. It took many decades for those phrases to be interpreted by the Supreme Court as providing specific protections for suspects and defendants in state criminal justice cases.

The Warren Court era (1953–69), under the leadership of Chief Justice Earl Warren, provided the most significant changes in the definition and expansion of constitutionally protected rights in the criminal justice system. The Warren Court used the Due Process Clause of the Fourteenth Amendment to apply rights from the Bill of Rights to state and local criminal cases. In the 1920s and 1930s, the Supreme Court had applied to the states various rights from the First Amendment, but the Warren Court of the 1960s was largely responsible for expanding the protective reach of criminal justice rights from the Fourth, Fifth, Sixth, and Eighth Amendments. For example, the Warren Court required states to respect the Eighth Amendment's Cruel and Unusual Punishments Clause (*Robinson v. California*, 1962) and imposed the requirement of Miranda warnings to protect the Fifth Amendment privilege against compelled self-incrimination during custodial questioning by police (*Miranda v. Arizona*, 1966). These warnings obligate police to tell suspects in custody that they have a right to remain silent and a right to have an attorney present during questioning. The Warren Court also expanded the protections for the right to counsel (*Gideon v. Wainwright*, 1963), the right to trial by jury (*Duncan v. Louisiana*, 1968), and other criminal justice rights.[5] Thus, the Warren Court era profoundly affected criminal justice by expanding the definitions of constitutional rights for suspects and defendants while also simultaneously limiting the discretionary authority of police and prosecutors.

When Chief Justice Warren retired in 1969, President Richard Nixon appointed Warren Burger to be the new chief justice of the United States. Nixon had campaigned on a "law and order" platform in the 1968 presidential election by using accusations that the Warren Court's rights-protective decisions had harmed police officers' efforts to stop crime. Nixon vowed to nominate new justices to the Supreme Court who would be less protective of constitutional rights in criminal justice, and Chief Justice Burger's selection was Nixon's first action in fulfillment of that campaign promise. The appointment of Burger initiated a period of more than twenty years in which the timing of justices' deaths and retirements meant that only Republican presidents enjoyed the opportunity to fill vacancies on the Supreme Court.

Over the course of his first term in office, Nixon gained the opportunity to appoint three additional justices who were less rights-protective in criminal justice than their predecessors. These new associate justices, Lewis Powell, William Rehnquist, and Harry Blackmun, when combined with the earlier Senate confirmation of Chief Justice Burger, changed nearly half of the court's composition by 1972.[6] President Gerald Ford's selection of Justice John Paul Stevens in 1975 installed a new proponent of rights to replace another rights advocate, Justice William O. Douglas. Subsequent appointments by President Ronald Reagan added new justices with restrictive views of rights in 1981 (Justice Sandra Day O'Connor), 1986 (Justice Antonin Scalia), and 1988 (Justice Anthony Kennedy).

The Burger Court era (1969–86), which ended with the Senate confirmation of Justice Scalia and the simultaneous elevation of Associate Justice Rehnquist to chief justice, generally limited the expansion of rights in criminal justice. For example, the Burger Court's decisions diminished the effect of the exclusionary rule that the Warren Court had applied nationwide to all law enforcement officers in *Mapp v. Ohio* (1961). The exclusionary rule generally requires that any evidence acquired from an improper search or improper questioning of a suspect must be excluded from use by the prosecution against the defendant whose rights were violated. The Burger Court created exceptions to the exclusionary rule, including the inevitable discovery rule (*Nix v. Williams*, 1984) and the public safety exception to Miranda warnings (*New York v. Quarles*,

1984), permitting the use of evidence that the Warren Court would have excluded as improperly acquired. These rulings gave police officers greater freedom to violate previously recognized legal protections. Similar decisions favoring law enforcement authority continued in the Rehnquist Court era (1986–2005), when a majority of justices continued to be appointees of Republican presidents.

Except for Justice John Paul Stevens, who was appointed in 1975 during the brief accidental presidency of Gerald Ford, the nine justices placed on the Supreme Court by Republican presidents from 1969 to 1991 were selected with the specific intention to choose judicial decision-makers who would be less rights-protective than their Warren Court predecessors. As a result, many of the decisions during the Burger Court and Rehnquist Court eras were arguably conservative reactions against liberal Warren Court era precedents.

In his autobiography, Justice Stevens described conservative justices' agenda aimed at reversing many rights-expanding Warren era precedents. As recounted by Stevens concerning the later years of the Burger Court era, "A majority of the Court had formed the view that its mission was to roll back the Warren Court's procedural protections for criminal defendants." Justice Stevens also referred to criminal justice "decisions retreating from Warren Court precedents" and "the injudiciousness of the [Burger] Court's forced march against the exclusionary rule."[7]

In analyzing the Warren Court and its successor eras, scholars look closely at continuity and change. Continuity and change in Supreme Court decisions shape society's rules and the governmental policies that impact people's lives. In the realm of criminal justice, the court's decisions shape people's interactions with police officers as well as individuals' fates when drawn into the justice system. The Warren Court's expansion of constitutional rights in criminal justice and its skepticism about excessive discretionary authority for criminal justice officials created a baseline for comparison with decisions and impacts produced by later court eras. A much-discussed book in the 1980s was *The Burger Court: The Counter-Revolution That Wasn't.*[8] The book's title alone conveys the idea that the immediate successors to the Warren Court era merely altered but did not eliminate the rights-protective impacts from decisions in the 1950s and 1960s.

Assessments of the Rehnquist Court era's impact are quite similar. One examination of that era's criminal justice decisions concluded that the "Rehnquist Court did not engage in a wholesale dismantling of rights in the criminal justice process, despite the expressed desire of some of its members to move in that direction."[9] An important challenge posed for scholars by broad generalizations about the conservatism of succeeding eras is to move beyond the expectation of wholesale changes in Warren Court–established doctrines. Instead, analysts must also think carefully about the cumulative impacts of modest doctrinal changes during later eras.

Many new developments in legal doctrine emerge through incremental changes rather than abrupt reversals of established precedents. Even seemingly modest changes can have important impacts for the experiences and fates of people in the justice system. Examples of such changes include the expanded use of improperly obtained evidence through Burger Court decisions creating exceptions to the exclusionary rule (for example, *Nix v. Williams*, 1984) and the Rehnquist Court's grant of flexibility to police officers concerning the words used to convey Miranda rights to suspects being questioned (for example, *Duckworth v. Eagan*, 1989). In considering developments during the Roberts Court era, it is important to note impactful incremental changes as well as the global question of whether this twenty-first-century court era can be characterized as one that substantially diluted or dismantled the rights-protective doctrines developed by the Warren Court.

Debates About Constitutional Interpretation

Disagreements between Supreme Court justices do not merely reflect differing views about the definitions of specific constitutional rights. Within the court, there are also debates about approaches to constitutional interpretation. Specific approaches utilized by justices in their analyses of issues and legal reasoning have major implications for the ultimate definitions of constitutional rights and governmental authority. In the Roberts Court era, these debates became especially visible and important. The second decade of the Roberts Court era saw increased representation and power for the advocates of interpreting the Constitution according to the original intentions of those who wrote and ratified its provisions. Initially, Justice Scalia was the lone supporter of originalism when he was appointed in 1986. He had been the leading advocate of this approach in academia when he was law school professor at the University of Chicago,[10] and his arguments were supported by officials in the Reagan administration in the 1980s.[11] However, this approach initially did not have other advocates or adherents among justices on the Supreme Court.

On the Rehnquist Court and continuing into the era of the Roberts Court, Scalia was joined in his advocacy of originalist interpretation by Justice Clarence Thomas, who was appointed to the court in 1991.[12] Moreover, Thomas's strident assertion of the originalist interpretive approach appeared to fortify Scalia's resolve to promote and utilize this approach.[13] Other justices, both liberal and conservative, referenced original intent in specific cases as one of the tools employed to justify their reasoning. But they did so without claiming that this was the lone proper way to engage in constitutional interpretation.

Scalia and Thomas scored a major victory for the originalist approach three years into the Roberts Court era by attracting the supporting votes of Chief Justice Roberts and Justices Kennedy and Samuel Alito to form a five-member majority that drastically changed the meaning of the Second Amendment in *District of Columbia v. Heller* (2008). The ruling established a right for individuals to own and keep handguns in their homes for self-defense. Previously, the Second Amendment's provision about a "right to keep and bear arms" was widely understood to support the opening words of the amendment, namely as a protection for states' authority to arm their "well-regulated militias." Scalia's majority opinion purported to find that historical evidence supported a complete reinterpretation of the Second Amendment's meaning.

In the year prior to the *Heller* case, Justice Scalia wrote a foreword to a book analyzing constitutional interpretation by his preferred means of focusing on "what the text was thought to mean when the people adopted it." He celebrated the fact that in debates about constitutional interpretation, "originalism is in the game, even if it does not always prevail." He noted that, unlike in his first years on the court, by the early years of the Roberts Court era there were cases in which "even when what I would consider the correct originalist position has not carried the day, the debate between majority and dissenting opinions has been carried on in originalist terms."[14] When he wrote those words, little did he know that he was only months away from the opportunity for his greatest originalist triumph by gathering majority support for his use of history-based arguments to justify his conclusions about the Second Amendment.

Originalists claim that the definitions of rights for the federal system became fixed in 1791 when the Bill of Rights was ratified. They similarly claim that definitions of federal constitutional rights applicable in state systems became firmly established with the ratification of the Fourteenth

Amendment in 1868. Therefore, adherence to this approach would require reversal of Warren Court decisions that expanded the definitions of constitutional rights in criminal justice during the 1960s. In the second decade of the Roberts Court era, originalist viewpoints gained strength and influence through President Donald Trump's appointment of two avowed originalists, Justices Neil Gorsuch and Amy Coney Barrett. In addition, Chief Justice Roberts and Justices Alito and Brett Kavanaugh were sympathetic to originalist analysis but did not declare that they were committed to using it as their sole approach to constitutional interpretation. Thus, their votes were potentially available to provide support for majority opinions based on originalism.

The originalist justices claim that their approach to constitutional interpretation prevents judges from asserting their own values and policy preferences into judicial decisions. This claim rests, however, on several flawed assumptions.[15] It assumes that constitutional provisions have a single definite meaning that was intended and understood by those who wrote and ratified the Constitution, the Bill of Rights, and subsequent amendments. Actually, these provisions were written by multimember legislative bodies whose members did not necessarily agree on a single specific meaning. The originalist approach also assumes that contemporary judges can use history to identify these precise meanings from the limited evidence of debates and declarations that occurred more than a century ago. There is also an assumption that these precise meanings can be accurately applied to modern contexts and technologies that were unimaginable by people in the eighteenth and nineteenth centuries. In specific Supreme Court opinions, however, originalist justices demonstrate the weakness of their approach by disagreeing with each other in their interpretations of history.[16] Moreover, there is simply no way to know what James Madison and his contemporaries would have thought about surveillance technology, semi-automatic weapons, and other modern devices that pose challenges to the definition of rights and governmental authority in contemporary times.

In a famous speech at Georgetown University, Justice William Brennan, who retired during the Rehnquist Court era, criticized the originalist approach as "a view that feigns self-effacing deference to the specific judgments of those who forged our original social compact. But it is little more than arrogance cloaked in humility." He noted the impossibility of knowing either the original intentions of multimember legislative bodies or how officials from centuries past would apply their ideas to contemporary problems. He also pointed out that originalism "establishes a presumption of resolving textual ambiguities against the claim of constitutional right," which he called a political choice reflecting antipathy to rights claims by political minorities. In sum, he called originalists "those who would restrict claims of right to the values of 1789 . . . [and] turn a blind eye to social progress and eschew adaptation of overarching principles to changes of social circumstance."[17]

Brennan advocated a flexible approach to constitutional interpretation that begins with the question, "What do the words of the text mean in our time?" In the view of Brennan and other justices, such as John Paul Stevens, Stephen Breyer, and Thurgood Marshall, "the genius of the Constitution rests not on any static meaning it might have had in a world that is dead and gone, but in the adaptability of its great principles to cope with current problems and current needs."[18] The justices who use flexible approaches in seeking to answer the question posed by Brennan will undoubtedly be influenced by their own values and policy preferences. Yet, the observation applies to the originalists. The originalists' use of history consistently demonstrates that they select, characterize, and manufacture historical evidence in ways that advance their own values and policy preferences.[19]

In most Supreme Court opinions in recent decades, both liberal and conservative justices have used Brennan's approach of seeking to determine what constitutional provisions should mean for contemporary issues and contexts. They have also considered the potential consequences of specific decisions to address modern problems. However, the expanded representation and influence of originalists on the Roberts Court increased the visibility of debates about the proper approach to constitutional interpretation. More importantly, the use of originalism began to shape the definitions of constitutional rights and raise the prospect of potential future changes in the legal protections for suspects and defendants in American criminal justice.

Overview of Topics

This book's chapters are organized into standard topics, such as search and seizure issues under the Fourth Amendment and trial rights under the Sixth Amendment. However, there is also a broader conception of "criminal justice–related cases" than that employed in most books examining Supreme Court decisions. One chapter examines the importance for criminal justice of Roberts Court decisions that restricted legislative authority to criminalize conduct related to First Amendment freedom of expression and Second Amendment gun rights. Judicial interpretations of these amendments are often treated as separate freestanding topics. Yet, the court's decisions on these topics have important connections to and impacts on criminal justice.

The book's analysis begins by presenting the development of the Roberts Court through the appointment of new justices in the twenty-first century. Chapter 2 describes the timing of each appointment and the impact of new justices based on their political backgrounds, priorities, and approaches to constitutional interpretation. A clearer picture of each justice, their patterns of decision-making, and their alignments with each other emerges through the systematic examination of empirical evidence presented in chapter 3. The use of data on decision-making helps to reveal which justices were especially influential in criminal justice cases through both their decisive votes when the court was divided and their opportunities to write opinions explaining the court's reasoning.

Subsequent chapters move through relevant amendments in the Bill of Rights in numerical order. Chapter 4 focuses on the First and Second Amendments with attention to the Roberts Court's decisions limiting legislative authority to criminalize certain communications and expressive actions. The First Amendment analysis reviews cases concerning prosecutions involving forms of expression, such as website access for people previously convicted of sex offenses and social media posts perceived as threatening. Of particular importance were decisions limiting legislative authority to regulate and criminalize election campaign contributions and spending by corporations and wealthy individuals. The Second Amendment material analyzes the court's major shift by defining an individual right to own firearms instead of treating the amendment as protecting states' ability to arm their "well regulated Militia."

Fourth Amendment search and seizure issues and the evolution of the exclusionary rule receive attention in chapter 5. The Supreme Court receives many different cases that raise both familiar and emerging issues on these subjects. Roberts Court decisions on Miranda warnings, police questioning of suspects, and the right to representation by a defense attorney are discussed in coverage of the Fifth and Sixth Amendments in chapter 6. Additional trial rights issues, including the Fifth Amendment protection against double jeopardy and the Sixth Amendment right to trial by jury, are examined in chapter 7. In chapter 8, the analysis turns to sentencing and corrections with attention to issues arising from rights in the Sixth and Eighth Amendments. The concluding chapter, "Incremental Conservatism or Accelerated Change?," highlights the Roberts Court's most impactful decisions affecting criminal justice as well as the prospects for future changes in law based on the court's composition and approach to decision-making.

1. THE ROBERTS COURT

On July 1, 2005, Sandra Day O'Connor, the first woman to serve on the US Supreme Court, announced her retirement from the nation's highest court after twenty-four years of influential service as an associate justice. The announcement caught many observers by surprise because Chief Justice William Rehnquist was known to be ill with thyroid cancer and was predicted to be the next person to retire from the court. Although O'Connor did not give a reason for her retirement, observers presumed that she felt the need to direct her time to caring for her husband, who suffered from Alzheimer's disease.[1] Less than three weeks later, President George W. Bush announced that he was nominating accomplished attorney and federal appellate court judge John G. Roberts to replace O'Connor as one of the eight associate justices on the nine-member court.

Had events moved forward as they appeared to be going in mid-2005, there would have been no "Roberts Court" era. Supreme Court eras are named after the chief justices who led the court during a specific period, and Roberts was slated to replace O'Connor as an associate justice. However, Chief Justice Rehnquist passed away in the first week of September 2005, and President Bush immediately reacted by nominating Roberts to be chief justice of the United States. Justice O'Connor announced that she would remain on the court until her new replacement could be nominated by President Bush and confirmed by the US Senate.[2]

The Roberts Court era began on September 29, 2005, when Roberts was confirmed by the Senate and took his oath of office.[3] As a practical matter, there is no reason to regard the first months of the Roberts Court era as any different from the final decade of the Rehnquist Court era. The eight associate justices were the same people who had served together as a group since the confirmation of President Bill Clinton's appointee Justice Stephen Breyer in 1994. In addition, Roberts was not expected to differ dramatically from Rehnquist in his approach to judicial decision-making.

Roberts had served as a law clerk to Rehnquist and then spent his career in Republican administrations and private practice prior to appointment to the US Court of Appeals for the District of Columbia Circuit in 2003. Like Rehnquist, he had developed a reputation as a conservative jurist.[4]

A more significant change occurred when appellate court judge Samuel Alito was confirmed to replace Justice O'Connor on January 31, 2006.[5] Justice Alito proved to be more conservative than O'Connor. Thus, the Roberts Court's identity and decision-making patterns began to take shape within months of the era's initiation when a distinctively conservative justice joined the divided court and began to cast votes in a manner that differed from his predecessor's votes.[6]

Throughout this book, the terms "liberal" and "conservative" with respect to Supreme Court justices and their decisions will be used in a manner consistent with usage in judicial studies. In criminal justice cases, liberal decisions are those that support claims by individuals, including criminal suspects, defendants, and those serving sentences after conviction. By contrast, conservative decisions endorse the authority and actions of police, prosecutors, judges, and corrections officials.[7] Obviously, these definitions do not apply neatly for all issues, such as the issue of gun owners' Second Amendment rights, for which political conservatives often support individuals' rights and political liberals seek to expand the government's regulatory authority.

The chapters of this book examine the Supreme Court's criminal justice decisions from the appointment of Chief Justice Roberts in 2005 through the retirement in 2022 of Justice Breyer, the last Democratic appointee from the Rehnquist Court era. At the time of Breyer's retirement, Republican appointee Justice Clarence Thomas was the last remaining justice from the Rehnquist era. The Roberts Court's decisions over this period illuminated societal developments affecting criminal justice in the first decades of the twenty-first century as well as the ways in which the institutional dynamics of the Supreme Court reflect the country's political divisions. The Roberts Court era coincided with important developments affecting criminal justice. For example, aggressive stop-and-frisk practices by police in many communities led to disproportionate searches and uses of force against people of color. These practices heightened awareness of racial profiling by police, raised questions about the legal justification for such practices, exacerbated tensions between the police and communities of color in many cities, and produced lawsuits over rights violations.[8]

The trends in severe sentencing practices from the 1990s pushed mass incarceration to its peak during the Roberts Court years, affecting more than two million people held each day in American prisons and jails and nearly five million more under correctional supervision on probation and parole.[9] The foregoing developments occurred amid heightened concerns about homeland security in the post-9/11 era. In addition, the Roberts Court era coincided with new technological developments that gave justice system officials quick access to computerized records, including those with erroneous information, as well as increased abilities to test evidence using scientific methods. At the same time, the proliferation of camera-equipped smartphones in the hands of the public served to publicize incidents of legally questionable police practices. In the worst incidents, officers were filmed using lethal violence without compelling justifications, triggering public protests and contributing to several fatal attacks on police officers.[10] Indeed, the protests across the United States in 2020 after the bystander-filmed video of George Floyd dying from a Minneapolis police officer kneeling on his neck led to a push for police reform and an increased awareness of abusive policing.[11]

Controversies also regularly emerged about governmental surveillance authority with respect to Americans' electronic communications as well as the targeting of specific ethnic and religious groups for suspicion and scrutiny. Thus, along with perennial debates about police authority to conduct searches and the legality of capital punishment, controversies about racial discrimination, police violence, and aggressive policing swirled around discussions of criminal justice. Some of these issues were directly addressed by the Roberts Court. Others emerged in the opinions of individual justices who feared that their colleagues did not adequately understand the contexts and consequences of Supreme Court decisions affecting criminal justice.

The Roberts Court also coincided with a period of stark political divisions within the country. The presidency of Barack Obama (2009–17) was characterized by partisan polarization as Republican members of Congress sought to prevent the Obama administration from gaining credit for success in the pursuit of policy goals. Indeed, the Supreme Court was affected by an extraordinary act of naked partisanship when Republican senators kept open a Supreme Court vacancy for fifteen months after the death of Justice Antonin Scalia in February 2016. They refused to consider the respected appellate judge Merrick Garland, who was nominated by

President Obama, because they hoped a Republican could win the White House in 2016 and appoint a staunch conservative to fill the Supreme Court vacancy instead. Ultimately, Donald Trump won the presidency and appointed Judge Neil Gorsuch to replace Scalia in 2017.[12] President Trump subsequently appointed two more justices, Brett Kavanaugh in 2018 and Amy Coney Barrett in 2020, and thereby succeeded in altering the composition and dynamics of the high court by completing the formation of a six-member supermajority of conservatives.[13]

At specific moments in history, the Supreme Court received praise as an important unifying force and source of stability for a divided country. For example, in *United States v. Nixon* (1974), the unanimous Supreme Court required President Richard Nixon to provide special prosecutors with tapes of Oval Office conversations relevant to an investigation of the president's involvement in the criminal cover-up of a burglary at Democratic Party headquarters. The court's decision ultimately led Nixon to resign rather than face the prospect of a bipartisan impeachment effort against him. The Burger Court's justices, including both Republican and Democratic appointees, avoided replicating the country's partisan divide and, instead, advanced shared notions of constitutional principles.

By contrast, the Roberts Court often reflected rather than overcame societal divisions. In an era of increasing partisan polarization, the Roberts Court faced several "hot button" issues, such as abortion and affirmative action, that divided Republicans and Democrats. Far from being a unifying institutional force for the nation, the Roberts Court's internal divisions highlighted many of the nation's deep disagreements about values and policy preferences. In many controversial cases, Justice Anthony Kennedy, as the most moderate of the conservative justices, was positioned to have a major impact by casting a decisive vote as he sat in the ideological center of a deeply divided court.

The Roberts Court issued numerous unanimous decisions, but such decisions did not typically occur in significant cases about the issues that divided American society. Instead, reflecting their political era, the Roberts Court's justices spanned a relatively wide spectrum, from consistent adherence to a deeply conservative ideology by Justices Thomas and Alito to outspoken advocacy of liberal judicial outcomes by Justices Ruth Bader Ginsburg, Sonia Sotomayor, and John Paul Stevens. The polarization within the Roberts Court was especially notable for such issues as racial discrimination,[14] abortion,[15] health care reform,[16] accommodation of religious beliefs,[17] and environmental regulation.[18] As this book's chapters will discuss, this polarization was also evident for a variety of criminal justice issues.

Chief Justice–Defined Supreme Court Eras

The study of the US Supreme Court's history is typically divided into segments defined by and named after the chief justice who served during specific years. This mechanism for dividing Supreme Court history is used by scholars as a matter of convenience. These dividing points between eras vary in their substantive importance.[19] Chief justices possess certain powers that potentially enable them to assert influence over decision-making, albeit without necessarily determining the outcomes of cases.[20] Chief justices create the tentative lists of cases to be considered for full hearing by the court and simultaneously communicate the initial recommendations about which cases should be turned aside without any presentation of arguments by attorneys. As the administrative leader of the court, the chief justice guides the flow of oral arguments and attempts to keep individual justices from dominating the questioning of attorneys when other justices wish to speak. Chief justices also present their viewpoints first when the justices meet in conference to discuss cases. Eventually, the chief justice determines which justice writes the opinion for the court whenever the chief justice is a member of the majority in a case. Despite inevitable differences in the ways that successive chief justices exercise these limited powers, the departure of one chief justice and the appointment of a new one may have little impact on creating a "new era" in any meaningful way. Continuity between eras is likely when the new chief justice decides cases and influences decision-making in a manner similar to that of the preceding chief justice. In fact, differences may be discernible within rather than between chief justice–named eras. These differences occur when there are significant changes in the Supreme Court's decisions within the tenure of a single chief justice through the appointment of new associate justices, consideration of new issues, or changes in the way specific justices make decisions.[21] In sum, the arrival of a new chief justice to lead the justices' discussions and assign the authorship of majority opinions does not automatically mean that the justices' interactions and decision-making will change significantly.

A useful way to think about changes in the Supreme Court's composition and attendant impacts on decision-making is to consider the concept of a "natural court." In the scholarly literature, a "natural court" for the Supreme Court is a period in which the same set of justices interact and decide cases together.[22] Supreme Court justices' retirements and deaths occur periodically but, obviously, not on any predictable schedule. Given that the justices, in the words of Article III of the US Constitution, serve "during good Behaviour" rather than for a specific term in office, they decide for themselves when to retire. They cannot be easily pressured to step down, even when they are well beyond the age at which most Americans retire from their jobs. Thus, a "natural court" era can be very short, such as the one-year period between the appointment of Justice Sotomayor in 2009 and the appointment of Justice Elena Kagan in 2010. By contrast, the final eleven years of the Rehnquist Court era constituted an especially long natural court period between the appointment of Justice Stephen Breyer in 1994 and the death of Chief Justice Rehnquist in 2005.

The first natural court period of the Roberts Court era was extraordinarily short, from the confirmation of Chief Justice Roberts in September 2005 until the confirmation of Justice Alito in January 2006. In fact, in less than seventeen calendar years, the Roberts Court comprised eight separate natural court periods. As indicated by table 1, only three justices—Chief Justice Roberts and Justices Thomas and Breyer—were on the court together for the entire initial seventeen years of the era.

When one discusses these years of the Roberts Court era, there must be awareness that this era includes interactions, decisions, and results that involved a total of fifteen different justices from September 2005 to June 2022. This period included an unusual fourteen-month span with only eight justices after the death of Justice Scalia and prior to the beginning of the sixth natural court period with the confirmation of Justice Gorsuch. Obviously, the depiction of change in table 1 raises an important question: How useful is it to speak of "the Roberts Court" as an entity? In fact, it is merely a traditional label that marks the outer boundaries of a number of meaningful entities known as natural court periods. In addition to the eight natural court periods preceding the retirement of Justice Breyer in 2022, there may be more retirements and replacements in future years beyond the ninth natural court that began with the appointment of Justice Ketanji Brown Jackson to replace Breyer in 2022. The number of natural courts within the Roberts Court era will depend on how many new justices are appointed while John Roberts continues to serve as chief justice. Despite the potential complications that changing natural courts' compositions

Table 1. Membership During the First Eight Natural Court Periods of the Roberts Court Era, 2005–2022

September 2005–January 2006	*Roberts*	Stevens	O'Connor	Scalia	Kennedy	Souter	Thomas	Ginsburg	Breyer
January 2006–August 2009	Roberts	Stevens	*Alito*	Scalia	Kennedy	Souter	Thomas	Ginsburg	Breyer
August 2009–August 2010	Roberts	Stevens	Alito	Scalia	Kennedy	*Sotomayor*	Thomas	Ginsburg	Breyer
August 2010–February 2016	Roberts	*Kagan*	Alito	Scalia	Kennedy	Sotomayor	Thomas	Ginsburg	Breyer
February 2016–April 2017	Roberts	Kagan	Alito	*[vacant]*	Kennedy	Sotomayor	Thomas	Ginsburg	Breyer
April 2017–October 2018	Roberts	Kagan	Alito	*Gorsuch*	Kennedy	Sotomayor	Thomas	Ginsburg	Breyer
October 2018–October 2020	Roberts	Kagan	Alito	Gorsuch	*Kavanaugh*	Sotomayor	Thomas	Ginsburg	Breyer
October 2020–June 2022	Roberts	Kagan	Alito	Gorsuch	Kavanaugh	Sotomayor	Thomas	*Barrett*	Breyer

Note: A change is indicated by italics.

pose for characterizations of the Roberts Court, there are good reasons to continue the tradition of analyzing the Supreme Court according to chief justice–defined eras.

At the simplest level, past analyses of Supreme Court history have used chief justice–defined eras.[23] Thus, analyzing the Roberts Court era as a defined period is consistent with and comparable to past scholarly efforts. Moreover, each era is shaped by the influence of the chief justice whose tenure defined the era's span. As Justice Stevens discussed in his book about the five chief justices whom he knew personally, each one brings a different style of leadership that can affect the court's organization, the justices' interactions, and the assignment of majority opinions.[24] Since the early 1950s, each chief justice's era has spanned approximately two decades, a time period that for other purposes might be more commonly called a "generation." In effect, the issues presented to the court during each of these eras has reflected the social contexts, world events, political developments, and technological innovations of a particular generation or two-decades-long period in history. As a result, there is utility in considering the court's institutional operations and policy impact in a period of American history that is comparable to other generation-long periods affected by different events and issues. Moreover, natural court periods are often simply too short to be useful for analyses and comparisons with other similarly defined time periods. Not only can natural court periods last for a year or less, but these short time periods often do not give a true picture of a particular justice's decision-making, as newcomers take time to find their footing in the organizational context of the court. Experienced justices may only gradually show signs of changing their approaches to decision-making, so these changes may not be evident within a single natural court period. Therefore, decades-long chief justice–defined eras can be especially useful for documenting development and change in individual justices' decision-making and voting alignments.

Supreme Court Eras and Criminal Justice

Many of the Supreme Court's constitutional cases concerning criminal justice since 1969 involved reactions to the breadth of rights protections established by the liberal Warren Court majority. Actions by state and local law enforcement officials tested the boundaries of the Warren Court's rulings concerning searches, Miranda warnings, and other matters. In response, the increasingly conservative majorities serving on the Burger

Court, the Rehnquist Court, and the Roberts Court issued decisions that incrementally diminished the legal protections mandated by the Warren era precedents.

Arguably, the shift in orientation from the Warren Court era to the Burger and Rehnquist Court eras can be encapsulated in the distinguishable initial questions they posed as a threshold consideration in constitutional rights cases. The Warren Court majority seemed to ask, "Were any rights violated by the police or prosecutors?" If the answer was "yes," then the Warren Court acted to remedy the rights violation. By contrast, the majority of justices in the Burger and Rehnquist Court eras seemed to begin by asking, "Did the police do anything wrong?" This is a very different question because it indicated that most justices in these later court eras would tolerate certain rights violations that were committed by police through ignorance, negligence, or reliance upon the mistakes of other officials. Thus, despite the existence of rights violations, these justices would permit police to use the evidence acquired in these situations. For example, when a judge made a mistake by issuing a search warrant without proper evidence to establish probable cause, the police could use the evidence obtained from the resulting search anyway, despite it being discovered through the use of a defective, rights-violating warrant (*United States v. Leon*, 1984). Thus, the Burger Court created the "good faith" exception to the exclusionary rule that tolerated Fourth Amendment rights violations when judges, rather than police, were responsible for the errors that led to an improper search. The Warren Court majority would have excluded the evidence in order to protect people against violations of Fourth Amendment rights.

Alterations of Warren Court precedents primarily involved incremental changes in constitutional rights, mostly in the direction of expanded governmental authority and diminished protections for individuals. The incremental nature of change was evident in the fact that the Burger and Rehnquist Court eras' justices kept intact the significant underlying precedents of the Warren Court era. For example, rather than overturn the Warren Court's requirement of Miranda warnings, the later justices chipped away at the protective impact of *Miranda v. Arizona* (1966). They granted greater flexibility to police concerning when and how the warnings could be delivered (*Duckworth v. Eagan*, 1989) and identified situations in which officers could use incriminating evidence despite violating the original Miranda principles (*New York v. Quarles*, 1984). The Rehnquist

Court justices, by a 7-to-2 vote, explicitly rejected a request that they directly overturn the original *Miranda* precedent (*Dickerson v. United States*, 2000). In preserving the iconic Warren Court decision, Chief Justice Rehnquist wrote that the warnings were constitutionally required and were not merely rules created by judges. Moreover, his majority opinion declared that "*Miranda* has become embedded in routine police practice to the point where the warnings have become part of our national culture."[25] Thus, the protective impact of Miranda warnings were reduced without eliminating the Warren Court precedent entirely.

Similarly, the exclusionary rule from the Warren Court's famous decision in *Mapp v. Ohio* (1961) was never eliminated despite political conservatives' arguments advocating its demise. With respect to both Miranda warnings and the exclusionary rule, it appeared that the majorities from the Burger and Rehnquist Courts apparently concluded that those protections were beneficial in some circumstances, albeit with more limited applications than those intended by the Warren Court. Instead of eliminating these rules, the later court eras produced decisions that narrowed definitions and created exceptions from the previously mandated requirements.[26]

Why was the Warren Court majority so different from its successors in its orientation toward defining the breadth and strength of constitutional rights in criminal justice? A primary factor was the justices' values and policy preferences. The Warren Court was dominated by appointees from Democratic Presidents Franklin Roosevelt, John F. Kennedy, and Lyndon Johnson. There were also two key justices, Chief Justice Earl Warren and Justice William Brennan, who turned out to be far more liberal than their appointing president, Dwight Eisenhower, had assumed.[27] By contrast, the outcomes of presidential elections and timing of justices' departures subsequently permitted Republican presidents to choose all ten new appointees over the period from 1969 to 1991. Several of these presidents—Presidents Nixon, Ronald Reagan, and George H. W. Bush—specifically intended to please their conservative political constituencies and advance their own policy preferences by appointing justices with narrower conceptions of rights than those of their Warren Court predecessors.

In addition, there were arguably generational differences between most of the Warren Court justices and their replacements who filled the Burger and Rehnquist Courts. The Warren Court justices came of age prior to the professionalization of policing. When they came into adulthood in the first decades of the twentieth century, there were few educational requirements for police officers. In addition, police officers had limited training. Widespread racial discrimination, abusive use of force, and limited conceptions of rights contributed to the unjust treatment of many people drawn into the criminal justice system. Several Warren Court justices had personal exposure to issues of police abuse.[28] Justice Brennan had seen his father, a labor union organizer, beaten bloody by police officers during the era when violence was often used to prevent workers from organizing unions. Chief Justice Warren reportedly observed abusive police interrogation practices when he was county prosecutor. Justice Thurgood Marshall narrowly escaped being lynched by Tennessee police officers when he was a crusading civil rights attorney in the South. Justice William O. Douglas wrote in his autobiography about seeing police officers harass poor people in his hometown. Justice Hugo Black was a local judge in Alabama at a historical moment that was particularly horrific for racial discrimination and violent victimization of Black residents in his community and elsewhere in that state.[29] These life experiences could very well have contributed to these justices' shared conclusions about the need to create clear, strong rules that would limit the risk of abusive actions by police.[30]

By contrast, many of the later appointees came into adulthood in the 1950s and thereafter, when police departments were developing training, standardized policies, and the aspiration to fulfill professional standards in their treatment of community residents. These justices were less likely to have observed the police abuses that were so common in the early twentieth century, and therefore their opinions about rights issues in criminal justice evinced much greater trust in police. In other words, their life experiences may have contributed to their willingness to grant greater authority and flexibility for investigative actions. With the exception of Justice Stevens, the justices of the Roberts Court era were too young to have experienced the horrifically abusive practices by unprofessional police that were accepted and routine in the early twentieth century.[31]

Justices of the Roberts Court Era

Supreme Court justices' votes and written opinions are influenced by their values and policy preferences as well as by their conception of a judicial officer's appropriate role in deciding cases. Justices' values and policy preferences can be affected by their life experiences, their understanding of societal conditions, and their predictions about the consequences of specific decisions. Other factors affecting decision-making can include specific justices' approaches to constitutional interpretation and the interactive processes in which members of the court seek to persuade their colleagues. Thus, Supreme Court justices do not merely "follow the law." Instead, they make law through the personal attitudes, values, and policy preferences that they bring to the court and place into the justices' interactive processes.[32] As a result, in order to understand the patterns of decision-making during the Roberts Court era, it is necessary to have familiarity with the backgrounds of the individual justices who served during this era.

The descriptions of the Roberts Court justices that follow do not include Justice O'Connor, who served on the Roberts Court for only a few months while awaiting the appointment and confirmation of her successor, Justice Alito. In addition, it should be noted that the Roberts Court era was shaped by individual justices' decisions to retire during the tenure of a president whom the justices presumably considered as most likely to appoint a successor with views comparable to their own. For example, despite being lifelong Republicans before appointment to the court, Justices John Paul Stevens and David Souter both chose to retire during the administration of Democratic President Obama. In so doing, they implicitly communicated a view that the Republican Party and Republican presidents had become too conservative to appoint successor justices with viewpoints compatible with their own.

The Holdovers from the Rehnquist Court

Justice John Paul Stevens was the only member of the Burger Court who also served throughout the Rehnquist Court era and remained on the court for the initial years of the Roberts era. Stevens was born in Chicago in 1920. He served as a US Navy officer during World War II, analyzing Japanese military communications and codes at a base in Hawaii. After the war, he was the top student at Northwestern University School of Law in Chicago, leading to a clerkship at the US Supreme Court with Justice Wiley Rutledge in 1947–48. He spent most of his legal career in private practice before being appointed to the US Court of Appeals for the Seventh Circuit by President Nixon in 1970. When President Gerald Ford appointed him to the Supreme Court in 1975, he quickly established himself as an independent thinker, a prolific opinion writer, and a defender of rights in criminal justice. Stevens was fifty-five years old at the time of his appointment. At the start of the Roberts Court era, Stevens had served on the Supreme Court for thirty years and was considered the court's most liberal justice with respect to criminal justice issues. He retired from the Supreme Court in 2010 at the age of ninety after five years on the Roberts Court and was replaced by President Obama's appointee, Justice Elena Kagan.[33]

Justice Stevens sought opportunities to explicitly criticize the originalists' approach to constitutional interpretation. He regularly highlighted how an originalist approach would produce undesirable consequences, such as the subjugation of women's decision-making authority to the preferences of their husbands[34] and the imposition of death sentences on children.[35] He openly advocated a flexible approach consistent with Justice Brennan's observations about the need for constitutional principles to reflect society's changing conditions and values.

President Reagan appointed Justice Antonin Scalia in 1986. He was fifty years old at the time of his appointment. A graduate of Harvard Law School, Justice Scalia was a former law professor, attorney in the Ford administration, and judge on the US Court of Appeals for the District of Columbia Circuit. Scalia established a reputation as a justice with strong views and sharply written opinions. He did not hesitate to criticize his colleagues in his judicial opinions. He advocated interpreting the Constitution according to the text and original meaning of the document. As an originalist, he believed that contemporary judges would avoid improperly creating law if they followed the framers' intentions rather than apply their own values in determining the Constitution's meaning. During his nearly thirty years on the Supreme Court, Scalia was an outspoken defender of capital punishment, and he advocated limiting rights for imprisoned people. He was generally consistent in arguing for limiting the recognition of constitutional rights in criminal justice and for expanding the authority of police. However, there were a few specific issues, such as the Confrontation Clause and specific search contexts, for which his understanding of the Constitution's original meaning led him to join his more liberal colleagues in supporting broader protection of constitutional rights.[36] His sudden death of an apparent heart attack in 2016 marked the end of an important natural court era for the Supreme Court and generated a partisan battle over which president would appoint his successor. Ultimately, the seat was filled in 2017 by Justice Gorsuch, a conservative Trump appointee.

Another Reagan appointee was Justice Anthony Kennedy, confirmed by the Senate in 1988 at the age of fifty-one. In Kennedy, a Harvard Law

School graduate, Reagan hoped he had found an experienced federal appellate judge who would be a dependable conservative vote in the Supreme Court's contentious cases. Justice Kennedy produced a generally conservative record. However, he gained influence and analytical attention by sitting in the ideological middle of the court and casting decisive votes for certain liberal decisions concerning such issues as abortion, capital punishment, juvenile justice, and legal equality for gays and lesbians. Upon the retirement of O'Connor at the dawn of the Roberts Court era, Kennedy became the most closely watched justice by news media and commentators for cases concerning issues that were likely to split the court. Justice Kennedy's retirement in 2018 facilitated President Trump's appointment of Justice Kavanaugh, a former Kennedy law clerk.[37]

Justice David Souter, also a Harvard Law School graduate, was appointed to the Supreme Court by President George H. W. Bush in 1990 as the replacement for the legendary liberal Justice William Brennan. Souter was fifty-one when he joined the court. Souter's views on controversial issues were largely unknown at the time of his appointment. He had served as New Hampshire's attorney general and then as a justice on the New Hampshire Supreme Court. He also served for a few months on the US Court of Appeals for the First Circuit prior to his nomination to the US Supreme Court. Republican officials in New Hampshire reassured Bush that Souter would be consistently conservative in his judicial decision-making. However, that prediction proved to be inaccurate. Souter was more liberal than Republicans expected. The political conservatives who had supported his nomination expressed dismay about his support for broad constitutional rights, including rights in the context of criminal justice. He was not as consistently liberal as Justice Stevens. Indeed, if he had served in the Warren Court era, Souter might have been labeled as a "moderate" in contrast to that era's half-dozen most liberal justices. During his four years on the Roberts Court, prior to his retirement in 2009, Souter was regarded as a member of the liberal wing of the court.[38] He was replaced by President Obama's first appointee, Justice Sonia Sotomayor.

Souter used a flexible approach to constitutional interpretation that included an emphasis on legal reasoning and the contemporary facts underlying each case. He did not directly confront and criticize the originalists' approach as Justice Stevens did. After his retirement, however, Souter delivered a commencement address at Harvard University to demonstrate clearly that he did not accept the originalists' approach. Souter did not use the term "originalism" in his speech's critique of the notion that there is a simple correct way to find the Constitution's meaning. Instead, he emphasized that the Constitution contains values that can be in tension with each other, and therefore judges must make decisions about what values and consequences to prioritize in specific cases. In saying that constitutional interpretation should occur "by relying on reason, by respecting all the words the Framers wrote, by facing facts, and by seeking to understand their meaning for living people," he clearly endorsed a flexible approach to interpretation.[39] Souter made plain his view that judges must interpret the Constitution in ways that reflect contemporary issues and problems.

Justice Clarence Thomas was confirmed for a seat on the Supreme Court in 1991 after being nominated by President George H. W. Bush. A Yale Law School graduate, he was only forty-three years old when he began his service as a Supreme Court justice after a very brief tenure as a judge on the US Court of Appeals for the District of Columbia Circuit. Previously, he was an administrator in two federal agencies. His performance in voting and writing opinions differed markedly from that of the justice he replaced, Thurgood Marshall, one of the foremost advocates of constitutional rights in criminal justice. Thomas claimed that he adhered to an originalist approach to constitutional interpretation, and he was consistently conservative in deciding criminal justice issues, though specific issues occasionally led him to part company with his conservative colleagues. Justice Thomas was resistant to the recognition of prisoners' rights, defended capital punishment, and sought to expand police authority.[40] Prior to the Roberts Court era, he and Justice Scalia often agreed with each other and sometimes dissented together in opposition to the rest of the justices. In the Roberts Court era, Justice Alito and Chief Justice Roberts frequently joined them when the majority issued a liberal decision.

Democratic President Bill Clinton appointed two justices, Ruth Bader Ginsburg in 1993 and Stephen Breyer in 1994. Ginsburg graduated from Columbia Law School after spending her first two years of law school at Harvard. She was a well-known civil rights lawyer and law professor prior to serving for a dozen years as a judge on the US Court of Appeals for the District of Columbia Circuit. She was appointed to the Supreme Court at the age of sixty. As a lawyer, she was especially famous for arguing key sex discrimination cases in the Supreme Court that established Equal Protection Clause coverage in the 1970s against laws mandating differential treatment by gender. Her overall record, especially during the Roberts

Court era, placed her among the court's most consistent defenders of clear, strong rights for suspects, defendants, and prisoners.[41] Her death less than two months before the 2020 presidential election enabled President Trump to make a last-minute third appointment to the Supreme Court. The replacement of Justice Ginsburg by Trump's conservative appointee Justice Amy Coney Barrett significantly shifted the court's composition by giving the conservatives a 6-to-3 supermajority. The shift also reflected the replacement of a justice who used flexible interpretation by one who claimed to adhere to an originalist approach to constitutional interpretation.

In contrast to Ginsburg, Breyer, a former law professor, US Senate staff attorney, and federal appellate judge, established a more moderate record. He was a graduate of Harvard Law School who was appointed to the Supreme Court at age fifty-six. While he often joined his most like-minded colleagues in criminal justice cases, he was the liberal justice who most frequently parted company with his liberal colleagues to support recognition of authority for police or prosecutors against claims of right by individuals.[42] When Justice Breyer retired in 2022, his replacement, Justice Ketanji Brown Jackson, President Joe Biden's appointee and the court's first Black woman to serve as a justice, seemed likely to establish a more liberal voting record in criminal justice than did Breyer. In her initial cases, she joined Justice Sotomayor in being outspoken on issues concerning alleged rights violations affecting criminal defendants.[43]

Breyer, a former Harvard Law professor, regularly appeared at university events to debate Scalia, a former University of Chicago professor, about constitutional interpretation. In a book written after his retirement, Breyer expressed the hope that audiences would see that justices could have strong disagreements while remaining friends and maintaining cordial interactions when discussing their disagreements. Breyer used the book to criticize originalists' approach to constitutional interpretation and make the case for his flexible approach.[44]

New Appointees During the Roberts Court Era

Chief Justice John Roberts, a former appellate judge and accomplished attorney in both government and private practice, became the court's administrative leader at the age of fifty. He was appointed by President George W. Bush to replace the man for whom he had served as a law clerk, Chief Justice William Rehnquist. Like several of his colleagues, he graduated from Harvard Law School. Although he was much younger than the other justices at the time of his appointment—the associate justices ranged in age from fifty-seven to eighty-five at that time, with the average age of seventy—Roberts won praise for the way in which he fulfilled the chief justice's leadership duties. In his book on chief justices, Justice Stevens praised Roberts as "always a well-prepared, fair, and effective leader" in leading the justices' discussions of cases.[45] In voting on cases, Roberts was a consistent member of the court's conservative wing. Although he became reviled by some conservative Republicans for his decision to support the constitutionality of President Obama's Affordable Care Act ("Obamacare"),[46] his decisions in criminal justice cases generally endorsed expansive authority for police and a limited conception of constitutional rights. In those cases when Roberts endorsed an individual's claim of right for a criminal justice issue, he was unlikely to be the lone conservative to conclude that a right was violated in the case.[47]

Justice Samuel Alito was appointed by President Bush in 2006 to replace Justice O'Connor. Thus, he served for all but the first few months of the Roberts Court era. He was fifty-five years old at the time of his appointment. Alito, a graduate of Yale Law School, served during the 1970s as an officer in the US Army Reserve, including a few months on active duty. Prior to his appointment to the Supreme Court, his career was spent as a federal prosecutor, a government attorney in the Reagan administration, and a judge on the US Court of Appeals for the Third Circuit.[48] On the Roberts Court, Alito quickly established himself as one of the most consistently conservative justices, especially in criminal justice cases. His opinions raised concerns about crime control, the need for broad police authority, and risks posed to public safety by lawbreakers. Observers speculated that his years as a prosecutor may have shaped the lens through which he analyzed criminal justice cases. In most years of the Roberts Court era, he was the justice least likely to support claims by individuals in criminal justice–related cases.[49]

Upon the retirement of Justice Souter in 2009, President Obama appointed Justice Sonia Sotomayor. She was fifty-five years old at the time of her appointment. Much was made of the fact that Sotomayor, who grew up in modest circumstances in New York City, was the first Latinx justice on the Supreme Court. Her parents had moved to New York from Puerto Rico. In her autobiography, she described experiencing discrimination in her life,[50] and her sensitivity to issues of race and discrimination was evident in her judicial opinions. A graduate of Yale Law School, she had the broadest professional experience within the criminal justice system among the Roberts Court justices. She was both a state and federal prosecutor as well as a federal trial court judge and a judge on the US Court of Appeals for the Second Circuit. Her experience as a prosecutor in state courts and time spent as a trial judge gave her closer contact with a wider array of aspects of the justice system than did the experiences of the other Roberts Court former prosecutor, Justice Alito. Alito's service as a prosecutor was limited to the narrower context of federal court. In the twelve-year period between the retirement of Justice Stevens and President Biden's appointment of Justice Jackson, Sotomayor stood out on the Roberts Court as the justice who was most protective of constitutional rights and willing to speak out in noticeable ways in questions from the bench during oral arguments and in sharp written opinions.[51] Like the court's other liberals, she used a flexible approach to interpretation that considered the nature of contemporary problems and the practical consequences of the court's decisions.

In 2010, President Obama appointed Justice Elena Kagan when Justice Stevens retired. She was fifty years old at the time of her appointment. She was an unusual nominee as the first Supreme Court appointee since the early 1970s who had not previously served as a judge. Yet, the Yale Law School graduate had served in impressive positions as the dean of Harvard Law School and the solicitor general of the United States, responsible for the federal government's arguments before the Supreme Court.[52] Her appointment meant three women served simultaneously on the court for the first time in history. Later, after the replacement of Justice Ginsburg by Justice Barrett in 2020 and the appointment of Justice Jackson in 2022, there were four women on the court. Justice Kagan was part of the liberal wing on the Roberts Court that regularly supported the rights claims of individuals in cases that divided the court.

Justice Neil Gorsuch was appointed by President Trump in 2017 at age forty-nine. He became a justice after a controversial process in which Republicans in the US Senate kept the Supreme Court at only eight members for more than a year while waiting to see if Trump would win the 2016 presidential election. Gorsuch earned degrees from Columbia University, Harvard Law School, and Oxford University. He was a well-known advocate of originalist constitutional interpretation during his decade of service as a judge on the US Court of Appeals for the Tenth Circuit. Previously, he had been a law clerk for Justice Kennedy, an attorney for the US Department of Justice during the administration of President George W. Bush, and a partner in a Denver law firm. His arrival at the Supreme Court gave fellow originalist Justice Thomas an outspoken ally in the role previously filled by Justice Scalia.

Upon the retirement of Justice Kennedy in 2018, President Trump appointed another former Kennedy law clerk, fifty-three-year-old Brett Kavanaugh, as Kennedy's replacement. Kavanaugh, a graduate of Yale Law School, worked as an attorney for the independent counsel investigating President Clinton. Thus, he contributed to the effort that led to impeachment proceedings against Clinton stemming from the president's inappropriate sexual relationship with a White House intern. Subsequently, Kavanaugh worked on behalf of President George W. Bush, first in the effort to determine the disputed results of the 2000 presidential election and later as part of the White House counsel's office. At the time of his Supreme Court appointment, he had served for twelve years as a judge on the US Court of Appeals for the District of Columbia Circuit.[53] Kavanaugh was confirmed by a close 50–48 vote in the Senate. At the time of his appointment, based on his opinions as an appellate judge, commentators predicted that Kavanaugh would vote to move constitutional law in the direction preferred by political conservatives.[54] Kavanaugh did not call himself an originalist but was receptive to originalists' arguments. Thus, he was available as a potential vote in favor of originalist majority opinions.

When liberal Justice Ruth Bader Ginsburg died a mere forty-seven days before the 2020 presidential election, Senate majority leader Mitch McConnell ignored his previously stated principle that senators should not confirm new appointees during presidential election years until after they know the voters' next choice for president. Instead, McConnell and the Republicans rushed to gain confirmation for President Trump's third nominee to the Supreme Court, Amy Coney Barrett. If they had not done so, they would have left the seat open to be filled by an appointee of President Biden, the victor in the 2020 presidential election. Justice Barrett was a forty-eight-year-old Notre Dame Law School graduate and former Notre Dame law professor who served as a judge on the US Court of Appeals for the Seventh Circuit. Barrett was confirmed by a close 52–48 vote in the Senate just eight days before Election Day in an extraordinarily swift confirmation process.[55] Barrett, a former Scalia law clerk, was a self-declared originalist who gave conservatives on the Supreme Court a 6–3 supermajority.

Later, President Biden appointed fifty-one-year-old Harvard Law School graduate Ketanji Brown Jackson to the high court in 2022. Justice Jackson had been a law clerk for Justice Breyer, a lawyer for the US Sentencing Commission, a federal trial judge, and a judge on the US Court of Appeals for the District of Columbia Circuit. As the replacement for liberal Justice Breyer, her arrival did not impact the 6–3 split between conservatives and liberals that shaped the court's decisions after Justice Barrett's confirmation in 2020. Because this book's empirical analysis concludes with the retirement of Breyer, Justice Jackson's initial votes and opinions in cases are not included in the analysis of the Roberts Court.

Conclusion

The Roberts Court era is viewed as one with a Supreme Court deeply divided between liberals and conservatives. For the first fifteen years, the conservatives held a slight numerical advantage, albeit with divided cases regularly producing liberal outcomes when specific conservative justices provided votes in favor of individuals' claims. After the retirement of the two liberal Republican appointees, Justices Stevens and Souter, the division within the court reflected the reality of the country's divided political parties, with the Democratic appointees constituting the liberal wing and Republican appointees generally ruling against claims by individuals in criminal justice cases.

During this era of division, the Roberts Court addressed important controversies in criminal justice–related cases, including gun control, capital punishment, and search and seizure. Some of these matters reflected the inevitability of new issues arising as society changed, such as technological changes that raised new Fourth Amendment search and seizure issues. Other matters concerned familiar issues reignited by events in society, such as the risk of racial discrimination in policing and concerns about humane methods of execution in capital punishment.

2. AN OVERVIEW OF CRIMINAL JUSTICE DECISIONS

Commentators and analysts often describe the Roberts Court as the most conservative Supreme Court in decades, if not in modern history.[1] An examination of empirical evidence indicates that this depiction is not journalistic hyperbole. Comparative assessments of justices' voting records across multiple issue areas show that several members of the Roberts Court, including Justices Thomas, Scalia, and Alito and Chief Justice Roberts, rank among the ten most conservative justices since 1937.[2] Empirical evidence also reveals the ways in which divisions among the justices affect the production of liberal and conservative outcomes in criminal justice cases.

The Roberts Court has been not only strongly conservative but also deeply divided, as evidenced by the number of cases determined by a single vote. There has been an unparalleled frequency of sharply divided decisions during the tenure of Chief Justice Roberts. At the time of Justice Ginsburg's death in 2020, the Roberts Court era equaled the Rehnquist Court era) with the highest rate of five-member majorities in Supreme Court history, as 21 percent of its rulings ended in a minimum winning coalition.[3] By contrast, during the Burger Court era, only 14 percent of decisions divided the court so starkly. The proportion of Roberts Court cases concerning criminal justice issues decided by a single vote from 2005 to 2022 was higher than the proportion of divided votes for all issues.

The Roberts Court's 5–4 decisions frequently appeared to reflect the justices' political ideology. In short, justices whose voting records defined them as members of the court's conservative wing often aligned against those justices with liberal voting records. Numerous academic and popular accounts show how ideological divisions could erode the court's perceived legitimacy and jeopardize the public's acceptance of justices as impartial arbiters settling society's most divisive issues.[4] Indeed, Chief Justice Roberts acknowledged this danger after his first year in office during an interview with law professor Jeffrey Rosen. According to Rosen, "Roberts expressed frustration that his colleagues . . . [b]y handing down . . . decisions along predictable ideological lines . . . [were] making it harder [for the public] . . . to respect the judiciary as an impartial institution that transcends partisan politics."[5]

The likelihood of perceived partisanship increased in 2010 when President Obama's nominee Elena Kagan replaced the liberal Republican appointee John Paul Stevens, who had been placed on the court by President Ford. For the first time in court history, the five most conservative members of the court were appointed by Republican presidents, while the four Democratic appointees constituted the court's liberal wing.[6] In previous Supreme Court eras, several factors typically prevented such a party-affiliated alignment of justices, including the intentional selection of judicial moderates to vacancies on the high court. In addition, there was the occasional "nomination surprise," such as when a presumptively conservative nominee produced a liberal voting record, as was the case with lifelong Republicans Stevens and Souter.

As a result, in major cases from 1790 until 2010, justices almost never split completely along the lines of their nominating presidents' party affiliations.[7] For example, although the vote in the landmark *Miranda v. Arizona* (1966) case concerning constitutional protection against compelled self-incrimination was 5–4, the majority included three Democratic appointees and two Republican ones, while the dissenters included two of each type of appointee. By contrast, the Roberts Court produced splits among the justices along party-nomination lines. These included, among others, major decisions that eliminated the long-established right of choice concerning abortion (*Dobbs v. Jackson Women's Health Organization*, 2022) and expanded the Second Amendment's definition to include a right for otherwise qualified individuals to carry firearms in public (*New York State Rifle & Pistol Association v. Bruen*, 2022). This development reflected the diminishing overlap between the two parties in the moderate middle of the American political spectrum. It also heightened concerns that the Supreme Court would come to be viewed—and disparaged—as indistinguishable from political institutions that appear to be arenas for partisans to advance their political party's interests. When the court's Democratic appointees and Republican appointees divide themselves with no overlap between them in major cases, it may invite the public to recognize the extent to which decisions are based on political ideology rather than on legal reasoning.

Case Selection, Coding, and Metrics

We begin our empirical analysis by identifying and reviewing criminal justice decisions issued by the Roberts Court from the 2005–6 term through the 2021–22 term. Typically, such issues represent approximately one-third of the decisions issued by the court.[8] Case decisions are excluded from the analysis if they were consolidated with another case,[9] were dismissed as improvidently granted, or resulted in unsigned (per curiam) opinions. Ultimately, we analyze 396 criminal justice decisions identified from the first seventeen terms of the Roberts Court era. The analysis examines the court as a whole, as well as individual justices, using metrics commonly employed by judicial researchers. These metrics include measures of voting agreements among subsets of justices, majority opinion authorship, and majority participation rates, including membership in minimum winning coalitions.

Scholars have relied on the labels "liberal" and "conservative" to categorize court decisions, voting patterns of justices, and entire court eras for over seventy years.[10] These labels often provide insight into a justice's philosophical approach and the likelihood that he or she might support certain outcomes. These labels also facilitate analysis of the extent to which the Roberts Court manifested ideological divisions. As analysts have observed, although justices are not necessarily politicians in robes, "it is well established that much judicial behavior can be predicted on the basis of the standard left-right ideological divide."[11]

With respect to criminal justice cases, the term "liberal" applies to decisions favoring claims by suspects, defendants, and convicted offenders, while "conservative" votes and rulings endorse government authority to investigate, prosecute, and punish criminal conduct. A few cases were classified as exceptions to these definitions. Four exceptions concerned the lawfulness of gun ownership, weapons purchases, or licenses to carry a concealed firearm. Typically, political liberals advocate gun control laws and political conservatives support broad rights protection for gun ownership and carrying firearms in public places. Thus, we coded the cases to reflect widely recognized political values and policy preferences rather than adhered to a strict treatment of pro-individual rights decisions as "liberal." Specifically, the court's decisions expanding rights under the Second Amendment in *District of Columbia v. Heller* (2008) and *McDonald v. City of Chicago* (2010) are coded as conservative. So, too, is the coding for the court's ruling in *New York State Rifle & Pistol Association v. Bruen* that a state's proper-cause requirement for obtaining a concealed carry permit was unconstitutional. The converse applies to the court's rights-restricting decision in *Abramski v. United States* (2014), which upheld a conviction for the straw purchase of a firearm for another individual otherwise lawfully eligible to own a gun, which is treated as a liberal outcome. By aligning the coding of these four cases with prevailing political values, the data better reflect an understanding of case outcomes and justices' votes along a liberal-conservative dimension.

The tables and discussion in this chapter also draw upon other well-established metrics of judicial decision-making, including the frequency with which pairs of justices voted together. These dyadic scores not only indicate the degree to which pairs of justices agreed in selected cases but also help identify possible voting blocs comprising a larger number of justices. Bloc voting analysis is a primary methodology for detecting conflict and consensus on the Supreme Court and other appellate courts. Past studies of shared voting patterns among pairs and larger groupings of justices advanced our understanding of whether "freshman" justices join existing blocs and how coalitions vary at different stages of the decision process. Bloc voting analysis can reveal important patterns in judicial behavior, such as unusually strong coalitions for certain issue areas, justices' majority participation rates, and presidential impacts when positions taken by justices support their nominating president's ideological goals.

A potential bloc exists when the average agreement scores for a set of justices exceed a given threshold. We adopt the Sprague criterion, which is the standard threshold in the field of judicial studies. A notable advantage of the Sprague criterion is how it accounts for the general degree of harmony or discord among justices at any given time by setting the minimum level for identifying voting blocs at a percentage relative to the average agreement rate on the court.[12] Otherwise, blocs that distinguish justices' voting tendencies and reveal meaningful differences between groups of justices could be obscured by those cases on which there is broad consensus. Justices in a particular bloc are not assumed to trade votes or consciously seek to vote with one another. Rather, their frequency of reaching shared conclusions in cases suggests possible commonalities in their experiences, values, judicial philosophies, and policy preferences.

Cases decided by a single vote attract disproportionate attention from journalists and scholars. Scholars generally regard 5–4 decisions as susceptible to being overturned by later Supreme Court decisions when the court's composition subsequently changes through the arrival of new appointees.[13] Scholars also focus on such split decisions to determine the fluidity or rigidity of minimum winning coalitions. In addition, these split decisions can reveal subtle but important philosophical differences among justices as an explanation for what otherwise appears to be inconsistent coalition formations. Analyses of cases that deeply divide the justices can identify critical swing votes and the justices most likely to cast them.[14]

A swing vote is defined as a justice's outcome-determining vote that deviates from the expected vote in light of his or her typical pattern of voting.[15] Based on the voting records of Roberts Court justices until Justice Barrett's appointment in 2020 created a six-justice conservative supermajority, the expected vote in 5–4 criminal justice decisions predicted that the five most conservative justices would constitute the majority with the four most liberal justices dissenting. A swing vote, then, is any vote from the conservative camp that helps produce a 5–4 liberal outcome, or one from the liberal wing that secures a five-member conservative majority when one or more conservative justices defect from their usual allies.

The Roberts Court possessed characteristics that were conducive to detecting swing votes because of its relatively cohesive and well-defined blocs that were close in size. Moreover, the Roberts Court era began with the departure of a key swing justice, Sandra Day O'Connor. Just prior to O'Connor's retirement, leading judicial scholars observed, "On virtually all conceptual and empirical definitions, O'Connor is the Court's center— the median, the key, the critical, and the swing Justice."[16] The changing composition on the Roberts Court increased the importance of analyzing criminal justice cases decided by the narrowest of margins in the years following O'Connor's retirement.

Patterns in the authorship of majority opinions in criminal justice cases provide additional insights into the court's decision-making dynamics. The choice of a specific opinion author can affect several things, including the scope and clarity of the ruling. The majority opinion author also influences whether a majority coalition is preserved, expanded, or lost during the opinion drafting process. For example, a draft majority opinion circulated among the justices that is too forceful can cause justices to switch their votes and withdraw from the majority if they believe the opinion goes too far in defining the law.[17] Analyses of opinion writing can also test the equitable distribution of the court's workload as well as the degree to which the decisions emphasize the policy preferences of the justice who selected the majority opinion author.[18] The chief justice wields the influential power of assigning the majority opinion if he is in the majority at the initial conference vote. Otherwise, the most senior associate justice in the majority makes the assignment.

Rehnquist Court Redux?

The advent of the Roberts Court era in 2005 seemed to signal a continuation of the Rehnquist Court's preference for law-and-order values and case outcomes. During his nomination process, many analysts pegged John Roberts as a younger version of his predecessor. Like Rehnquist, Roberts was seen as an intelligent, conservative, and strategic jurist. A few months after Roberts took his seat as chief justice, another strong conservative joined the court when the Senate confirmed Samuel Alito, a former prosecutor with a staunchly conservative record.

Not only did these early appointments preserve a conservative majority, but they also increased the prospects for a more robustly conservative court. Commentators at the time depicted Alito as a far more dependable advocate of law-and-order principles than his predecessor, the moderately conservative Justice O'Connor. She was known for occasionally providing the critical swing vote supporting liberal criminal justice outcomes, and she moved somewhat to the left in her final years' decisions on the court.[19] By contrast, a review of Alito's circuit court tenure concluded, "In 15 years on the bench, Alito has filed more than a dozen dissents in criminal cases. . . . Not one of those dissents urges a position more protective of individual rights than the majority['s position]."[20] Alito's prior record indicated that he might be the eventual heir to Justice Scalia's mantle as the court's conservative intellectual leader.

President Obama followed President Bush's appointments with two of his own, Justices Sotomayor and Kagan, who replaced Justices Souter and Stevens, two retiring justices considered to be among the most liberal members of the court. Consequently, initial changes in the court's composition provided little reason to expect major shifts in the fundamental balance of ideological power on the court. Conservative newcomers replaced two departing conservatives, and new liberal appointees filled the seats of two liberal retirees.

President Trump appointed Justice Gorsuch to fill Scalia's seat in 2017. This action maintained the five-member conservative majority on the court, a majority that otherwise would have shifted to a five-member liberal majority if President Obama's nominee had not been blocked from consideration in the Senate one year earlier. A year later, Trump's second court appointee, Justice Kavanaugh, was approved by a historically close 50–48 confirmation vote. Most analyses at the time depicted Kavanaugh as more conservative than retiring Justice Kennedy. An attorney for the Brennan Center wrote about Kavanaugh's record as a federal appellate judge: "Based on Kavanaugh's limited criminal jurisprudence, there is no indication that Kavanaugh falls to the left of Kennedy on *any* aspect of criminal justice."[21] Later, the death of the most senior member of the court's liberal wing, Justice Ginsburg, in September 2020 prompted the most dramatic shift in the Roberts Court's composition. Her replacement, Justice Barrett, was considered among the most conservative judges on the US Court of Appeals for the Seventh Circuit.[22] Her confirmation expanded the court's conservative majority to six members.

It is not surprising, then, that the distribution of the Roberts Court's criminal justice decisions shown in tables 2 and 3 demonstrates a continuation of the court's rightward tilt. The number of rulings favoring government interests in investigating and prosecuting criminal cases markedly outnumbered those favoring the claims of suspects and defendants during both the last decade of the Rehnquist Court era and the first seventeen terms of the Roberts Court era. Moreover, a notable percentage of cases in each period ended with unanimous or near-unanimous decisions, while an almost equally large percentage of cases addressed issues for which the justices split sharply and generated at least three dissenting votes.

General patterns in criminal justice decisions handed down by the Roberts Court diverge from those of the final decade under Chief Justice Rehnquist in an important way. The percentage of rulings favoring individuals ticked upward under Roberts, especially in the most divided cases. Indeed, nonunanimous decisions from 2005 to 2022 split almost evenly between conservative and liberal outcomes, and just over half of the cases decided by a single vote went against law enforcement interests. These initial results appear to be at odds with the widespread portrayal of the first several years of the Roberts Court as being dominated by five conservative members and therefore simply an extension of the Rehnquist Court era. Although specific issues differ from case to case, simplistically applying rates from the Rehnquist Court would predict thirty fewer liberal

Table 2. Detailed Distribution of Criminal Justice Cases by Vote and Liberal / Conservative Outcome, Roberts Court, 2005–2022

Vote[a]	Liberal	Conservative	Total
Unanimous	52	82	134 (33.8%)
Nonunanimous	132	130	262 (66.2%)
8–1	18	13	31 (7.8%)
7–2/7–1	30	25	55 (13.9%)
6–3/6–2	29	40	69 (17.4%)
5–4/5–3	55	52	107 (27.0%)
Totals	184 (46.5%)	212 (53.5%)	396

[a] "5–4/5–3" includes the 4-to-2 conservative decision in *Ziglar v. Abbasi* (2017) in which Kagan and Sotomayor recused and Gorsuch was not yet on the court. A vacancy and/or a justice's recusal caused 72 criminal justice cases to be decided by fewer than nine justices during the first seventeen terms of the Roberts court. This produced 31 decisions ending 8–0, 8 ending 7–1, 13 ending 6–2, 19 ending 5–3, and 1 ending 4–2. The 396 analyzed criminal justice decisions include 6 cases decided during the 2005–6 term when Sandra Day O'Connor was still on the court, before being replaced by Samuel Alito. O'Connor's votes are included for most calculations in this chapter but are insufficient to analyze separately.

Table 3. Criminal Justice Cases by Vote and Outcome, Final Decade of Rehnquist Era Compared with Roberts Era

N dissenters	% of decisions		% liberal outcome	
	1995–2005	2005–2022	1995–2005	2005–2022
0–1	44.5	44.7	37.6	43.4
2	13.2	15.2	40.5	47.5
3–4	42.3	40.2	39.5	49.4
Total % liberal			38.8	46.5

Sources: Data for the last ten years of the Rehnquist Court are drawn from Madhavi M. McCall and Michael A. McCall, "Chief Justice William Rehnquist: His Law-and-Order Legacy and Impact on Criminal Justice," *Akron Law Review* 39, no. 2 (2006): 323–72; and Christopher E. Smith, "The Rehnquist Court and Criminal Justice: An Empirical Assessment," *Journal of Contemporary Criminal Justice* 19 (2003): 161–81.

criminal justice outcomes than were actually produced by the Roberts Court through the 2021–22 term.

However, two considerations caution against overestimating the liberalness of the Roberts Court. First, while there have been slightly more liberal decisions in highly divided criminal justice cases over the entire period analyzed, most 5–4 decisions after Scalia's death in early 2016 have sided with the interests of law enforcement. Thus, when the justices were most divided about an issue, the direction of such decisions moved increasingly toward conservative outcomes. Second, the recently constituted supermajority of six conservative justices was just beginning to flex its judicial muscles after the appointment of Justice Barrett in 2020. In criminal justice cases decided during the 2020 and 2021 terms, most of the nonunanimous conservative decisions ended with the entire conservative wing voting together against all members of the liberal wing. This may suggest an increased desire and ability of the six-member majority to advance conservative outcomes more frequently.

Wings, Dyads, and Blocs

The simplistic metric of "percent liberal/conservative voting" clusters the justices into two distinct camps in a manner that corresponds with typical portrayals of a divided court. The voting records in criminal justice cases summarized in table 4 locate Roberts, Scalia, Kennedy, Thomas, Alito, Gorsuch, Kavanaugh, and Barrett in the court's conservative wing and place Stevens, Ginsburg, Breyer, Souter, Kagan, and Sotomayor in the liberal wing. In nonunanimous cases, members of the court's conservative wing, on average, supported law enforcement interests over those of individuals almost 3.5 times more often than did their liberal colleagues (71.8 percent to 20.6 percent).

Both camps demonstrated strong internal cohesion, at least by some measures. Criminal justice questions dividing the court most sharply often ended with all or nearly all members of the conservative wing arrayed against all members of the liberal one. More generally, as shown in table 4, when a nonunanimous decision produced a liberal outcome, about 95 percent of the votes by members of the liberal wing supported the majority. A similar percentage of votes from the conservative camp (92 percent) backed nonunanimous, conservative decisions.

Naturally, the voting records contrast most distinctly when comparing justices from each end of the table. In the nonunanimous criminal justice

Table 4. Justices' Support for Conservative Outcomes in Criminal Justice Decisions and Majority Participation Rates by Majority Size and Type, 2005–2022

Justice (n total votes)	% voted conservative		% voted with majority when majority was			
	all	(nonunanimous)	6 to 9 members	5[a] members	nonunanimous and conservative	liberal
Alito (381)	79.5	(88.3)	82.7	51.0	100.0	23.3
Thomas (396)	75.8	(83.2)	76.8	54.2	89.2	22.7
Barrett (28)	67.9	(75.0)	100.0	40.0	100.0	62.5
Scalia (269)	66.9	(67.4)	87.4	47.1	81.8	47.1
Kavanaugh (62)	64.5	(68.9)	100.0	73.7	100.0	73.7
Roberts (395)	64.3	(65.9)	97.6	51.9	93.8	61.8
Kennedy (332)	59.1	(55.8)	95.1	82.6	93.2	82.1
Gorsuch (86)	54.7	(57.1)	84.7	63.0	77.4	62.5
Breyer (395)	38.7	(27.2)	87.2	56.1	45.0	90.2
Souter (111)	35.1	(23.0)	85.0	51.6	38.1	96.9
Ginsburg (364)	34.1	(19.6)	85.0	56.0	35.9	95.9
Stevens (140)	32.9	(20.0)	77.9	50.0	29.6	92.7
Kagan (241)	32.0	(19.3)	88.4	57.4	37.5	95.5
Sotomayor (282)	29.8	(13.0)	85.1	55.4	26.7	99.0
Court wing[b]						
Conservative	*68.3*	*(71.8)*	*88.3*	*57.9*	*92.0*	*48.2*
Liberal	*34.1*	*(20.6)*	*85.8*	*55.3*	*36.4*	*94.8*

[a] "5 members" includes 4-to-2 majority in *Ziglar v. Abbasi* (2017).
[b] Percentages for wings are weighted means. Conservative wing rates include six votes by O'Connor.

cases analyzed, Justice Alito supported government interests in investigating, prosecuting, and punishing criminal conduct 88 percent of the time, while 87 percent of Justice Sotomayor's votes favored the individual. By the end of the 2021–22 term, the court had handed down more than 200 conservative criminal justice decisions since Alito's confirmation. Notably, he did not dissent from any of these decisions. Sotomayor's only dissent from a liberal criminal justice decision came when the court held that the Double Jeopardy Clause prohibited Puerto Rico and the United States from prosecuting the same individual for the same conduct under equivalent criminal laws (*Puerto Rico v. Sanchez Valle*, 2016). Sotomayor joined Breyer's dissent asserting that Puerto Rico had independent authority to prosecute its own criminal laws and that under the dual sovereignty doctrine, the Double Jeopardy Clause does not bar such successive prosecutions. In light of the issue's focus on jurisdictional authority rather than on constitutional rights, this was not the typical dissent from a liberal criminal justice decision.

Other patterns in the justices' voting are less obvious. For example, despite being considered an intellectual leader of the conservative wing, Scalia accounted for nearly half of all dissents by a conservative justice from a conservative criminal justice decision during his years on the Roberts Court. Similarly, among the court's liberals, Breyer cast nearly half of all dissenting votes from a liberal decision in his seventeen years on the Roberts Court. It is striking that during Scalia's time on the Roberts Court, he joined every liberal criminal justice majority from which Breyer dissented. All but three of those cases presented Fourth or Sixth Amendment claims. These were issue areas for which Scalia tended to be more supportive of the accused's rights than he was with respect to other criminal justice issues. Furthermore, Breyer joined over two-thirds of the conservative majorities from which Scalia dissented. In a sense, the two justices "traded places" in one of every eight nonunanimous criminal justice decisions in which they both participated during the Roberts Court era.

These cases help explain why Scalia was less likely to agree with Breyer than with Ginsburg, Souter, Sotomayor, or Kagan, despite Breyer's more moderate overall voting record. The issue areas causing both Scalia and Breyer to defect from their respective camps also reveal sharp interpretational differences between Scalia and Alito. In these cases, Alito almost always agreed with Breyer rather than with Scalia. By contrast, Scalia's particular originalist approach often led him to support a defendant's Sixth

Amendment right to confront accusing witnesses and to take a narrower view of police authority in certain Fourth Amendment cases.[23]

At the time of Alito's nomination, some observers described the similarities of Alito and Scalia, but others focused on contrasts. The latter observers accurately predicted, "There will be no one to the right of Sam Alito on this Court,"[24] and "While Alito goes to conservative places Scalia won't, the more telling point is that Scalia goes to liberal places Alito won't."[25] Alito's criminal justice voting record quickly put him not only to the right of his colleagues but also to the right of every other justice since World War II except for consistently conservative Chief Justice Rehnquist.[26]

Other individual voting tendencies summarized in table 4 illustrate that Kennedy joined many more majorities producing nonunanimous liberal outcomes than did any of his conservative colleagues. He also posted the court's highest rate of majority membership in criminal justice cases decided by a single vote. These empirical conclusions support numerous scholarly discussions of his role as the median justice, especially after the retirement of O'Connor at the dawn of the Roberts Court era.[27] Overall, Justice Kennedy was quite conservative on the Rehnquist Court. Yet, when serving on the Roberts Court, as one commentator observed, he "was much more likely than in the past to vote in a liberal direction on cases involving criminal-justice issues, civil rights and due process."[28]

Justice Kennedy joined a higher percentage of conservative criminal justice majorities during his time on the Roberts Court than did either Thomas or Scalia, despite having a conservative voting "score" considerably lower than those of his two fellow conservatives. The willingness of Thomas and Scalia to break from large conservative majorities explains most of this puzzling observation. From 2005 through 2022, forty-seven conservative criminal justice decisions ended with one or two dissenters. Most of the dissenting votes predictably came from liberal justices. Yet, Scalia and Thomas each dissented seven times in these cases, while no other member of the conservative wing dissented more than twice. Such findings indicate that a single ideological dimension does not always capture a justice's philosophical values and interpretive approach. For example, Thomas's and Scalia's opposition to broadening congressional power under the Necessary and Proper Clause took priority in some cases over their general inclination to endorse crime-control measures.[29]

Justice Thomas, a prolific dissenter, wrote almost half of the solo dissents filed by Roberts Court justices in criminal justice cases decided through the

2021–22 term and three times as many as the next closest justice. Thomas presented the lowest participation rate (55.7 percent) in nonunanimous criminal justice majorities despite being a staunch conservative on a solidly conservative court. Throughout his career going back to the Rehnquist Court, Thomas seemed to write dissenting and concurring opinions for an audience of conservative lawyers and potential future judicial appointees rather than as an effort to persuade his colleagues to share his conclusions. These opinions enabled Thomas to express highly idiosyncratic views about constitutional and statutory interpretation. However, Thomas's views appeared to find a more receptive audience among his colleagues after President Trump appointed three new conservative justices. For example, the court's opinion in *Dobbs v. Jackson Women's Health* (2022) overturning *Roe v. Wade* (1973) was replete with references to some of Thomas's earlier dissenting and concurring opinions. Similarly, Thomas harshly criticized the court in 2017 for its "treatment of the Second Amendment as a disfavored right" when his fellow justices refused to hear a case challenging a state's prohibition on carrying firearms in public spaces for self-defense.[30] Just five years later, Thomas wrote for the majority, including the three Trump-appointed conservative justices, a decision expanding opportunities to carry a concealed firearm in public for self-defense in *New York Rifle & Pistol Association v. Bruen* (2022). As one observer put it, "After decades of writing alone from the conservative fringe, [Thomas] seems to have more power and more support."[31]

The findings in table 4 show Chief Justice Roberts stood out for his role in closely divided decisions. Roberts voted with the majority frequently in criminal justice cases as well as in other cases. Only relative newcomers Kavanaugh and Barrett, who participated in significantly fewer cases, joined more criminal justice majorities of six or more members than the chief justice, who voted with the winning side in 282 of 289 such decisions. However, Roberts's dominant presence in the majority dropped precipitously when the analysis narrows to cases decided by a single vote. The chief justice dissented from almost as many of these closely divided decisions as he joined.

His role in deeply divided decisions was ironic given two statements by Roberts early in his chief justiceship. In one statement, he announced a goal of forging consensus on the court through narrow rulings.[32] He also said, "I do think the rule of law is threatened by a steady term after term after term focus on 5–4 decisions."[33] The chief justice's voting behavior raised questions about whether he could fulfill the spirit and intent of his statements when participating in the court's actual divided decisions about criminal justice issues.

Interpreting the voting records of President Trump's three additions to the conservative wing requires considerable care to avoid overstating the significance of any early patterns during their initial Supreme Court careers. One possible early conclusion is that Justice Barrett's presence and voting record generated an increase in the number of 6–3 decisions favoring law enforcement interests. Although a shift was expected given the enlarged size of the conservative wing after Barrett replaced Ginsburg, the magnitude of the surge in these decisions was striking. A 6–3 conservative outcome appeared in fewer than 10 percent of nonunanimous criminal justice decisions handed down during the first fifteen years of the Roberts Court era. By contrast, this figure jumped to 41 percent of such cases decided during Barrett's first two years on the court.

Since joining the court in 2018, Justice Kavanaugh rarely cast a vote against the majority. When the entire court docket is considered, for example, Kavanaugh's frequency of voting with the majority led all justices during three of his first four terms and slightly trailed only Roberts in the 2019–20 term.[34] Of the criminal justice cases in which he participated during those four years, Kavanaugh joined over 90 percent of the majorities. It is notable that Trump-appointee Justice Gorsuch provided a critical fifth liberal vote in each of the five criminal justice cases in which Trump-appointee Kavanaugh dissented.

There was no basis for predicting Justice Kagan's likely decision-making patterns for criminal justice issues.[35] Unlike the other justices, all of whom had previously decided criminal justice cases as judges on US courts of appeals, Kagan's prior experience was in academia and federal government service. As solicitor general of the United States, Kagan bore responsibility for presenting arguments to the Supreme Court, not based on her own views of legal issues but based on policy decisions by the Obama administration and its Department of Justice.

Because Justices Sotomayor and Alito both previously served as prosecutors, it was especially difficult to anticipate that Sotomayor's liberal criminal justice voting patterns would produce a near mirror image of Alito's conservative record.[36] She emerged as a potent liberal voice on and off the bench by emphasizing the practical human consequences of the Supreme Court's decisions.[37] One observer wrote in 2019 that Sotomayor "is not only its most outspoken questioner [during oral arguments]. . . . Her voice, in all its forms, has become the liberal conscience . . . that speaks out in defense of minorities, immigrants, criminal defendants and death row inmates."[38]

In the individual decision-making rates summarized in table 4, justices from the court's liberal wing recorded more consistent "scores" than their conservative counterparts, even after excluding the three most recently confirmed conservatives whose numbers were affected by their participation in relatively few case decisions. For example, the spread in the percentage of conservative voting in all criminal justice cases is about ten points from Sotomayor to Breyer among the court's liberals, while the gap is over twice as large between the rates for Kennedy and Alito among the conservative justices.

Each of the liberal justices, except Stevens, joined approximately two of every three nonunanimous majorities examined. Thomas's majority participation rate, which was lower than the rates of his fellow conservatives, reflected his willingness to dissent from both large conservative and liberal majorities. By contrast, Stevens's rates were almost exclusively a function of his dissents from conservative criminal justice decisions. On the Roberts Court, Stevens broke with a large majority producing a liberal criminal justice outcome only once. This occurred when the majority held that a court of appeals could not, on its own initiative, vacate a shorter sentence based on a sentencing error by a district court and then impose a longer corrected sentence. This case, *Greenlaw v. United States* (2008), had limited impact given that such sua sponte sentence increases are rare. The case might be remembered most as the one instance that Stevens joined an Alito-authored dissent from a liberal criminal justice decision.

Individual voting records and distinctions between the court's ideological wings can be instructive. However, they shed only limited light on the dynamics of group decision-making. To explore other possibilities, the analytical lens must shift to interagreement rates among justices. For ease of presentation, table 5 provides interagreement rates for nonunanimous criminal justice decisions handed down by the Roberts Court prior to Scalia's death in early 2016, while subsequent rates through the 2021–22 term are shown in table 6. To account for changes in the court's composition, we identified voting blocs for each natural court period defined by the arrival of a new justice. We analyzed rates in nonunanimous cases because, presumably, such rulings illuminate most clearly differences in justices' philosophical approaches, attitudes, and values.

Table 5. Interagreement Percentages for Paired Justices in Nonunanimous Criminal Justice Decisions, 2005–2016

	Alito	Scalia	Thomas	Kennedy	Breyer	Souter	Stevens	Ginsburg	Sotomayor	Kagan
Roberts	78.6	77.6	69.5	74.1	51.4	41.1	37.2	43.2	51.5	48.0
Alito		68.6	75.7	62.7	39.9	34.8	29.2	32.0	27.6	29.3
Scalia			78.3	54.9	33.9	36.5	32.6	38.9	39.4	49.3
Thomas				51.4	28.7	29.7	22.1	26.3	28.3	30.7
Kennedy					66.1	54.1	54.7	58.9	58.6	68.0
Breyer						73.0	69.5	71.8	79.6	75.7
Souter							74.3	82.4	--	--
Stevens								73.7	63.2	--
Ginsburg									80.8	84.0
Sotomayor										82.7

Court mean, 2005–9: 54.4
Sprague criterion: 77.2
Voting blocs: Roberts, Scalia, Alito (80.9)
    Stevens, Ginsburg, Souter (79.3)[a]

Court mean, 2010–16: 54.3
Sprague criterion: 77.2
Voting blocs: Ginsburg, Sotomayor, Kagan (82.6)
    Ginsburg, Sotomayor, Kagan, Breyer (79.1)[a]

Cohesion score, 2005–16[b]
    Conservative wing: 69.1
    Liberal wing: 76.2

Note: N = 175 nonunanimous decisions prior to Scalia's death.
[a] Denotes a near bloc.
[b] Cohesion scores are weighted mean interagreement rates with all other subgroup members. Rates for Justice O'Connor are not included in these calculations.

Table 6. Interagreement Percentages for Paired Justices in Nonunanimous Criminal Justice Decisions, 2016–2022

	Gorsuch	Alito	Thomas	Kennedy	Kavanaugh	Barrett	Breyer	Sotomayor	Kagan	Ginsburg
Roberts	57.1	69.0	58.6	80.0	93.3	90.0	51.7	46.5	51.2	55.4
Gorsuch		58.7	63.5	62.5	62.2	70.0	42.9	41.3	44.4	43.9
Alito			75.9	57.5	77.8	85.0	29.5	17.4	26.7	29.2
Thomas				47.5	66.7	65.0	24.1	18.6	18.6	18.5
Kavanaugh						95.0	46.7	33.3	37.8	39.1
Kennedy							65.0	64.1	74.4	65.0
Barrett							35.0	25.0	30.0	--
Breyer								82.6	84.9	80.0
Sotomayor									79.1	84.4
Kagan										79.7

	Court mean	Sprague criterion	Voting blocs
2016 before Gorsuch	59.6	79.8	none
2016–18 before Kavanaugh	53.0	76.5	Breyer, Ginsburg, Sotomayor, Kagan (93.0)
2018–20 before Barrett	50.6	75.3	Breyer, Ginsburg, Sotomayor (83.1); Roberts, Alito, Kavanaugh (81.3); Breyer, Ginsburg, Sotomayor, Kagan (79.2)[a]; Alito, Thomas, Kavanaugh (78.7)[a]
2020–22	53.3	76.7	Roberts, Alito, Kavanaugh, Barrett (88.3); Breyer, Sotomayor, Kagan (93.3)

Cohesion score, 2016–22[b]

Conservative wing: 68.1
Liberal wing: 81.8

Note: N = 87 nonunanimous decisions after Scalia's death.
[a] Denotes a near bloc.
[b] Cohesion scores are weighted mean interagreement rates with all other subgroup members.

Only a few coalitions of three or more members met or nearly met the threshold to be labeled as "voting blocs." Most of those blocs involved justices with liberal voting records. The average agreement rate (cohesion score) among members of the smaller liberal wing substantially exceeded that for the more numerous conservative justices in the time period from 2005 through 2022. Indeed, the entire liberal wing qualified as a voting bloc or a "near bloc" in divided criminal justice cases for most periods analyzed from 2010 to 2022. A "near bloc" is a coalition whose average agreement exceeds the Sprague criterion but with one or more paired justices' rates falling just short of that threshold.[39] Although the average interagreement rate for Roberts, Scalia, and Alito satisfied the Sprague criterion for the existence of a voting bloc during the first five years of the Roberts Court era, the interagreement rate for that trio dropped sharply after 2009. The increased frequency of Alito and Scalia breaking separately from large majorities accounts for over half of the decline in the agreement rate for this trio.[40] Chief Justice Roberts agreed less often with Alito and Thomas in criminal justice cases decided by a divided court after Scalia's passing than he did in his first decade on the court. Roberts's support for claims by individuals increased slightly, as did the willingness of Alito and Thomas to dissent from large majorities.

Both the liberal and conservative wings demonstrated strong internal cohesion overall across the seventeen Supreme Court annual terms reviewed. Nearly all justices were about twice as likely to agree with a member of their own wing in these cases rather than to agree with a justice in the opposing camp. Justices Gorsuch and Kennedy were the two exceptions, with Kennedy's record proving the most notable. Remarkably, Kennedy's 215 votes in nonunanimous cases were almost as likely to align with positions taken by a more liberal justice (62 percent) as to agree with a fellow member of the conservative wing (63 percent). Although Kennedy was more moderate than his fellow conservatives, that alone cannot explain this anomaly. Instead, as clarified later in this chapter, the conditions under which Kennedy voted to support the interests of individuals drawn into the criminal justice system are what make his record distinctive.

Minimum Winning Coalitions: When Every Vote Counts

Over one-fourth of all criminal justice cases during the first seventeen terms of the Roberts Court era hinged on a single vote (see table 2). These cases include several major 5–4 rulings discussed in later chapters on issues such as gun rights, prison overcrowding, and capital punishment. Studies of judicial behavior often focus on such split decisions as indicators of ideological polarization on the Supreme Court and to demonstrate the potential power of a single vote.

Justice Kennedy's regular presence in five-member criminal justice majorities was unmatched on the Roberts Court (see also table 4). He joined ten more such majorities than did the liberal centrist Breyer, and that edge was *after* Breyer served an additional four years following Kennedy's retirement. In many of those cases, Kennedy provided a critical "swing vote." A swing vote is an outcome-determining vote from a conservative justice that supports a liberal decision or from a liberal justice that supports a conservative decision. Outcome-determining votes are those in which the direction of the outcome would change if a given justice had voted differently. Thus, all votes in a five-member majority are outcome-determining ones but not necessarily swing votes.

Although the justices aligned in different configurations to produce various minimum winning coalitions, as shown in table 7, these groupings often broke along perceived ideological lines. Among the 107 five-member majorities indicated in table 2, 40 percent involved all of the justices from the court's conservative wing lined up against all of those from the liberal wing. These cases included notable decisions concerning such issues as gun rights, capital punishment, and search and seizure.

The most notable finding concerns Kennedy's unrivaled role as the court's swing voter. With respect to criminal justice cases decided by the Roberts Court before he retired in 2018, Kennedy supplied 40 percent of all outcome-determining swing votes. He was *the* swing voter in over three-fourths of cases decided by a single swing vote. Kennedy's regular presence in criminal justice majorities (see table 4) and his leading role in providing decisive fifth votes in several cases (see tables 4 and 7) prompted some court observers to suggest the high court should have been characterized as the "Kennedy court" in light of his influence.[41]

Justice Kennedy's votes in minimum winning coalitions account for his high interagreement rate with members of the court's liberal wing (see tables 5 and 6). Had he voted like his fellow conservatives in these cases decided by a single vote, his mean interagreement rate with liberal justices would have been about average for a member of the conservative wing. In addition, his rate of agreeing with other conservatives would have been

Table 7. Minimum Winning Coalition Types in Criminal Justice Cases, Highlighting Swing Voters and Majority Opinions Authored by Swing Voter, 2005–2022

Type of Coalition by Wing Membership / Swing Voter(s) (Cases)

A. All Members of Conservative Wing v. Members of Liberal Wing (42)
No swing voter:[a]

> *United States v. Tsarnaev* (2022), *New York State Rifle & Pistol Association v. Bruen* (2022), *Vega v. Tekoh* (2022), *Brown v. Davenport* (2022), *Shinn v. Ramirez* (2022), *Egbert v. Boule* (2022), *Edwards v. Vannoy* (2021), *Jones v. Mississippi* (2021), *Pereida v. Wilkinson* (2021), *Hernandez v. Mesa* (2020), *McKinney v. Arizona* (2020), *Kansas v. Garcia* (2020), *Barton v. Barr* (2020), *Nielsen v. Preap* (2019), *Bucklew v. Precythe* (2019), *Murphy v. Smith* (2018), *Currier v. Virginia* (2018), *Davila v. Davis* (2017), *Ziglar v. Abbasi* (2017), *Davis v. Ayala* (2015), *Glossip v. Gross* (2015), *Clapper v. Amnesty International* (2013), *Salinas v. Texas* (2013), *Florence v. Board of Chosen Freeholders* (2012), *Chamber of Commerce v. Whiting* (2011), *Cullen v. Pinholster* (2011), *Connick v. Thompson* (2011), *Berghuis v. Thompkins* (2010), *McDonald v. City of Chicago* (2010), *Montejo v. Louisiana* (2009), *Herring v. United States* (2009), *Ashcroft v. Iqba* (2009), *Dist. Attorney's Office v. Osborne* (2009), *District of Columbia v. Heller* (2008), *Bowles v. Russell* (2007), *Lawrence v. Florida* (2007), *Schriro v. Landrigan* (2007), *Uttecht v. Brown* (2007), *Ayers v. Belmontes* (2006), *Kansas v. Marsh* (2006), *Brown v. Sanders* (2006), *Hudson v. Michigan* (2006)*

B. One Conservative and Four Liberal Justices (39)
Kennedy:

> *McWilliams v. Dunn* (2017), *Moore v. Texas* (2017), *Pena-Rodriguez v. Colorado* (2017), *City of Los Angeles v. Patel* (2015), *Brumfield v. Cain* (2015), *Kingsley v. Hendrickson* (2015), *Hall v. Florida* (2014), *Abramski v. United States* (2014), *Peugh v. United States* (2013), *Trevino v. Thaler* (2013), *McQuiggin v. Perkins* (2013), *Missouri v. Frye* (2012), *Lafler v. Cooper* (2012), *Miller v. Alabama* (2012), *Dorsey v. United States* (2012), *J. D. B. v. North Carolina* (2011), *Turner v. Rogers* (2011), *Freeman v. United States* (2011), *Brown v. Plata* (2011), *Corley v. United States* (2009), *United States v. Denedo* (2009), *Kennedy v. Louisiana* (2008), *Boumediene v. Bush* (2008), *Smith v. Texas* (2007), *Panetti v. Quarterman* (2007), *Abdul-Kabir v. Quarterman* (2007), *Brewer v. Quarterman* (2007), *Hamdan v. Rumsfeld* (2006), *Georgia v. Randolph* (2006), *House v. Bell* (2006)*

Table 7 (continued)

Type of Coalition by Wing Membership / Swing Voter(s) (Cases)

Roberts:
    Madison v. Alabama (2019), *Carpenter v. United States* (2018)

Gorsuch:
    McGirt v. Oklahoma (2020), *United States v. Haymond* (2019), *United States v. Davis* (2019), *Sessions v. Dimaya* (2018)

Scalia:
    United States v. Gonzalez-Lopez (2006)

Thomas:
    Alleyne v. United States (2013)

Alito:
    Gundy v. United States (2019)

C. One Liberal and Four Conservative Justices (8)
Breyer:
    Stokeling v. United States (2019), *Mitchell v. Wisconsin* (2019), *Navarette v. California* (2014), *Maryland v. King* (2013), *Williams v. Illinois* (2012)

Ginsburg:
    Mont v. United States (2019), *Hemi Group v. City of New York* (2010)

Stevens:
    Irizarry v. United States (2008)

D. Two Conservative and Three Liberal Justices (16)
Scalia and Thomas:
    Florida v. Jardines (2013), *Bullcoming v. New Mexico* (2011), *Magwood v. Patterson* (2010), *Arizona v. Gant* (2009), *Melendez-Diaz v. Massachusetts* (2009), *United States v. Santos* (2008)

Scalia and Kennedy:
    Missouri v. McNeely (2013)

Thomas and Gorsuch:
    Concepcion v. United States (2022), *Borden v. United States* (2021)

Roberts and Kavanaugh:
    Nance v. Ward (2022), *Torres v. Madrid* (2021)

Roberts and Kennedy:
    Arizona v. United States (2012)

Table 7 (continued)

Type of Coalition by Wing Membership / Swing Voter(s) (Cases)

Roberts and Alito:
  Yates v. United States (2015)

Kennedy and Alito:
  Paroline v. United States (2013), *Oregon v. Ice* (2009)

Alito and Thomas:
  Dolan v. United States (2010)

E. Two Liberal and Three Conservative Justices (2)
  Ginsburg and Breyer:
  <u>*Chavez-Meza v. United States*</u> (2018)

Breyer and Souter:
  James v. United States (2007)

Note: <u>Underlined case</u> denotes majority opinion authored by a swing voter (*n* = 26).
[a] Eight of these cases ended with all six justices from the court's conservative wing lined up against the three justices from the liberal wing. Consequently, they are included here, although the majority in each was not a minimum winning coalition. Those cases are *United States v. Tsarnaev* (2022); *New York State Rifle & Pistol Association v. Bruen* (2022); *Vega v. Tekoh* (2022); *Brown v. Davenport* (2022); *Shinn v. Ramirez* (2022); *Egbert v. Boule* (2022); *Edwards v. Vannoy* (2021); and *Jones v. Mississippi* (2021).

near that of Chief Justice Roberts. In other words, what most distinguished Kennedy's criminal justice voting record was not just that he supported rights of individuals more often than his fellow conservatives, but that when he did, he typically agreed with the entire liberal wing, and often in the court's most divided cases.

Justice Kennedy cast decisive votes for liberal outcomes in cases concerning a range of criminal justice issues. For example, he supported rights of the accused in cases concerning Fourth Amendment search and seizure (for example, *Georgia v. Randolph*, 2006), Fifth Amendment self-incrimination (for example, *J. D. B. v. North Carolina*, 2011), Sixth Amendment right to counsel (for example, *Lafler v. Cooper*, 2012), and Eighth Amendment cruel and unusual punishments (for example, *Kennedy v. Louisiana*, 2008). Yet, in several other cases raising related issues, Kennedy favored conservative positions. Consequently, some analysts portray Kennedy's criminal justice voting record as having been guided more by a pragmatic, case-by-case approach than by a consistent approach to constitutional interpretation.[42]

Although Scalia and Thomas provided fewer decisive votes for liberal criminal justice outcomes than did Kennedy, their pro-defendant positions were somewhat more predictable. For example, Scalia routinely supported individuals' claims in Sixth Amendment Confrontation Clause cases during both the Roberts Court and Rehnquist Court eras.[43] Similarly, Thomas's liberal swing vote in *Alleyne v. United States* (2013) requiring that any fact that increases a mandatory minimum sentence be submitted to the jury was an extension of his earlier positions concerning the Sixth Amendment right to trial by jury.[44] Justices Scalia and Thomas cast the only two swing votes in six criminal justice cases. This was more than any other duo, and most of those cases raised questions regarding searches or the Confrontation Clause. As noted earlier, Scalia and Thomas also voted together in dissent from several large conservative majorities. It is not surprising, then, that they were frequent allies in criminal justice cases when judged by their voting interagreement rates (see table 5).

Justice Scalia's passing undoubtedly affected the internal dynamics of the court in several ways, including altering Thomas's role. In a case involving a prohibition on firearms possession that was argued just weeks after Scalia's death (*Voisine v. United States*, 2016), Thomas asked his first question during oral arguments in over a decade. Adam Liptak, the *New York Times* reporter who covered the Supreme Court, observed, "Perhaps Justice Scalia's death was a sort of passing of the baton, leaving Justice Thomas as the only member" to defend the type of originalist interpretive approach he shared with Scalia.[45] Shortly after Scalia's death, Thomas for the first time began citing Scalia's nonjudicial writings in dissenting and concurring opinions.[46] It is unclear whether this was simply an homage to a like-minded ally or a signal of Thomas's intent to advance forcefully the originalist approach that he shared with Scalia.

Several commentators predicted Chief Justice Roberts would cast the most frequent swing votes after Kennedy retired.[47] However, the rate at which Roberts provided a pivotal fifth liberal vote increased only modestly. It was not until his thirteenth year on the court that Roberts cast his first solo swing vote in a criminal justice case (*Carpenter v. United States*, 2018).

Notably, Trump-appointee Justice Gorsuch supplied swing votes in six criminal justice cases during his first five full terms on the court. That was almost twice as many as the Roberts Court's numerical average for a justice over a five-year period. In addition to twice defecting from the conservative camp with Thomas to produce 5–4 liberal outcomes in cases affecting sentence lengths (*Concepcion v. United States*, 2022; *Borden v. United States*, 2021), Gorsuch provided the lone swing vote in four other criminal justice cases. He also wrote the majority opinions in three of those cases.[48]

Assigning the task of writing the court's majority opinion to the swing or median justice is recognized as a particularly attractive tactic to reward support from the pivotal voter and to preserve or expand a fragile majority.[49] By assigning the majority opinion to the justice viewed as potentially least committed to the majority's position, others in the majority hope the opinion writer will convince himself or herself to avoid second thoughts when bearing the responsibility for generating the rationale and reasoning for the majority's position.[50] For the 2005–22 period, the justice providing a swing vote authored the court's majority opinion in twenty-seven of the sixty-five criminal justice cases ending in a five-member majority that included at least one swing vote.

Majority Opinion Authorship: The Voice of the Court

Few observers doubt the importance of the justice who is chosen to write the reasoning for the court's majority opinion. While the assigned author's opinion must reflect the viewpoints of other justices in the majority, the author's particular approach, tone, and arguments can shape jurisprudence and, more broadly, public policy and policy debates. Justices varied significantly in their opportunities to write for the court. The differences in opportunities to write majority opinions were shaped by several factors. For example, not all justices served during all terms reviewed, and therefore some participated in fewer case decisions. In addition, some justices were much more likely to vote with the majority than were other justices.

To account for such differences, we utilize an opinion authorship ratio (OAR) for each justice by majority type. An OAR exceeding 1.0 indicates that a justice wrote more majority opinions than expected given that justice's presence in majorities of different sizes. By contrast, a score under 1.0 shows that the justice received fewer majority opinion assignments than expected. This measure accounts for differences in the probability of being assigned a majority opinion for a unanimous court (1/9) versus a minimum winning coalition (1/5). The high percentage of criminal justice cases decided by the Roberts Court without a single dissenter and another notable portion decided by a single vote (see table 2) underscore the importance of controlling for such differences.

Most judicial research using an OAR measure seeks to examine how chief justices assign majority opinions. Consequently, those OARs refer to "opinion *assignment* ratios." The focus here on majority opinion authorship (regardless of assigner) leads to a slight change in the label and construction of the opinion *authorship* ratio. Specifically, the OAR is the observed number of majority opinions written by a justice divided by the expected number of majority opinions written by that justice. The expected number of authored opinions is the sum of the probabilities of writing any given majority opinion, as determined by the justice's presence in the majority and the size of the majority. For example, we would expect a justice who joined ten majorities, each with five members, to author two of those court decisions.

Overall, criminal justice majority opinion assignments were equitably distributed, as most Roberts Court justices posted a total OAR of between 0.9 and 1.1. Several nonideological considerations affect who writes a particular criminal justice decision for the court, such as a specific justice's interest or expertise in the legal issue examined in the case. Assignments are also affected by the relative availability of each majority member to tackle writing an opinion for the court given his or her pending workload of previous opinion assignments in other cases. As it turned out, the distribution of criminal justice majority opinion assignments over the first seventeen years of the Roberts Court era could hardly be more equitable between the court's two ideological camps. If one randomly assigned to a member of a given majority the task of writing for the Roberts Court in each criminal justice case, we would expect the liberal justices collectively to have authored 170 majority opinions. They actually wrote 169 of these opinions.

Closer examination of findings shown in table 8, however, reveals that some justices significantly outperformed expectations in terms of their frequency of being selected to write for the court in certain contexts while receiving fewer assignments than expected with regard to other sizes of numerical majorities. For example, it is noteworthy that less than 20 percent of Sotomayor's majority criminal justice opinions were for a unanimous court and that she was assigned fewer than half of the unanimous decisions one would expect (OAR = 0.45). Chief Justice Roberts's rate of assigning

Table 8. Majority Opinion Authorship in Criminal Justice Cases, 2005–2022

| | All maj. opinions | | | N assigned by | | | Unanimous | | | N liberal-conservative opinions (OAR)[a] | | | | | |
| | | | | | | | | | | 5-member | | | All others | | |
Justice	N	(lib.)	OAR	Roberts	self	other	L	C	OAR	L	C	OAR	L	C	OAR
Breyer	47	(21)	1.06	41	0	6	6	14	(1.30)	6	2	(0.67)	9	10	(1.11)
Alito	47	(9)	1.17	46	0	1	7	13	(1.40)	0	12	(1.13)	2	13	(0.97)
Kennedy	45	(29)	1.01	29	9	7	5	5	(0.74)	14	8	(1.57)	10	3	(0.75)
Thomas	43	(10)	1.07	40	2	1	7	11	(1.17)	2	11	(1.12)	1	11	(0.91)
Ginsburg	39	(17)	0.96	34	0	5	3	16	(1.34)	4	1	(0.44)	10	5	(0.99)
Roberts	38	(18)	0.78	38	—	0	7	5	(0.78)	3	4	(0.63)	8	11	(0.86)
Scalia	33	(12)	1.14	29	1	3	3	10	(1.22)	4	4	(1.21)	5	7	(1.03)
Kagan	32	(21)	1.16	26	0	6	7	4	(1.20)	7	2	(1.15)	7	5	(1.12)
Sotomayor	26	(19)	0.83	20	0	6	2	3	(0.45)	6	0	(0.73)	11	4	(1.27)
Stevens	15	(11)	1.08	10	5	0	1	0	(0.20)	4	1	(1.39)	6	3	(1.73)
Souter	10	(9)	0.85	8	0	2	4	0	(0.96)	2	0	(0.63)	3	1	(0.90)
Gorsuch	10	(5)	1.00	6	0	4	0	0	(0.00)	3	4	(2.06)	2	1	(0.74)
Kavanaugh	9	(2)	1.03	9	0	0	0	1	(0.52)	0	3	(1.07)	2	3	(1.25)
Barrett	2	(1)	0.55	1	0	1	0	0	(0.00)	0	0	(0.00)	1	1	(0.85)
Totals	396	(184)		337	17	42	52–82			55–52			77–78		

[a] OAR = opinion authorship ratio. O'Connor did not author a majority opinion in any of the six cases in which she participated during this period.

majority opinions to Stevens in unanimous criminal justice decisions was lower still (OAR = 0.20). Remarkably, despite being two of the most consistent liberal justices on the court, Sotomayor and Stevens authored only three of the fifty-two liberal unanimous criminal justice opinions handed down during the period analyzed.

Chief Justice Roberts's apparent reluctance to assign unanimous criminal justice opinions to Stevens and Sotomayor may reflect his perception that these justices were too likely to espouse broader interpretations of defendants' rights than he preferred. If true, this would be consistent with his reliance on Ginsburg and Breyer, the more cautious members of the liberal wing, to write for the full court. Ginsburg and Breyer tended to favor narrower rulings, which may have appealed to Roberts's sensibilities and policy preferences. Moreover, it is striking that thirty of the thirty-nine unanimous criminal justice decisions assigned by Roberts to Ginsburg and Breyer were conservative rulings that supported law enforcement interests. Such strategic choices may demonstrate Roberts's willingness to forgo certain opportunities to advance the articulation of conservative legal reasoning, at least in the short term, in exchange for maintaining consensus. Moreover, no justice during the first seventeen years of the Roberts Court era authored more unanimous liberal criminal justice opinions than did Roberts, Alito, and Thomas, who each wrote seven. Justice Kagan, the other liberal who seemed less doctrinaire than Stevens and Sotomayor, also received seven unanimous liberal opinion assignments. These choices suggest the chief justice may have acted on a desire to maintain consensus, limit the scope of the reasoning, and avoid the articulation of expansive liberal ideas.

With respect to other formal powers of a chief justice, the preceding analysis illustrates the one power for which it is possible to document influence over the court's production of law and policy. Certainly, the chief justice's powers over making initial recommendations about which cases to consider for hearing and ensuring that justices have fair opportunities to speak during oral arguments influence the decisions ultimately issued by the court. However, the nature and extent of influence from the exercise of these powers are subtle, uncertain, and unmeasurable. Conclusions about the chief justice's precise motives for making each majority opinion assignment are necessarily speculative. Yet, observers familiar with the unique interpretive approaches, priorities, and tone in individual justices' opinions can readily recognize the impact of choosing one justice instead of another for writing the court's opinion on a specific issue.

The motivations behind other assignments made by Roberts seem clearer. For instance, no justice agreed with Roberts in more criminal justice cases than did Alito, and Alito led all justices in the number of criminal justice opinion assignments from Roberts. Alito wrote a disproportionate number of unanimous opinions and, like Thomas, also frequently authored conservative majority opinions in cases decided by a single vote. Roberts could choose Alito to write for the court with confidence that their thinking was aligned for many issues. Aside from relative newcomers Kavanaugh and Barrett, Alito was the only justice to write just once for a criminal justice case majority that did not include Chief Justice Roberts (*Ocasio v. United States*, 2016). That opinion was assigned by Justice Kennedy in the role of senior associate justice in the majority. Few other justices had an opportunity to assign criminal justice majority opinions to Alito. He was part of only eight majorities from which Roberts dissented. Thus, there were very few cases in which Alito was eligible to receive a majority opinion assignment from a senior associate justice.

Many of the changes over time in the justices' majority opinion authorship rates were modest and expected. For example, it was not surprising that the authorship ratios with respect to unanimous conservative criminal justice decisions increased slightly for most remaining justices after Scalia's death. Scalia had been something of a specialist in that area, authoring almost 50 percent more than his expected share of unanimous conservative decisions. Other shifts were more dramatic, such as the diverging trajectories of Kagan and Sotomayor writing for five-member majorities in criminal justice cases. These justices often were part of the same minimum winning coalitions, and Kagan joined the court just a year and a day after Sotomayor. Kagan's authorship rate in such cases continued to languish through her fifth term. By then, she had been a member of twenty-one minimum winning coalitions but had written for the majority only twice in these cases (OAR = 0.48). Over the subsequent seven terms, Kagan was part of eighteen such majorities and authored the court's opinion in seven of those cases (OAR = 1.94). Meanwhile, Sotomayor wrote five majority criminal justice opinions in cases decided by one vote in her first six years on the court, followed by a gap of over six years without any such assignments.

The mix of issues examined in different cases and the demands of the court's full docket likely explain these trends. However, the importance of the court's changing composition and configuration of majority alignments should not be discounted as possible influential factors. In his role as senior associate justice in the majority, Kennedy assigned several of the court's majority opinions in 5–4 criminal justice cases during Sotomayor's and Kagan's first years on the court. Kennedy tended to tap Breyer or Sotomayor for the task when he did not assign the opinion to himself. Most of Kagan's later criminal justice opinions for five-member majorities came after Kennedy retired, and almost all were assigned by Roberts or Ginsburg. Whether a product of interpersonal dynamics or the idiosyncrasies of case issues, these contrasting experiences demonstrate the value of looking beyond simple statistics to identify behavior patterns or relationships that may affect opinion assignment.

Decades of judicial research indicate that chief justices often assign to themselves majority opinions in particularly important cases and in cases decided by the slimmest of margins.[51] Despite voting with the majority in over 85 percent of the cases reviewed from 2005 through 2022, Roberts self-assigned relatively few criminal justice majority opinions, including those in 5–4 decisions. Chief Justice Roberts's overall OAR in criminal justice cases ranks lowest among all justices except for O'Connor and Barrett, who, collectively, participated in fewer than 10 percent of the cases reviewed. Similarly, Roberts's OAR in 5–4 cases surpasses only that of Ginsburg, O'Connor, and Barrett. Chief Justice Roberts's most notable self-assigned majority opinions tended to come in other issue areas, such as free speech and free exercise of religion under the First Amendment, partisan gerrymandering claims, and his landmark 2012 opinion upholding key elements of the Affordable Care Act.[52]

The types of criminal justice majority opinions written by Roberts changed dramatically after Scalia's death in 2016. Only nine of Roberts's first twenty-seven such opinions explained a liberal outcome, but nine of his next eleven criminal justice opinions for the court did so. The apparent shift becomes less striking upon closer inspection. For example, almost all were for cases with large majorities, as seven of Roberts's later liberal opinions produced a total of only eight dissenting votes. The only dissenters in these seven cases were Thomas (five times) and Alito (three times). Moreover, one case (*Ramirez v. Collier*, 2021) regarding a death-row resident's request to have his pastor lay hands on him during his execution concerned the exercise of religious practices, a topic for which Roberts tended to interpret individual rights broadly. Elsewhere, a pair of Roberts's liberal court opinions in 2017 diverged from the typical direction of his votes in cases raising claims of ineffective assistance of counsel. However, both cases included highly unusual circumstances that were unlikely to be replicated in subsequent disputes before the court.[53]

One would expect that in a politically potent case in which a sitting president is the petitioner, a chief justice would likely self-assign and write for the court in order to place the prestige of his office visibly behind the court's announced reasoning. Chief Justice Roberts did just that in *Trump v. Vance* (2020), a case concerning a local prosecutor's access to a president's business records. Somewhat more unexpected were two liberal Fourth Amendment majority opinions authored by Roberts. He wrote for a narrow winning coalition in *Torres v. Madrid* (2020) in which the court defined "seizure" under the Constitution in ways that may have important ramifications for regulating police use of force. In *Carpenter v. United States* (2018), Roberts and other members of the majority ruled that police officers generally need a warrant before accessing a person's cell phone location data collected by wireless carriers. This was a landmark case with potentially far-reaching privacy implications that prompted Roberts's first solo swing vote in a criminal justice case. Previously, Roberts wrote for the court when it held that the warrantless search of an arrestee's cell phone violated Fourth Amendment protections. That decision in *Riley v. California* (2014) was for a unanimous court and, unlike in *Carpenter*, involved data maintained by the individual in his phone rather than by a third-party service provider. As the analysis of Fourth Amendment cases in chapter 5 will discuss, it appears that Roberts and other justices may be particularly sensitive to emerging privacy concerns affecting society in the fast-changing digital age of the twenty-first century.

Because he voted so often with the majority, Roberts made majority opinion assignment decisions in nearly seven of every eight criminal justice cases during his first seventeen years as chief justice. Consequently, experienced associate justices enjoyed relatively few opportunities to choose who would write majority opinions for the court. There was a specific type of case for which Roberts was most likely to be a dissenter and thereby relinquish the majority opinion assigner role: cases sharply dividing the court in which a five-justice majority supported the interests of the individual accused or convicted. Of the fifty-nine criminal justice majorities without Roberts during his first seventeen years as chief justice, forty-six had minimum winning coalitions producing a liberal outcome. Justice Kennedy emerged as the dominant voice of the court in these instances, authoring more 5–4 opinions for the Roberts Court than any other two justices combined. All but one of Kennedy's fourteen liberal majority opinions for a five-member majority were assigned by someone other than the chief justice, namely by Stevens or by Kennedy himself as the most senior member of liberal majorities after Stevens's retirement in 2010.

Justice Stevens and Chief Justice Roberts often ended up on opposing sides of decisions. Indeed, the chief justice's lowest agreement rate through the 2015 term in nonunanimous criminal justice cases was with Stevens, who became the senior associate justice during the Rehnquist Court era following the retirement of Harry Blackmun in 1994. Remarkably, Roberts and Stevens agreed only twice in the thirty-six criminal justice cases ending in 5–4 decisions during their years together on the court. Of the five criminal justice majority opinions that Steven self-assigned, four were in cases decided by a single vote.[54]

With respect to criminal justice cases that deeply divided the Roberts Court, Gorsuch penned more than twice as many opinions for five-member majorities in criminal justice cases than his presence in such majorities would predict (OAR = 2.06). Nearly half of these opinions, including the landmark decision in *McGirt v. Oklahoma* (2020), were in cases in which Gorsuch provided the sole swing vote. *McGirt* concerned the authority of tribal courts over criminal charges applied against tribal members across a large area of Oklahoma, thus precluding parallel prosecutions in state courts.

The period in which outcome-determining swing votes characterized a large portion of the Roberts Court's criminal justice decisions ended, at least temporarily, with Barrett's confirmation in 2020. As a result of President Trump's three appointments, the balance between the two ideological wings on the Roberts Court shifted from a one-justice conservative advantage to a three-justice conservative advantage. Justices will continue to defect from their usual ideological allies in individual cases, but it remains to be seen how frequently these defections will occur and how often such defections determine the direction of the court's future decisions. After Barrett's confirmation, it would take the defections of two usually conservative justices to create a majority with the three liberal justices. Since late 2020, this situation was quite different from the earlier years of the Roberts Court, in which Justice Kennedy alone could determine the outcome of a case by departing from his usual conservative allies to vote with the then four-member liberal wing of the court.

Conclusion

The descriptive statistics presented in this chapter verify certain themes common in other analyses of the Roberts Court while also revealing nuances overlooked in many portrayals of the court's criminal justice decision-making. For example, the examination of the Roberts Court justices' voting patterns demonstrated that the court was indeed divided between a majority of members occupying the law enforcement–supportive conservative wing and those justices of the liberal wing who tended to favor individuals' rights. The strong voting cohesion within each camp for nonunanimous decisions painted a picture of a polarized Supreme Court for criminal justice issues. The possibility exists that this ideological polarization could affect the public's view of the Supreme Court. Judicial scholars, and Supreme Court justices themselves, often express fears about a loss of legitimacy, respect, and compliance if the public views the high court's decisions as driven by political motives rather than by legal reasoning.

After the retirements of liberal Republican appointees Stevens and Souter in the early years of the Roberts Court era, the voting records of justices on criminal justice issues became highly associated with the prior political affiliations of each justice and especially the political party affiliation of each justice's appointing president. Republican appointees, except for Stevens and Souter, were members of the court's conservative wing, and Democratic appointees were part of the liberal wing. Thus, the definition of rights and corresponding limits on law enforcement officials can be viewed as largely the product of political developments that shape the court's composition rather than as the products of constitutional principles, legal reasoning, and respect for prior case precedents. Indeed, studies of Supreme Court decision-making identify the ways in which individual justices' political values shape their decision-making.[55] To counter perceptions of the court's partisan division, Chief Justice Roberts sought to reassure the public that the Supreme Court was not driven by politics when he made statements defending the court's legitimacy and justices' purported roles as "umpires" rather than policymakers when deciding legal issues.[56]

Yet, the data also reveal broad agreement among the justices in most criminal justice cases heard by the Roberts Court, with nearly three of

every five cases through the 2021 term generating no more than two dissenters, and 134 out of 396 cases decided unanimously. Furthermore, the
court's narrowest majorities favored the rights of individual defendants
slightly more often than they upheld law enforcement interests. Both the
large percentage of unanimous or near-unanimous decisions and the
frequency of the Roberts Court ruling in a rights-affirming fashion are
important but often overlooked characteristics of this era's criminal justice jurisprudence. Even in a politically polarized era with justices whose
decisions are shaped by their political values and policy preferences, there
can be a strong consensus among frequently divided justices concerning
the existence and definition of specific rights in criminal justice.

With Kennedy's retirement, the court lost one of the most influential
median justices in Supreme Court history. He was also the Roberts Court's
primary author of split criminal justice decisions. Will the post-Kennedy
transformation of the court's majority through the appointments by
President Trump lead conservative justices to accept for hearing criminal
justice cases intended to alter existing legal principles and public policies?
As a law professor said shortly after the announcement of Kennedy's
retirement, "With a more reliably conservative replacement, it's possible
we'll see more aggressive efforts by right-wing advocacy groups to upset
precedents they were willing to live with under Kennedy."[57] The choices
that justices make about which cases to accept for decision are shaped by
the specific cases presented to them by advocacy groups and individual
attorneys. In the post-Kennedy era, the Roberts Court issued controversial decisions that dramatically altered legal doctrines concerning such
matters as a right of choice for abortion, affirmative action in college admissions, and environmental protection.[58] Specific justices' opinions make
suggestions about potential changes they wish to consider. For example,
Justices Thomas and Gorsuch asserted in a dissenting opinion that an
originalist interpretation of the Sixth Amendment right to counsel should
eliminate both the requirement of state-provided attorneys for indigent
defendants and minimum standards for defense attorneys' performance
(*Garza v. Idaho*, 2019). It remains to be seen, however, whether and how
the Roberts Court will make such significant conservative changes in the
realm of criminal justice.

Will Gorsuch assume a variation of Kennedy's role and continue to
offer occasional support for liberal outcomes in certain divided decisions? If so, will he be able to persuade at least one other member of the

now-larger conservative wing to join him in order to have five votes for that outcome? Could Kavanaugh turn out to be the new median justice for some issues in light of his unwillingness to describe himself as a devotee of originalist constitutional interpretation? The Trump appointees will make clearer over time whether they share Alito's consistent favoritism for law enforcement interests or whether, like Kennedy, they see reasons to part company with their usual conservative allies for specific issues affecting constitutional rights in criminal justice. Ultimately, the data tables and discussion of voting tendencies can only suggest the potential importance of compositional change and other influences on the Roberts Court's criminal justice decision-making. Clearer understanding of the court's impact on specific criminal justice issues requires analysis of the justices' decisions and reasoning.

3. BLOCKING LEGISLATIVE DEFINITIONS OF CRIMES

In news reports and scholarly literature, analyses of the Supreme Court's decisions affecting criminal justice typically focus on cases concerning the definition of constitutional rights in the justice process. This focus reflects the central debates about the Supreme Court's role in shaping the justice system that emerged through the Warren Court's decisions expanding the definitions of rights and limiting the authority of police in the 1960s. Because of the scholarly and journalistic attention to Supreme Court decisions concerning the constitutional rights of suspects, defendants, and imprisoned individuals, the high court's decisions on First and Second Amendment issues are less frequently included in analyses of the court's impact on criminal justice.[1] These two amendments are often discussed as independent topics separate from criminal justice,[2] even though commentators can readily acknowledge the ways in which they can intersect with and affect criminal justice.[3] During the Roberts Court era, decisions concerning the First and Second Amendments assumed new importance for their potential impacts on criminal justice. In particular, the court addressed issues concerning the definition of the First Amendment's protection for free speech. With respect to the Second Amendment's words about the right to "keep and bear arms," the Roberts Court era saw the high court make unprecedented new decisions about gun rights. The common element that links these two amendments together when analyzing Roberts Court decisions is that their greatest impacts occur when the court is blocking legislatures from criminalizing specific conduct. Certain decisions in which the Roberts Court invalidated statutes as violative of First Amendment or Second Amendment rights may ultimately prove to be the most significant decisions of this era in Supreme Court history.

Criminal Laws and Free Speech

The First Amendment does not always come to mind as a component of the Bill of Rights that is connected to criminal justice. Yet, legislatures have used criminal laws to block or limit expressive conduct throughout American history. Moreover, without constitutional protections, there are risks that criminal laws could be used without proper justification to block free exercise of religion. In contemporary times, First Amendment debates related to criminal justice focus primarily on expressive conduct, including the technological expansion of expression through social media.

The Roberts Court's decisions produced competing perspectives about the court's impact on the First Amendment. There were free speech advocates who found this court to be a strong defender of individual rights, while others saw it as creating an era with severe limits on speech perceived to be threatening to social order.[4] For example, one free speech advocate argued that the Roberts Court was more protective of unpopular speech than any other in history,[5] but another claimed that the court does not have an expansive view of the First Amendment.[6] The difference in opinion was understandable. The Roberts Court was responsible for liberal decisions expanding the rights of criminal defendants under the First Amendment, including the rights of animal cruelty video producers (*United States v. Stevens*, 2010) and the rights of those lying about their military service (*United States v. Alvarez*, 2012). These decisions led First Amendment lawyer Floyd Abrams to claim, "It is unpopular speech, distasteful speech, that most requires First Amendment protection, and on that score, no prior Supreme Court has been as protective as this."[7]

On the other hand, the Roberts Court was also responsible for two of the most controversial campaign finance cases in US history, both decided on First Amendment grounds. *Citizens United v. Federal Election Commission* (2010) and *McCutcheon v. Federal Election Commission* (2014) declared that corporations have First Amendment expression rights embodied in their political campaign contributions, thereby virtually eliminating campaign contribution limits for corporations. These cases implicated criminal justice by precluding Congress and state legislatures from creating criminal laws that would significantly restrict the role of corporations and other organizations in using their substantial financial assets to affect elections and influence elected policymakers.

Contexts of Expressive Conduct

During the Rehnquist Court era, the high court issued several decisions limiting the application of federal statutes by protecting free speech interests. In *Reno v. ACLU* (1997), *Ashcroft v. Free Speech Coalition* (2002), and *Ashcroft v. ACLU* (2004), the Rehnquist Court examined such matters as laws to prevent minors from gaining online access to certain materials. The Rehnquist Court's majorities in these cases took a critical view of content-based federal statutory restrictions and found the coverage in their wording to go beyond the narrow harms that the government could legitimately target with a prohibition. The Roberts Court subsequently continued that approach when individuals raised First Amendment claims as a means to resist the imposition of prosecution and punishment.

In *United States v. Stevens*, the court ruled that the First Amendment protects the rights of individuals to buy and sell depictions of animal cruelty. The case concerned a man who sold dog fighting videos over the internet and was indicted for violating federal law. Defendant Stevens argued that the Animal Welfare Act violated his First Amendment right to free speech. Writing for eight justices, with only Justice Alito in dissent, Chief Justice Roberts's majority opinion declared that the congressional statute that criminalized depictions of animal cruelty was overly broad and therefore violated the First Amendment. The majority concluded that speech will be deemed as unprotected by the First Amendment only in instances in which its use is linked to human abuses or the production of such expressions is itself illegal across the nation, such as in the case of child pornography.[8] In the eyes of those intent on limiting governmental authority to impose content-based restrictions on videos, this was considered a notable liberal victory.[9]

Similarly, the unanimous eight-member court struck down a state law that prohibited people previously convicted of sex crimes from accessing social networking sites that are open to minors (*Packingham v. North Carolina*, 2017). The case was argued while one seat on the court remained vacant after the death of Justice Scalia. The law was intended to prevent certain individuals from using social networking sites to cultivate or contact potential child victims. The justices unanimously concluded that the law was overly broad by barring access to an important contemporary arena for obtaining information about current events, jobs, and other benign communications. The justices presumed that a narrowly tailored law might survive review if it focused solely on prohibiting communications with minors rather than on closing off social networking sites entirely.

The pervasive use of social media sites and text messages developed during the twenty-first-century Roberts Court era. As a result, the justices faced new challenges in determining when computer and cell phone communications could be considered as threats eligible for prosecution. In *Elonis v. United States* (2015), the court reversed the conviction of a man who used Facebook to post graphically violent rap music lyrics and other communications perceived as threatening by his coworkers and estranged wife. He was convicted under a federal law criminalizing threats in interstate commerce. The jury was instructed that he could be convicted of a crime if a reasonable person perceived the communications to constitute a threat. Chief Justice Roberts wrote the majority opinion in the 8–1 decision. The majority insisted that there must be a greater showing of intent, either because the individual intended to make a threat or was aware that the communication would be received as a threat.

The Roberts Court later considered a related case in which a man had been sentenced to prison under a state's stalking law for sending hundreds of Facebook messages to a stranger that the targeted individual perceived as threatening. The state stalking law authorized conviction for communications that would cause a reasonable person to suffer serious emotional distress and that did, in fact, cause emotional distress. In *Counterman v. Colorado* (2023), Justice Kagan's opinion for a seven-member majority overturned the individual's conviction. The opinion reiterated that a reasonable person's perception of a threat did not adequately establish the level of intent required for a criminal stalking conviction. Instead, there must be proof that the communicator had a subjective understanding of the threatening nature of the messages. The court clarified that recklessness, namely the conscious disregard of a substantial risk that the conduct causes harm, is sufficient as proof of intent. Justices Thomas and Barrett dissented. In the aftermath of the decision, stalking victims and their advocates were gravely concerned that the court's decision significantly weakened potential legal protections against communications that make people live in constant fear for their safety.[10]

As indicated by the foregoing case decisions, the Roberts Court supported certain First Amendment claims when confronted with statutes criminalizing unpopular and distasteful forms of expression. One the most notable aspects of these decisions was the high degree of consensus among the Roberts Court justices from both sides of their ideological divide. One case was unanimous (*Packingham*), two cases were 8–1 decisions (*Stevens* and *Elonis*), and one was a 7–2 decision (*Counterman*). None of these cases created the 5–4 divisions that, with respect to other issues, gained significant attention as illuminating the stark differences between the court's liberal and conservative wings.

In *United States v. Alvarez*, the court considered a different form of expressive conduct in a context separate from government efforts to regulate online activity. A six-member majority held that telling lies about one's military service is a form of protected expression. Alvarez was charged with violating the Stolen Valor Act, a federal law that made it illegal to lie about receiving certain medals for one's military service. Specifically, the act was violated when someone "falsely represents himself or herself, verbally or in writing, to have been awarded any decoration or medal authorized by Congress for the Armed Forces of the United States."[11] While running for office in a local election, Alvarez falsely claimed to be a retired Marine who was awarded the Congressional Medal of Honor, the military's highest award for valor. When charged with a crime for violating the Stolen Valor Act, Alvarez claimed the act was an unconstitutional infringement on his free speech rights under the First Amendment.

In a plurality opinion written by Justice Kennedy, the court found the law to be unconstitutional. Justice Kennedy noted that laws imposing content-based speech restrictions are rarely permissible. Making false statements is not one of the historical categories of expression that sit outside the boundaries of First Amendment protection. As Kennedy concluded, "The Nation well knows that one of the costs of the First Amendment is that it protects the speech we detest as well as the speech we embrace."[12]

In dissent, Justice Alito, joined by Justices Scalia and Thomas, asserted that the First Amendment should not protect lies that cause actual harm. The dissenters saw the tolerance of lies about awards for military valor as undermining the value and legitimacy of military honors. Justice Alito said that the statute did not threaten free speech because it was narrowly tailored to address knowingly false statements about a factual matter within the knowledge of the speaker. To Alito and the dissenters, there was no legitimate interest to be protected in applying the First Amendment to such false expressions.

In the foregoing cases, specific justices stood out as more likely than others to support the criminalization of expression. Two justices were the notable dissenters in the cases in which the majority invalidated criminal statutes on First Amendment grounds. Justice Thomas dissented in three cases (*Alvarez, Elonis,* and *Counterman*). In *Elonis,* Thomas was the sole dissenter when the other justices, who spanned the ideological spectrum, supported the First Amendment claim concerning Facebook posts of violent lyrics that referenced the individual's estranged wife and coworkers. Justice Alito dissented in the cases concerning animal cruelty videos (*Stevens*) and lies about military medals for valor (*Alvarez*). In so doing, they stood out from their colleagues as the justices least inclined to protect First Amendment expressions that the government sought to criminalize.[13]

By contrast, one of the noteworthy aspects of free speech cases during the Roberts Court was the sheer number of such cases and the percentage of majority opinions that Chief Justice Roberts assigned to himself for authorship. Some commentators pointed to this as evidence that Roberts was a strong defender of the First Amendment.[14] According to the Supreme Court Judicial Database, Chief Justice Roberts wrote majority opinions in more than one-third of the Roberts Court's forty-one free speech cases through the end of the 2019 term.[15] This doubled the number of majority opinions authored by the next most prolific author on free speech issues, Justice Kennedy.[16] The number of majority opinions written by the chief justice invited the inference that these issues were of importance to Roberts and a topical area in which he perhaps hoped to create a legacy.[17]

In general, the Roberts Court limited the scope of potential criminal liability when analyzing content-based government restrictions that collided with First Amendment protections for free expression. There were, however, certain aspects of communicative content that the court majority viewed as especially harmful and therefore permissibly subject to criminalization. In *United States v. Williams* (2008), the Roberts Court identified a specific subject for which it was willing to reject First Amendment protections. A seven-member majority produced a conservative outcome that declined to provide First Amendment protections for child pornography. In addressing the harms from producing and transmitting such images, Congress enacted the Prosecutorial Remedies and Other Tools to End the Exploitation of Children Today Act of 2003 (PROTECT Act). The PROTECT Act made it illegal to traffic in child pornography, whether or not the pornography depicted actual children rather than adult actors portraying teens. The law criminalized the act of trafficking if the individual believed it to be child pornography or sought to convince others of the same.

Writing for the majority, Justice Scalia upheld the PROTECT Act because the statute prohibited transactions, commercial or otherwise, of material that the distributor knowingly communicated as including child pornography. As Scalia stated, "Offers to engage in illegal transactions are categorically excluded from First Amendment protection" because "offers to give or receive what it is unlawful to possess have no social value and thus, like obscenity, enjoy no First Amendment protection." Justice Scalia took great pains to distinguish this decision from other cases that provided First Amendment protections for speech. He noted that advocacy, in the abstract, of criminal behavior is protected by the First Amendment. As he explained, "The Act before us does not prohibit advocacy of child pornography, but only [prohibits] offers to provide or requests to obtain it." Thus, he concluded that, "in sum, we hold that offers to provide or requests to obtain child pornography are categorically excluded from the First Amendment."[18] Justices Souter and Ginsburg dissented.

The Roberts Court majority approved other content-based restrictions in *Holder v. Humanitarian Law Project* (2010). A majority of justices endorsed the constitutionality of a federal statute prohibiting organizations from providing "material support" to "foreign terrorist organizations." Thus, Congress could criminalize communications related to those activities. The statute in question prohibited various forms of assistance, including training, expert advice, and personnel, as well as financial assistance. American groups that provided humanitarian aid to organizations labeled by the United States government as "foreign terrorist organizations" challenged the statute as an unconstitutional violation of their First Amendment free speech and association rights. The groups provided expert advice and assistance in conflict resolution and peace negotiations. The two "terrorist" groups in question receiving assistance were organizations of ethnic or religious minorities in Turkey and Sri Lanka that sought to establish their own independent states within the borders of those countries. The court issued a 6–3 decision with the court's most liberal justice, Stevens, joining the five most conservative justices. The majority opinion by Chief Justice Roberts concluded that the statute was not unconstitutionally vague because it clearly identified the types of prohibited "material support," such as training and expert advice.

Chief Justice Roberts noted that the government has a compelling interest in enacting statutes aimed at reducing support for terrorist organizations. The majority opinion noted that peace groups are free to say or write anything that they wish about the conflicts in those countries as well as advocate for these groups at the United Nations. However, the court rejected the claim that if the assistance to the designated organizations is in the form of speech, such as training, advice, and expertise, then this communication is automatically protected by the First Amendment as political speech. In applying a strict scrutiny analysis, Roberts stated that courts traditionally must give significant weight to the considered judgments of the executive and legislative branches of government concerning issues of foreign affairs and national security.

In a dissenting opinion, Justice Breyer, joined by Justices Ginsburg and Sotomayor, argued that the government did not make the necessary showing that advocacy and teaching aimed at facilitating peace adversely affected American security interests. Moreover, Breyer argued that the statute could still stand if it was read to imply that violations require a knowing contribution to the terrorist activities of a foreign group, rather than teaching and advocacy aimed at advancing peaceful resolution of international conflicts.[19]

The Roberts Court's approval of legislative criminalization of speech in the *Williams* and *Holder* cases made clear that the majority viewed certain statements in the topical areas of child pornography and terrorism as more than merely objectionable expression. Unlike distasteful expression, such as animal cruelty videos and lies about military honors, child pornography and terrorism threats were characterized as sufficiently harmful to society that criminalization of expression was justified. In the eyes of the court, the government's interest in protecting society from these harms outweighed individuals' interests in advancing these particular forms of communication.

Corporate Speech

The Roberts Court's majority produced a significant impact on American society through interpretations of free speech doctrine in the realm of campaign finance laws. The court's critics described the campaign finance decisions as enabling the growth of significant and undesirable influences on elections. In effect, the Roberts Court's interpretations of the First Amendment enhanced the wealth-based power imbalance among individuals and organizational entities seeking to influence the election of public officials.[20]

Although campaign finance cases are not typically considered to be part of criminal justice jurisprudence, they define the limits of legislators' authority to regulate and criminalize financial contributions to political campaign efforts. The most striking and controversial aspect of judicial decisions on this topic concerned the Roberts Court's declaration that corporate entities' financial expenditures on elections are "free speech" that deserves the same protection as individuals' spoken expressions. To many observers, the idea that corporate entities possess constitutional rights clashed with the widespread understanding that constitutional rights are exclusively intended to protect individual human beings.

Although the court examined several cases dealing with campaign finance and the rights of corporations, two major cases stood out in particular: *Citizens United v. Federal Election Commission* (2010) and *McCutcheon v. Federal Election Commission* (2014). These cases concern criminal justice because they prohibited the criminalization of campaign finance activities that many legislators seek to regulate through deterrence and punishment. Moreover, these decisions increased wealthy entities' ability to influence the selection and actions of elected officials whose decisions shape many aspects of criminal justice policy.

The most important and impactful case was *Citizens United*. This 5–4 decision divided the justices along the liberal-conservative fault line. Although technically a "liberal" decision extending First Amendment protections, commentators and critics generally regarded the case as having a "conservative" impact. It advanced corporate and organizational interests as well as the electoral success of politicians whose ideologies and actions focused on serving the desires of corporate entities.[21] The case raised a challenge to the constitutionality of the Bipartisan Campaign Reform Act of 2002. This act made it a felony for corporations, including nonprofit corporations, to use their general treasury funds to make independent expenditures for electioneering communication or for speech that expressly advocates the election or defeat of a federal elective office candidate within a specified number of days before an election.[22] A nonprofit corporation, Citizens United, produced a film presenting a negative view of Hillary Clinton, who was a Democratic presidential candidate. The film was released to theaters and on DVD, but the organization also wanted to make it available as an on-demand offering on cable television networks, the primary outlet for political advertising and a communication mechanism targeted by the Bipartisan Campaign Reform Act. Instead of looking for narrow grounds to decide the case, the Roberts Court majority saw the statute as having a chilling impact on political speech. Thus, the five-member majority issued a ruling that significantly strengthened corporate entities' mechanisms for political influence by characterizing such financial expenditures as protected by the First Amendment.[23]

The court majority used this case to overturn the Rehnquist Court's 1990 decision in *Austin v. Michigan Chamber of Commerce* (1990). The Rehnquist Court upheld corporate campaign expenditure limits in *Austin*. The *Austin* majority took note of "the corrosive and distorting effects of immense aggregations of wealth that are accumulated with the help of the corporate form and that have little or no correlation to the public's support for the corporation's political ideal."[24] The Rehnquist era majority regarded this as a compelling rationale for the government's restriction of corporate campaign activity. In *Citizens United*, the Roberts Court majority reversed course, holding instead that limitations on corporate expenditures violate corporations' First Amendment rights to free expression. Thus, the decision struck down legislative authority to criminalize significant campaign expenditures by organizational entities.

In the majority opinion, Justice Kennedy emphasized that campaign finance laws discriminated against certain disfavored speakers, specifically corporations.[25] He saw harm to the public when legislatures sought to limit the timing and nature of elections-related communications from corporate entities. Thus, a slim majority of justices concluded that the government could not show a sufficiently compelling interest to justify limiting corporate speech in the form of campaign expenditures. In Kennedy's words, "The Government may not suppress political speech on the basis of the speaker's corporate identity."[26] As a result, political action committees (PACs) operating separately from candidates' campaigns could raise and spend unlimited funds from corporations and wealthy individuals in support of specific candidates and political parties.

On behalf of the four dissenters, Justice Stevens was especially critical of the path the majority used to arrive at its conclusion, noting that the court's decision to overturn *Austin* ignored the importance of respecting case precedents. Justice Stevens reminded the majority that it had taken it upon itself to reconsider *Austin*, since the parties had not asked for such reconsideration of that precedent in the original filings and oral arguments. The original question in *Citizens United* was narrow, and thus, in Stevens's words, "essentially, five Justices were unhappy with the limited nature of the case before us, so they changed the case to give themselves an opportunity to change the law."[27] The decision had a major impact by opening a flood of corporate money into the electoral arena. After his retirement in 2010, Stevens continued to criticize the decision and its impact, calling it variously "a giant step in the wrong direction," "a disaster for our election law," and a "very, very bad case."[28]

The Roberts Court majority extended *Citizens United*'s impact in *McCutcheon v. Federal Election Commission*, a second campaign finance case decided by a 5–4 vote. In this case, the court examined the constitutionality of the Federal Election Campaign Act and its imposition of aggregate campaign contribution limits that had been upheld by the court in *Buckley v. Valeo* (1976). In *Buckley*, the Burger Court held that the government had a compelling interest in restricting how much people could donate to campaigns. The compelling interest concerned the need to avoid the appearance that campaign contributions led to corrupting influences on candidates and elected officials. In *McCutcheon*, the Roberts Court majority reversed course on that conclusion.

With Justice Thomas writing a separate concurring opinion, Chief Justice Roberts's plurality opinion for four justices declared that the government cannot restrict contributions by individuals to various campaigns using aggregate campaign limits. Rather, Roberts argued that there is no connection—or at least none that the government had shown—between campaign contributions and the type of unsavory quid pro quo behavior the government claimed to be trying to prevent. In short, Roberts dismissed the corruption argument and championed the notion that spending money on elections is a form of free speech protected by the First Amendment.

On behalf of the dissenters, Justice Breyer criticized the opinions by Chief Justice Roberts and Justice Thomas for failing to respect precedent and imposing their own judgment over the facts in the case. Combining his criticisms of *McCutcheon* and *Citizens United*, Breyer blasted the Roberts Court's dramatic shift in First Amendment jurisprudence that "eviscerates our Nation's campaign finance laws, leaving a remnant incapable of dealing with the grave problems of democratic legitimacy that those laws were intended to resolve."[29]

These Roberts Court decisions generated grave concerns about "dark money" in politics, namely, the opportunity for undisclosed individuals to make limitless contributions to "super PACs" that make unlimited expenditures to advance their political agendas. By using the First Amendment to eliminate the powerful threat of criminal prosecution for exceeding campaign contribution limits to PACs, the Roberts Court's decisions enhanced the power of wealthy individuals and organizations. These decisions gave wealthy interests increased opportunities to influence which individuals are elected as authoritative decision-makers. Moreover, these decisions guaranteed that many policymakers would seek to serve the policy preferences of significant donors in order to receive substantial funding for successful reelection campaigns.

Not only did these decisions preclude the creation of criminal laws to limit aggregate contributions and corporate expenditures, but they also helped influence the development of criminal justice policy in the legislative and executive branches of government. For example, an analysis by a watchdog group found that from 2015 to 2019 the GEO Group, the nation's largest private corrections company and a key contractor running immigration detention centers, gave at least $1.8 million to super PACs supporting President Trump and other politicians who expanded immigration detention and advocated the use of private prisons.[30] In another example, the National Rifle Association reportedly spent more than $50 million in the 2016 election cycle to support candidates opposed to firearms regulations.[31] With its funding support from companies that manufacture firearms and related accessories, the NRA had the capacity to far outspend pro–gun control interests during that election year.[32] With these types of consequences in mind, Justice Stevens concluded his *Citizens United* dissent by expressing his dismay and bewilderment that the majority would believe our democracy suffers in some way if corporate financial influence over elections is limited: "At bottom, the Court's opinion is thus a rejection of the common sense of the American people, who have recognized a need to prevent corporations from undermining self-government since the founding, and who have fought against the distinctive corrupting potential of corporate electioneering since the days of Theodore Roosevelt. It is a strange time to repudiate that common sense. While American democracy is imperfect, few outside the majority of this Court would have thought its flaws included a dearth of corporate money in politics."[33]

The Supreme Court and Gun Rights

The Second Amendment in the Bill of Rights contains language about legal protections related to possession of firearms. The amendment says, "A well regulated Militia, being necessary to the security of a free State, the right of the people to keep and bear Arms, shall not be infringed." There are intense debates about the proper interpretation and application of this constitutional language. The debates can be quite emotional because many Americans believe that private gun ownership, the proliferation of firearms throughout the population, and the ability to carry guns are essential for preserving liberty. They see widespread gun ownership as necessary to prevent governmental tyranny and the predations of violent criminals. On the other hand, tens of thousands of Americans lose their lives each year due to firearms through suicides, accidents, individual homicides, and mass shootings. The number of firearms per one hundred residents in the United States is nearly four times greater than that of Canada, and the rate of firearms homicides is nine times greater than Canada's. Compared to Great Britain, the number of firearms per one hundred residents in the United States is twenty-six times greater, and the rate of firearms homicides is one hundred times greater.[34] Thus, a large percentage of Americans believe that restrictions on firearms sales, gun ownership, and opportunities to carry weapons are necessary for a safer society.

Historically, the US Supreme Court stayed away from clarifying the meaning of the Second Amendment and thereby inserting itself into highly contentious debates about constitutional interpretation and gun policy. In effect, the development of laws and policies concerning firearms rested primarily in the hands of legislatures. By the time of the Roberts Court era, however, the National Rifle Association had mounted a sustained effort to promote the idea that the Second Amendment should be defined as protecting a right for individuals to own and carry a wide array of firearms with limited governmental regulation. This effort, which received significant financial support from companies that manufacture guns, included campaign contributions, advocacy information directed at the public, lobbying aimed at Congress and state legislatures, and litigation in the courts. Through strategic litigation, the NRA and allied interest groups mounted legal challenges to restrictive gun laws. In the first decade of the twenty-first century, they saw their efforts come to fruition when the Roberts Court justices directly addressed and changed the meaning of the Second Amendment for gun-owning individuals.

In *United States v. Miller* (1939), a man was charged with a federal crime under the National Firearms Act of 1934 for transporting an unregistered sawed-off shotgun across state lines. He argued that the law violated his Second Amendment right to "bear arms." In rejecting this argument, the unanimous Supreme Court discussed the Second Amendment as if it concerned the ability for members of the "militia" to keep firearms, but it rejected the argument that the shotgun was a weapon with military purposes. From 1939 onward, the *Miller* decision was regarded as the Supreme Court's foundational constitutional ruling that defined the Second Amendment and firearms rights. Two implications of the Second Amendment were made quite clear by this decision, as well as by the court's disinclination to revisit the issue for nearly seven decades. First, the Second Amendment focused exclusively on states' authority to arm members of the "Militia." And second, governmental entities possessed the authority to regulate the ownership, possession, and sale of firearms.

Nearly six decades later, the Rehnquist Court addressed the authority of Congress to regulate guns in a decision that did not address the meaning of the Second Amendment. One of the provisions of the Brady Handgun Violence Prevention Act (1994) required local "chief law enforcement officers" to conduct background checks on gun buyers within a few days of the initiation of a sale by a firearms dealer. Two sheriffs, one from Arizona and one from Montana, challenged the validity of the law. They argued that local executive officers cannot be required by Congress to fulfill these duties. In a 5–4 decision in *Printz v. United States* (1997), with the majority opinion written by Justice Scalia, the Rehnquist Court agreed with the sheriffs and declared that a specific portion of the law was unconstitutional.

In his concurring opinion, Justice Thomas provided a clue that he would be willing to question the *Miller* decision's treatment of the Second Amendment as focused solely on states' ability to arm their "Militia[s]." As Thomas wrote:

> The Court has not had recent occasion to consider the substantive right safeguarded by the Second Amendment. If, however, the Second Amendment is read to confer a *personal* right to "keep and bear arms," a colorable argument exists that the Federal Government's regulatory scheme, at least as it pertains to the purely intrastate sale or possession of firearms, runs afoul of that Amendment's protections. . . . Perhaps, at some future date, this Court will have the opportunity to determine whether Justice Story was correct when he wrote [in 1833] that the right to bear arms "has justly been considered, as the palladium of the liberties of a republic." (emphasis in original)[35]

This opportunity sought by Thomas to reconsider the meaning of the Second Amendment arrived a decade later during the Roberts Court era.

The Roberts Court's Monumental Decision

The Roberts Court's first close examination of the Second Amendment came in *District of Columbia v. Heller* (2008). By local law, the District of Columbia prohibited the possession of handguns. The local laws also required that long guns be stored disassembled or incapacitated with a trigger lock when not kept in a place of business or in use for recreational purposes. The police chief of the District of Columbia could issue one-year permits for the possession of a handgun. Dick Heller, a police officer who carried a handgun while on duty at a federal building, applied for a permit for a handgun in his home. When his application was denied, he filed a lawsuit to challenge the constitutionality of the District of Columbia's restrictive laws.

In *Heller*, the Roberts Court produced a blockbuster 5–4 decision that redefined the Second Amendment as providing a legal right for individuals to own and possess firearms. The decision rejected the underlying framework of the *Miller* decision that focused on the amendment as concerned with the arming of state militias. The majority opinion was written by Justice Scalia, who was joined by Chief Justice Roberts and Justices Kennedy, Thomas, and Alito. As an advocate of an originalist approach to constitutional interpretation, Scalia argued for years that the Constitution's meaning should be determined by following "what the text was thought to mean when the people adopted it."[36] However, he and fellow originalist Thomas rarely gained the support of enough justices to make this interpretative approach the basis for law-defining majority opinions. The *Heller* majority opinion was a breakthrough for the application and impact of originalist interpretation on a major issue of constitutional rights. It purported to rest entirely on originalist interpretation, but it drew abundant criticism from analysts who questioned whether it truly followed knowable elements of legal history or merely used historical examples to obscure and rationalize the assertion of justices' political values and policy preferences.[37]

In his majority opinion, Justice Scalia highlighted what he identified as the Second Amendment's "prefatory clause" ("A well regulated Militia, being necessary to the security of a free State") and its "operative clause" ("the right of the people to keep and bear Arms, shall not be infringed"). According to Scalia, the prefatory clause in founding-era documents was typically a "statement of purpose."[38] By emphasizing his conclusion that the original meaning of "Militia" encompassed all able-bodied men, he asserted that the Second Amendment protects a right for individuals to own firearms. In his view, the amendment did not solely protect states' ability to keep their organized "Militias," now known as the National Guard, free from being disarmed or eliminated by the federal government.

Two additional aspects of this re-characterization of the Second Amendment were especially notable. Justice Scalia acknowledged that the words of the first clause concern a "well regulated Militia" and not just the word "Militia." Moreover, he stated that "the adjective 'well-regulated' implies nothing more than the imposition of proper discipline and training."[39] The thrust of the opinion subsequently pivoted when discussing the second clause to emphasize, in effect, a constitutional right for law-abiding adults to keep a handgun in the home for purposes of personal self-defense. This pivot raised puzzling questions that seemed to separate the ultimate doctrine from the actual words, despite Scalia's long-standing claims to emphasize the importance of the constitutional text as well as its history. How does a personal right to self-defense in the home with handguns emerge from a single-sentence constitutional amendment that specifically presents the "well regulated Militia" as the purpose of the provision? Moreover, how does the possession of firearms for their personal self-defense by individuals who have no connection to the organized militia fit with the term "well regulated," which Scalia said concerned "proper discipline and training"? Stated more succinctly, did Scalia cast aside the concept of a "well regulated Militia" as if it was a mere slogan disconnected from the second clause in the Amendment's single sentence? This approach is plausible for judges who use flexible interpretation to advance the doctrinal conclusion and policy outcome that they believe will best apply a constitutional provision to the social context and issues of contemporary society. Justice Scalia always condemned such an approach. Yet, the conclusions of his opinion raised questions about whether his interpretation of the Second Amendment, in fact, demonstrated how the selective use of historical justifications can produce flexible interpretive results under the pretense of judicial restraint and fidelity to history.

Justices Stevens and Breyer each wrote dissenting opinions, supported by the other two dissenters, Justices Ginsburg and Souter. Stevens was a persistent critic of constitutional interpretation based on the Scalia–Thomas approach to originalism. Yet, the dissenting opinion by Justice Stevens relied on historical sources in order to contest Scalia's majority opinion on its own terms. Relying on constitutional history, Stevens reached a contrary conclusion about the purpose and effect of the Second Amendment. According to Stevens, "The Second Amendment was adopted to protect the right of the people of each of the several States to maintain a well-regulated militia. It was a response to concerns raised during the ratification of the Constitution [about] the power of Congress to disarm the state militias. . . . Neither the text of the Amendment nor the arguments advanced by its proponents evidenced the slightest interest in limiting any legislature's authority to regulate private civilian uses of firearms."[40]

Justice Stevens used originalism for this interpretation in order to demonstrate that Scalia could not accurately assert that history clearly justified the individual-right result produced by the majority.[41] Justice Stevens's lingering dissatisfaction with the *Heller* decision was evident in his post-retirement book that proposed six revised amendments for the Constitution. He argued that words should be added to the Second Amendment to clarify that the amendment was intended to protect the arming of state militias, not individuals in their homes. He proposed that the Second Amendment be changed to read, "A well regulated Militia, being necessary to the security of a free State, the right of the people to keep and bear Arms *when serving in the Militia* shall not be infringed."[42]

Justice Scalia, on behalf of the majority, concluded that the District of Columbia's law violated the Second Amendment rights of individuals, yet his opinion explicitly limited the scope of the right defined by the decision. His reasoning openly endorsed legislative authority to regulate private firearms without banning the possession of handguns kept in the home for self-defense by law-abiding citizens. Justice Scalia's critics pointed to his acknowledgment of government's specific regulatory authority as an aspect of his opinion that revealed he was not committed to justifying his stated conclusions with strong originalist evidence.[43] Specifically, Justice Scalia wrote, "Although we do not undertake an exhaustive historical analysis today of the full scope of the Second Amendment, nothing in our opinion should be taken to cast doubt on longstanding prohibitions on the possession of firearms by felons and the mentally ill, or laws forbidding the carrying of firearms in sensitive places such as schools and government buildings, or laws imposing conditions and qualifications on the commercial sale of firearms."[44] In the words of one critic, Scalia "provides zero originalist basis for these conclusions."[45]

Justice Scalia also invited criticism of his use of originalism when he rejected arguments claiming that the intentions of the Second Amendment's authors were necessarily limited to the slow-loading, single-shot gunpowder weapons, such as muskets, with which they were familiar. According to Scalia, "Some have made the argument, bordering on the frivolous, that only those arms in existence in the eighteenth century are protected by the Second Amendment. We do not interpret constitutional rights that way. Just as the First Amendment protects modern forms of communication . . . [citing *Reno v. ACLU*, 1997] and the Fourth Amendment applies to modern forms of search, . . . [citing *Kyllo v. United States*, 2001] the Second Amendment extends, prima facie, to all instruments that constitute bearable arms, even those that were not in existence at the founding."[46]

If the purpose and benefit of using originalist constitutional interpretation are to prevent modern judges from applying their own interpretive values in decision-making, how could Scalia possibly avoid this pitfall when rejecting the precise knowledge and intentions of the Second Amendment's framers who could never have envisioned modern weaponry? Indeed, the First Amendment case referenced by Scalia in the foregoing quote concerned an invalidated federal statute that sought to regulate "indecent" material on the internet. Certainly, the framers of the First Amendment could never have imagined the kinds of materials that would be available via computers, nor envisioned computers as ubiquitous personal devices. In addition, the First Amendment opinion cited by Scalia, *Reno v. ACLU*, was written by Justice Stevens, a harsh critic of using originalism to interpret the Constitution. Thus, Scalia relied on a non-originalist opinion to claim that the court applies originalism to modern technology and methods of free expression that were unknown in the eighteenth century. In effect, Justice Scalia sought to escape the box in which strict fidelity to originalism would place him if he really followed eighteenth-century knowledge and intentions. Thus, when Scalia wrote, "We do not interpret constitutional rights that way"—by limiting ourselves to the precise understanding and meaning of the eighteenth-century framers—he was really conceding that the justices, including himself, do not genuinely rely on originalism to define constitutional rights. Instead, they seek to obscure the assertion of their own political values by dressing up their preferences with history-based justifications.

Similarly, Justice Scalia dismissed, without careful discussion, the argument that any constitutional right recognized through originalist constitutional interpretation should have its definition based on the knowledge, understanding, and specific intentions of the eighteenth-century authors of the

Second Amendment. It is difficult to see how he could justify invalidating a law directed at modern rapid-fire, multi-shot firearms if he genuinely followed his own asserted principle that the Constitution's meaning should be determined by following "what the text was thought to mean when the people adopted it."[47] As a result, he opened the door to meanings of bearable "arms" that include a wide array of modern military-style weapons that were unimaginable in the eighteenth century and are frequently damaging to public safety in the hands of twenty-first-century civilians.

The biggest surprise in the *Heller* decision was Justice Kennedy's complete endorsement of Scalia's originalist analysis and conclusions. Justice Kennedy did not adhere to originalism in his own interpretations of the Constitution. Indeed, Scalia was critical of Kennedy's flexible approach to constitutional interpretation, especially in cases that provided constitutional protections for the privacy and equality of gay and lesbian Americans. Justice Scalia considered Kennedy's opinions on these subjects to be the antithesis of originalism and quintessential examples of the risk that judges will impose their own values and policy preferences on the nation. The *Heller* case was anticipated as one in which Kennedy would cast the decisive vote from the middle of the deeply divided court. In this case, unlike Kennedy's key liberal decisions legitimizing and protecting same-sex relationships, *Lawrence v. Texas* (2003) and *Obergefell v. Hodges* (2015), Kennedy cast the decisive vote to favor the outcome preferred by political conservatives.

Expanded Application of a Limited Individual Right

By the early years of the twenty-first century, there was only a short list of protections in the Bill of Rights that had never been interpreted as applying against state and local action through the Fourteenth Amendment's Due Process Clause. The Second Amendment was among these provisions that applied only to federal entities at the time of *Heller* in 2008. Because *Heller* concerned gun rights in the federal jurisdictional entity of Washington, DC, it did not settle the issue of the decision's impact on state and local laws regulating firearms.

Two years later, the case of *McDonald v. City of Chicago* (2010) addressed laws enacted by the Illinois cities of Chicago and Oak Park. The justices split in the same 5–4 vote as in *Heller* except that Justice Souter had retired and was replaced among the four dissenters by his successor, Justice Sotomayor. The majority opinion was written by Justice Alito, and there were dissenting opinions written by Justices Breyer and Stevens. Justice Alito's analysis concluded that the Second Amendment's individual right to keep guns in one's home is fundamental and therefore should be incorporated into the Fourteenth Amendment's Due Process Clause. One irony of this incorporation decision was that politically conservative justices over the years had raised doubts about whether states and localities should be obligated to respect the same rights as those imposed on the federal government by the Bill of Rights. Conversely, politically liberal justices often sought to expand the reach of the Bill of Rights to provide broad legal protections for individuals against actions by states and localities. With respect to the issue of gun rights, however, values and policy preferences move in opposite ideological directions. Political conservatives wanted expanded gun rights, and political liberals favored governmental authority to enact gun control legislation.

The *McDonald* ruling did not expand the scope of the Second Amendment's meaning. The decision merely expanded the amendment's application by imposing the rights-protective *Heller* rule against cities and states as a means to prevent them from creating certain gun safety laws. The *McDonald* majority did not seize the opportunity to expand the recognized constitutional right by including additional types of firearms or contexts outside of an individual's home. At the conclusion of the majority opinion, Justice Alito declared, "In *Heller*, we held that the Second Amendment protects the right to possess a handgun in the home for the purpose of self-defense. Unless considerations of *stare decisis* [adherence to case precedent] counsel otherwise, a provision of the Bill of Rights that protects a right that is fundamental from an American perspective applies equally to the Federal Government and the States. . . . We therefore hold that the Due Process Clause of the Fourteenth Amendment incorporates the Second Amendment right recognized in *Heller*."[48]

In commenting on the decisions in *Heller* and *McDonald* after his retirement, Justice Stevens emphasized that the decisions defined the gun ownership right narrowly. He noted that the majority opinions specifically limited themselves to protecting possession of handguns in the home, but they left open the possibility of governments regulating both other firearms and other contexts in which people might seek to possess firearms.[49] The NRA and other gun rights groups advocate a broader right for individuals under the Second Amendment, one that would encompass larger weapons that individuals could carry nearly anywhere in American society. Thus, localities throughout the country see gun rights advocates carrying military-style rifles at state capitols, inside public libraries, and at other locations.[50] These activists seek to assert their belief that the Second Amendment provides a right that does not limit the nature of the "arms" or the locations in which they can be borne.

Gun rights advocates continued to seek judicial nullification of additional gun regulations. Two cases worked their way through the court system in 2015. However, the Roberts Court declined to hear both cases. In *Jackson v. City and County of San Francisco* (2015), a local law required that handguns kept in the home be stored in containers or disabled with trigger locks. Lower courts refused to invalidate the restriction or otherwise prevent its imposition on gun owners. The Roberts Court's decision to turn the case away left the lower court decisions intact and indicated that there were not yet four justices on the court who wanted to decide the issue. It takes the votes of only four justices to accept a case for hearing. Justices Thomas and Scalia objected so strongly to the court's inaction that they issued an opinion dissenting from the decision to turn down the case. The opinion, written by Thomas and joined by Scalia, argued that the court should have accepted the case to examine lower courts' decisions that potentially impinged on the breadth of the not-yet-fully-defined Second Amendment right.

Six months later, the Roberts Court again declined to accept another case challenging a local law that prohibited possessing, owning, and selling military-style semiautomatic rifles. In *Friedman v. City of Highland Park* (2015), Justice Thomas, joined by Justice Scalia, wrote another dissent from the denial of certiorari and argued that the Supreme Court should accept the case. Justice Thomas was outspoken in his criticism of the court's refusal to examine the lower court decision that upheld the local law. According to Thomas, the Supreme Court was refusing to "review a decision that flouts two of our Second Amendment precedents," referring to *Heller* and *McDonald*.[51] Clearly, Thomas and Scalia believed that the principle of individual gun rights established in *Heller* should extend beyond the possession of handguns in people's homes. It seemed equally clear that there was an insufficient number of other justices who shared that view in 2015, thus leaving the Second Amendment right defined in a limited way.

Expansion of Gun Rights by Limiting State Authority

Opponents of gun regulations continued to file legal challenges to new and existing laws. These challenges began to receive favorable decisions from some judges, including a lower court decision in *Miller v. Bonta* (2021) to invalidate California's thirty-year-old ban on civilian ownership of military-style rifles.[52] A US court of appeals panel stayed the district judge's decision, but that kept the issue alive in litigation processes and increased the likelihood it would be presented to the US Supreme Court in the future.[53] As the Supreme Court's composition changed with the addition of the three Trump-appointed justices, there were greater incentives for opponents of gun regulations to use a litigation strategy with the hope that the increasingly conservative high court might accept these cases as a means to expand the definition of the Second Amendment right.

In 2020, the Roberts Court considered a challenge to an unusual New York City ordinance that restricted the ability of licensed gun owners residing in the city to transport their guns to second homes or shooting ranges outside the city. After the court accepted *New York State Rifle & Pistol Association v. City of New York* (2020) for hearing, the city revoked the ordinance with the hope of making the case moot and ineligible for decision by the court. The strategy worked. In a 5–4 decision in April 2020, the Supreme Court declared the case to be moot and declined to issue a decision. However, the two-page per curiam opinion for the majority was countered by a thirty-one-page strenuous dissent from Justice Alito, joined by Justice Gorsuch and, for the most part, by Justice Thomas. They disagreed with the court's conclusion that the case was moot and presented detailed reasons for deciding the case in favor of gun owners.

In a brief concurring opinion, Justice Kavanaugh expressed agreement with the majority's conclusion about mootness but also voiced his desire for the court to accept cases presenting Second Amendment issues. He wrote, "And I share Justice Alito's concern that some federal and state courts may not be properly applying *Heller* and *McDonald*. The Court should address that issue soon, perhaps in one of the several Second Amendment cases with petitions for certiorari now pending before the Court."[54] Justice Kavanaugh, in effect, announced that he would join the three dissenters in providing the fourth vote needed to accept future Second Amendment cases.[55]

Subsequently, the Roberts Court accepted *New York State Rifle & Pistol Association v. Bruen* for hearing in November 2021. In most states, individuals automatically received concealed carry permits if they qualified by passing state requirements for training, background checks, and other licensing rules. By contrast, in New York and seven other restrictive states, individuals were also required to provide a reason for their need to carry a gun outside the home. State officials used their discretionary authority to reject submitted reasons and thereby deny issuance of permits. Those who challenged New York's laws wanted permits to be issued automatically for people who were otherwise qualified for gun-carry licenses. To defenders of such restrictions, a decision to strike down discretionary denial laws as violating the Second Amendment could greatly increase the number of guns carried on the streets of New York, Los Angeles, Boston, Baltimore, Newark, Providence, and other cities within the eight states that restricted gun-carrying permits in this way.[56]

In June 2022, the Roberts Court issued a 6–3 decision striking down New York's law and, in effect, striking down similar laws in the other seven states. According to Justice Thomas's majority opinion in *Bruen*, "Consistent with *Heller* and *McDonald*, . . . the Second and Fourteenth Amendments protect an individual's right to carry a handgun for self-defense outside the home."[57] The majority opinion employed the same originalist interpretive approach as the prior two cases that expanded Second Amendment rights. This time, however, the majority opinion gave explicit instructions to lower courts about how to analyze the constitutionality of gun laws challenged in future litigation. Instead of giving consideration to public safety and other potentially detrimental policy impacts from invalidating gun safety laws, the lower courts were instructed to look solely at whether each challenged law "is consistent with this Nation's historical tradition of firearm regulation."[58] Given the originalist justices' purported focus on the intentions of the framers and ratifiers of constitutional amendments, this was understood to mean that judges must evaluate federal gun laws by seeing whether they are consistent with laws that existed in 1791 when the Bill of Rights was ratified. Alternatively, a judge might look for analogous state and local gun laws in existence in 1868, when the ratification of the Fourteenth Amendment opened the door to apply constitutional rights against actions by states and localities.

In a dissenting opinion on behalf of himself and Justices Sotomayor and Kagan, Justice Breyer objected to the majority's command that lower courts look at history and base decisions solely on whether analogous laws existed. Breyer argued that courts should consider governments' compelling interests underlying gun safety regulations in light of the significant problem of gun violence in contemporary American society. In Breyer's words, "When courts interpret the Second Amendment, it is constitutionally proper, indeed often necessary, for them to consider the serious dangers and consequences of gun violence that lead States to regulate firearms."[59]

Justice Breyer's dissenting opinion pointed out that judges are not historians and are poorly prepared for the task of identifying analogous laws in American history.[60] In addition, Breyer noted, "Indeed, the Court offers many and varied reasons to reject potential representative analogues, but very few reasons to accept them. At best, the numerous justifications that the Court finds for rejecting historical evidence give judges ample tools to pick their friends out of history's crowd. At worst, they create a one-way ratchet that will disqualify virtually any 'representative historical analogue' and make it nearly impossible to sustain common-sense regulations necessary to our Nation's safety and security."[61]

Very quickly, Justice Breyer's dissenting opinion proved to be prophetic. After the Roberts Court decision in *Bruen*, New York immediately enacted a new set of laws limiting where guns can be carried and other measures intended to increase gun safety. In October 2022, however, a federal judge in New York struck down most of the new laws' provisions, including invalidating prohibitions on guns at summer camps, stadiums, concert venues, and subways.[62] Because eighteenth- and nineteenth-century New York laws did not clearly prohibit people from carrying guns in these locations, twenty-first-century legislators are barred from enacting such laws in modern times. In a separate case, a different New York judge similarly blocked the treatment of religious institutions as "sensitive locations" where firearms could be banned by the government.[63] These decisions showed how difficult it will be for gun safety laws to survive when lower court judges follow the mandate to look for analogous historical antecedents as the justification for permitting gun safety laws.

The Roberts Court and Gun Policy

The Roberts Court's decision in *Heller* significantly shifted the interpretation of the Second Amendment. The court's decision emboldened and mobilized gun rights advocates by legitimizing arguments about the Second Amendment's protection of individual gun rights and by encouraging lawsuits to challenge additional government restrictions on firearms. In the aftermath of *Bruen*, gun rights advocates were invited to use litigation strategies to invalidate gun laws even in states where there was a strong consensus among the populace about the need for such laws.

As political polarization within the United States intensified during the years of the Trump administration and thereafter, divisions within the public over gun rights and the meaning of the Second Amendment became key elements of that polarization. As described by commentators, "The debate over gun rights isn't really about guns at all. It's about what they represent: cherished freedoms, a reverence for independence. . . . Even the most incremental move to constrain deadly weaponry seems to many Americans to cut against their rights."[64] With clashing valuations of gun rights so central to the country's political divisions, even horrific mass shootings have limited impacts on gun policies and individuals' views on gun rights. Significant national gun regulations were blocked in Congress for years with the exception of limited measures enacted in the aftermath of the mass shooting at the elementary school in Uvalde, Texas, in 2022. Public pressure after the shooting led some opponents of gun regulation in Congress to seek a way to claim that they "did something" about gun violence. The new law contained limited measures such as tightening restrictions on domestic abusers, funding mental health programs, and promoting efforts by interested states to temporarily remove firearms from people experiencing emotional or mental health crises.[65]

By limiting the authority of legislatures to regulate firearms, the Roberts Court set into motion legal battles over gun rights. In prior Supreme Court eras, such Second Amendment challenges to laws regulating individuals' ownership of firearms were doomed to fail. By contrast, the aftermath of the *Bruen* decision in 2022 appeared to guarantee that judges will look critically at every effort to enact gun safety laws. Unless changed in a subsequent Supreme Court decision, the mandate to use the existence of laws in prior centuries to determine the permissibility of twenty-first-century legislation will certainly lead to the invalidation of many contemporary gun safety laws.

Conclusion

The Roberts Court majority issued important decisions that blocked legislative authority to criminalize certain kinds of expressive conduct as well as specific restrictions on owning and carrying firearms. For example, in the realm of First Amendment jurisprudence, the Roberts Court decisions expanded protected speech rights for expression that was generally considered distasteful, such as violent video games and false claims about the receipt of military medals. Indeed, there was a high degree of consensus among the justices about the need to strike down the criminalization of most content-based restrictions on expression.

In its most impactful decisions, the Roberts Court majority invalidated several criminal statutes regulating financial contributions used to support political candidates and their campaigns. In so doing, the majority significantly expanded the definition of First Amendment rights for corporate entities in the realm of campaign contributions. In effect, a narrow Roberts Court majority significantly changed the meaning and use of the First Amendment in ways that advanced the politically conservative interests and policy preferences of wealthy individuals and corporate entities.[66] Viewed through the lens of criminal justice, the Roberts Court majority invalidated campaign finance laws that the people's elected representatives in Congress believed should define crimes and punishments related to the use of money in seeking to influence elections and elected officials. Moreover, by eliminating restrictions on expenditures, these decisions helped to open the way for undue influence affecting criminal justice and other policy areas by wealthy actors, such as private prison companies and the NRA. These cases caused one commentator to lament that "political organizations can speak more powerfully than a natural person in contemporary America."[67] With respect to criminal justice–related First Amendment decisions, this may be the Roberts Court's most impactful and enduring legacy.

Similarly, the Roberts Court completely changed the long-accepted meaning of the Second Amendment by invalidating laws that limited individuals' opportunities to own and carry firearms. In 2008, the *Heller* decision redefined the Second Amendment as a protection for individuals to own and keep firearms in their homes rather than as a protection for maintaining "well regulated" armed militias controlled by each state. In *McDonald*, the narrow majority expanded the individual-rights interpretation to invalidate city ordinances barring private ownership of firearms and, by extension, prohibiting states from enacting statutes that might do the same. After the arrival of the three Trump appointees, the court's *Bruen* decision in 2022 dramatically impacted the ability of states to criminalize firearms-related activities.

The *Bruen* decision purported to be modest in scope by merely striking down legislatively imposed rules in eight states. These rules prevented otherwise qualified individuals from obtaining permits to carry handguns outside their homes when they could not provide good reasons for wanting to carry a gun. In fact, however, the results of the *Bruen* decision were dramatic and far-reaching. By declaring that gun laws can survive judicial scrutiny only when judges can find analogous laws that existed centuries ago, the Roberts Court majority unleashed a wave of lower court decisions striking down a wide array of gun safety laws in states throughout the country.[68]

In 2024, the court decided *United States v. Rahimi*, a case challenging a lower court's invalidation of the federal law that barred gun acquisition and possession by individuals subject to protection orders for domestic violence.[69] Such a law did not exist in 1791, when legislators generally ignored husbands' abusive violence against their wives. Thus, the lower court judge said the contemporary law was not permissible. Commentators were eager to see if a majority of justices would conclude that their instructions to the lower courts had gone too far in limiting legislative authority to enact gun safety laws.

In *Rahimi*, the court upheld the federal law. In so doing, the justices further confused observers about what gun laws could survive the historical analysis mandated by the *Bruen* decision. Chief Justice Roberts wrote the majority opinion in the 8–1 decision, while five other justices wrote their own concurring opinions and Justice Thomas wrote a dissenting opinion. Such a large number of opinions by different justices seeking to present arguments and explanations can serve to make lower court judges less certain about how to decide subsequent cases. The majority opinion said lower court judges had been too rigid in seeking to identify analogous laws from earlier centuries. Instead, Roberts instructed them to ask whether contemporary laws facing legal challenges are "relevantly similar" to laws from our earlier traditions. This formulation did not provide clarity for lower court judges. Thus, observers anticipated a continued flow of cases into the federal courts as gun rights advocates challenge various laws and state governments experiment with gun safety laws that they hope will survive the Roberts Court's scrutiny.

Twenty-first-century American society's social conditions and firearms technology are far different from those in the eighteenth and nineteenth centuries. Yet, the *Bruen* majority rejected the idea that considerations of public safety could take precedence over fealty to laws developed centuries ago in a completely different societal and technological context. The *Rahimi* majority softened and complicated that stance by inviting judges to hunt for early laws that demonstrated a specific safety concern, as Chief Justice Roberts did in *Rahimi* by highlighting an eighteenth-century Massachusetts law authorizing the arrest of individuals who threaten the peace by carrying arms. Justices who purport to use originalism as the basis for their constitutional interpretation decisions seldom admit error when issues are revisited in later cases. Indeed, Chief Justice Roberts's *Rahimi* opinion blamed lower court judges for misunderstanding the guidance in *Bruen* rather than admitting that the *Bruen* formulation was too vague and difficult for those judges to apply. Thus, gun safety laws and the definition of the Second Amendment will continue to be developed through the use of malleable historical examples and rationalizations rather than through an emphasis on either constitutional principles or significant policy consequences.

4. SEARCH AND SEIZURE

The Fourth Amendment protects against unreasonable searches and seizures and describes the requirements for a judge-issued search or arrest warrant. The definition and application of these legal protections generated debates among the Roberts Court justices as they considered an array of claims from individuals. Throughout American history, Fourth Amendment issues illustrated tensions between society's need for safety and individuals' personal privacy and liberty. In the twenty-first century, for example, Americans' increasing use of social media, the internet, and cell phones have enhanced opportunities for new forms of governmental surveillance and searches to intrude into Americans' private lives.[1]

In Fourth Amendment cases, liberal justices often sided with individuals' claims, and conservative justices frequently found law and order arguments most persuasive. In light of the numerical advantage possessed by conservative justices, search and seizure cases most often favored the interests of police and prosecutors. Indeed, much like the Rehnquist Court, the Roberts Court handed down conservative rulings in three out of four Fourth Amendment cases.[2] While the overall vote totals are similar in the two eras, the cases in which a Roberts Court majority found liberal arguments persuasive were very different from those in the Rehnquist Court era.

Compared with the Rehnquist Court, the Roberts Court's decisions provided greater support for the warrant requirement and blocked certain law enforcement efforts to undertake warrantless investigations of individuals and property.[3] For example, while the Rehnquist Court upheld cases significantly limiting Fourth Amendment protections for car searches, certain Roberts Court rulings, such as *Arizona v. Gant* (2009), identified violations of Fourth Amendment rights in these contexts. The Roberts Court also required a warrant supported by probable cause to bring drug-sniffing dogs on the front porch of a home in *Florida v. Jardines* (2013)

94

and to place Global Positioning System (GPS) monitors on automobiles in *United States v. Jones* (2012).

The Roberts Court continued the Rehnquist Court's trend of reducing the protections of the exclusionary rule.[4] The exclusionary rule is the general legal principle that evidence obtained through improper searches or questioning of suspects should be excluded from use by the prosecution against defendants. Intended to deter and remedy police misconduct, the court's approval of the rule for federal cases in *Weeks v. United States* (1914) was extended to apply to state criminal justice systems in the Warren Court's landmark case of *Mapp v. Ohio* in 1961. Beginning in the Burger Court era of the 1970s and 1980s, the Supreme Court weakened this principle through the creation of exceptions that permitted the use of improperly obtained evidence in certain situations.

In *Herring v. United States* (2009), the Roberts Court diminished the applicability of the exclusionary rule even when officers rely on an inaccurate database controlled by the police themselves. Erroneous database reports about the purported existence of arrest warrants can lead to arrests and searches, yet the court says any evidence discovered in such illegally triggered searches can be used by the prosecution. Similarly, in *Hudson v. Michigan* (2006), a majority of justices declined to apply the exclusionary rule when police officers failed to follow required knock-and-announce procedures while entering a home to execute a search warrant. Several Roberts Court justices were highly critical of the exclusionary rule.[5] The creation of a supermajority of conservatives through President Trump's three appointments to the court raised questions about whether the court's critics of the exclusionary rule had gained sufficient support to eliminate long-standing precedents on the exclusion of evidence after improper searches.

Unlike other issues, such as abortion rights and federalism, in which the liberal-conservative voting patterns of justices can seem predictable, the voting patterns of justices in Fourth Amendment cases provide interesting variations.[6] In its first decade, when the Roberts Court handed down a significant liberal ruling on the Fourth Amendment, it was usually because Justice Scalia joined the liberal justices to render an outcome in favor of the civil liberties claim. On the other hand, there were times when, even without Justice Scalia's vote, the court ruled in a conservative manner because Justice Breyer provided a vote to create a conservative majority on an issue.

Defining a "Search" Under the
Fourth Amendment

An initial question under the Fourth Amendment is whether the police have conducted a "search" in a given situation. If the activities in question do not constitute a search, no Fourth Amendment protections apply. Thus, questions about what constitutes a search are important inquiries.[7] Generally, intrusions by government officials into people's "reasonable expectations of privacy" constitute searches. But questions remain about what defines the circumstances in which such an intrusion is identified as having occurred, especially with respect to surveillance and search contexts produced by new technological developments.[8]

In *United States v. Jones*, the court was asked to determine whether attaching GPS devices to cars in order to track the vehicles' movements are "searches" within the meaning of the Fourth Amendment. The Roberts Court unanimously concluded that the police use of GPS monitoring without a valid warrant violated the Fourth Amendment. The *Jones* case is regarded as a notable decision limiting the surveillance authority of law enforcement officials. Joan Biskupic, *USA Today*'s Supreme Court correspondent, called it a "major decision on privacy in the digital age."[9] Adam Liptak of the *New York Times* noted that the decision signaled that "a majority of the justices are prepared to apply broad privacy principles to bring the Fourth Amendment's ban on unreasonable searches into the digital age."[10] The decision was one example of how issues concerning technology and the Fourth Amendment could produce liberal decisions by the generally conservative Roberts Court.

In another major ruling defining searches for Fourth Amendment purposes, the court held in *Florida v. Jardines* that police may not use a drug-sniffing dog on the front porch of a suspect's home without a search warrant. The 5–4 ruling saw Justices Thomas and Scalia cast liberal rights-protective votes but Justice Breyer voted to support governmental authority. Police took a drug-sniffing dog to the porch of Jardines's home based on their suspicion that he was involved in illegal drug activity. The dog's signaling behavior indicated that there were illegal drugs in the house, and police used this information to obtain a search warrant.

In the majority opinion, Justice Scalia used historical analysis to conclude that a Fourth Amendment search had indeed taken place. Scalia noted that a front porch is part of the house itself and has long been considered as part of the protected area of a home. As such, the porch area was entitled to substantial constitutional protection and was covered by the Fourth Amendment's warrant requirement. In dissent, Justice Alito argued that people do not have a reasonable expectation of privacy concerning activities on their porch because the short duration of time spent on a porch by various categories of visitors does not constitute a trespass on private property. Door-to-door salespeople and others may ring the doorbell and stand on a porch briefly without necessarily committing the act of trespass.

While *Jones* dealt with new technology, *Jardines* also involved surveillance techniques based on a different element of science, namely training dogs for use by law enforcement. These decisions, coupled with the later Roberts Court's ruling in *Carpenter v. United States* (2018), suggested that the Roberts Court was cognizant of the need to adapt the Fourth Amendment to the changing technological landscape. In *Carpenter*, the court held that government acquisition of data from cell phone towers for law enforcement investigations constitutes a search and therefore requires a warrant. In each of the three instances noted here (*Jardines*, *Jones*, and *Carpenter*), the Roberts Court majority articulated a liberal, rights-protective position and provided protection against expanded investigatory techniques.

In *Collins v. Virginia* (2018), an eight-member majority reinforced the importance of providing greater Fourth Amendment protections for the home and its curtilage than that provided in other spaces. An officer suspected that a motorcycle in a home's driveway was stolen, and he walked up the driveway to look under the tarp covering the motorcycle to check the license plate. It was indeed the stolen vehicle being sought by the police. In a majority opinion by Justice Sotomayor, the Roberts Court declared that the diminished Fourth Amendment protection for vehicles as compared with homes did not justify the officer's warrantless invasion of the curtilage of the home by walking on the property to examine the motorcycle.

As he did with other issues, including Second Amendment gun rights (*Printz v. United States*, 1997) and the Sixth Amendment right to counsel (*Garza v. Idaho*, 2019), Justice Thomas used the occasion to write a concurring opinion suggesting that the court ought to consider overruling *Mapp v. Ohio*. *Mapp* was the landmark Warren Court decision that imposed the exclusionary rule on state and local law enforcement officials throughout the country. Thomas used such opinions to invite attorneys to initiate future challenges that might lead the court to overturn long-standing precedents.

Justice Thomas's desires may come to fruition later in the Roberts Court era in light of the conservative supermajority's assertive reconsideration of established precedents, such as those affecting abortion (*Dobbs v. Jackson Women's Health Organization*, 2022) and affirmative action (*Students for Fair Admissions v. Harvard*, 2023).

Exceptions to the Warrant Requirement

Consent searches are situations in which police are granted permission to search by someone possessing the actual or reasonably perceived authority to consent to the governmental intrusion. Scholarly estimates conclude that 90 percent of all searches without warrants are consent searches.[11] Thus, what constitutes consent and who can grant it are questions of significant constitutional importance.

In *Georgia v. Randolph* (2006), the Roberts Court clarified the conditions under which police may search a home when one resident of the property gives consent but another resident declines to consent to a search. The decision took a rights-protective approach to consent searches of a home. However, in a later decision, a different majority diminished the strength of the *Randolph* principle and broadened opportunities for police to search even when they know one resident refused to consent.

The Randolphs, a married but separated couple, both had access to the family residence. Although Mrs. Randolph had formally separated from her husband, at some point she returned to the home and informed the police of her husband's drug use. She gave police permission to search the residence. Mr. Randolph, who was present at the time, insisted he would not consent to a police search of the home. Nonetheless, based on Mrs. Randolph's consent, the police searched and found incriminating evidence. Mr. Randolph moved to have the evidence excluded because he had not consented to the search.

Writing for the five-member majority, Justice Souter found merit in Mr. Randolph's objection to the search and concluded that the search violated Mr. Randolph's rights. Souter's opinion held that because Mr. Randolph, a co-resident, was physically present when consent was requested and he explicitly refused consent, the police should have respected his denial of the request to search. All three dissenters, Thomas, Scalia, and Roberts, wrote individual dissenting opinions. In his opinion, Chief Justice Roberts argued that privacy within a home is reduced when one shares that space and thus the search with one occupant's consent should be deemed constitutionally permissible. In his opinion, Roberts warned that the majority's decision would harm victims of domestic violence if their abusers were able to hide evidence by blocking the victim's ability to consent to a search.

The Roberts Court's ruling in this case surprised observers. Indeed, as one analyst noted, "*Randolph* seems to alter . . . the holding of [prior precedents] by applying a bright-line, all-inclusive approach that does not acknowledge the reasonableness of the officer's conduct."[12] The perception that the court established a clear principle disappeared eight years later. The court heard a case with slightly different factual circumstances, and two justices in the *Randolph* majority, Kennedy and Breyer, regarded the new fact situation as sufficiently distinguishable to permit a search based on the consent of one resident.

In *Fernandez v. California* (2014), Fernandez refused police entry into an apartment that was shared with an intimate partner. At the apartment, the officers observed what they believed to be evidence of domestic violence when they spoke to a woman who answered the apartment door. Based on the observation of her possible injuries, they arrested Fernandez and removed him from the premises. Police later returned to the apartment and secured verbal and written consent to search the apartment from Fernandez's partner. The Roberts Court, in an opinion by Justice Alito, declared that it would not extend the logic of *Randolph* to instances in which the co-occupant was not physically present to deny consent to a search. Rather, Alito noted that generally a co-occupant can validly consent to searches of a residence except in the narrow circumstance carved out in *Randolph*, namely when the objection of a co-occupant who is physically present can block such a consent search. In effect, the majority's decision created a roadmap for police to gain the opportunity to search when they know that one co-resident objects to a search while another is willing to consent. The police can simply wait until the objecting co-resident leaves the premises or, as here, find a legal basis to remove that co-resident. The *Fernandez* case did not formally overrule the *Randolph* decision. However, the *Fernandez* decision likely rendered the purported *Randolph* principle ineffective whenever police wait until the resistant resident is away from home.

Exigent circumstances constitute another well-recognized exception to the warrant requirement. Exigent circumstances are urgent situations that, as described by one legal scholar, "make obtaining a warrant impractical, useless, dangerous, or unnecessary, and that justify warrantless arrests or entries into homes or premises."[13] Because these cases tend to concern the reasonableness of perceiving a situation to be urgent, the Supreme Court assesses such situations on a case-by-case basis. Thus, the high court has not created clear standards to aid lower courts and police in determining what constitutes an exigent circumstance that justifies a warrantless search. In its decisions, the Roberts Court attempted to clarify certain contexts in which the exigent circumstances doctrine may be used by police, and these decisions often supported police discretionary authority to search.

For example, Utah police officers responded to a noise complaint and observed underage drinking through a screen door in *Brigham City v. Stuart* (2006). From outside the house, the police also witnessed a fight between a juvenile and four adults inside the home. During the altercation, the police entered the home without a warrant and arrested the adults. Writing for a unanimous court, Chief Justice Roberts found the police entry into the home permissible under the Fourth Amendment because the violent altercation that police observed through a screen door and windows created exigent circumstances justifying their warrantless entry and intervention.

In *Kentucky v. King* (2011), the police entered a residence without a warrant and justified their entry based on their perception of exigent circumstances. While chasing a suspect who disappeared inside an apartment building, officers smelled marijuana coming from one apartment. They knocked loudly and announced their presence, heard what they thought were sounds consistent with the destruction of evidence, and entered the apartment by force. The suspect being sought was not inside this apartment, but the residents were in possession of marijuana. In an 8–1 decision explained by Justice Alito's majority opinion, the Supreme Court upheld the legality of the entry. This case resolved a question that had emerged from the lower courts. Prior to *King*, lower courts articulated a "police-created exigency doctrine."[14] Under this doctrine, if the urgent situation was created by the police, they could not enter without a warrant. In this case, the police arguably created an urgent situation. By pounding on the apartment door upon smelling marijuana, they presumably led the people inside to react by moving around inside the dwelling, thereby creating noises that the police later claimed as the justification for their exigent-circumstances entry. The narrow question answered in this case concerned whether the police action here constituted an improper police-created exigency. Justice Alito's majority opinion placed responsibility for the event on the people inside the apartment who reacted to police knocking on the door by moving around and creating suspicious sounds.

In cases concerning testing drivers for alcohol consumption, the Roberts Court's opinions appeared to shift as the court's composition changed. A divided court declined to accept an exigent-circumstances justification for a search in *Missouri v. McNeely* (2013). The case concerned a nonconsensual blood draw to conduct a blood alcohol test for a suspected drunk driver. Justices Scalia and Kennedy joined three liberal colleagues to create the majority, while generally liberal Justice Breyer joined three consistent conservatives to form the bloc of four dissenters.

In the *McNeely* case, a driver suspected of operating a motor vehicle while under the influence of alcohol refused to submit voluntarily to testing that would document his blood alcohol level. Police transported him to the hospital and ordered medical personnel to draw blood for testing. In an opinion by Justice Sotomayor, the majority held that when police stop suspected drunk drivers who refuse blood alcohol testing and there is time to obtain a warrant, the police should seek a warrant. The key factor is whether the time it takes to obtain a warrant would undermine the usefulness of the blood alcohol content test because the blood alcohol level naturally declines over time. Thus, if testing is delayed too long, a driver who exceeded state blood alcohol levels while behind the wheel might later test at a legally permissible level.

Although *McNeely* was a liberal ruling, it did not deviate from the exigent-circumstance analysis that the court generally uses. The analysis treats exigent circumstances assertions on a case-by-case basis.[15] That was the same approach applied here. Justice Sotomayor's majority opinion declined to endorse an across-the-board rule permitting nonconsensual blood tests. However, her opinion still left open the possibility of imposing such tests on suspected drunken drivers depending on the individual circumstances that police officers encounter.

In *Birchfield v. North Dakota* (2016), a decision issued shortly after the death of Justice Scalia, the court allowed breathalyzer tests to be administrated without a warrant because they are significantly less intrusive than the blood tests used in *McNeely* and serve important government objectives. This case was not litigated and analyzed as an exigent-circumstance case but instead relied on the "search incident to a valid arrest" exception to the warrant requirement. Thus, it distinguished the contested issue in *McNeely* by characterizing blood tests as significantly more intrusive and damaging to reasonable expectations of privacy than the imposition of breathalyzer tests. Justices Sotomayor and Ginsburg dissented, in part, by asserting that officers should seek warrants when practicable for all forms of blood alcohol testing. Justice Thomas dissented, in part, by asserting that all forms of blood alcohol testing should be imposed without warrants on suspected drunk drivers. As indicated by the divisions in the opinions, the justices viewed these kinds of cases from a variety of perspectives, especially with respect to the issue of whether blood alcohol testing for drivers is sufficiently intrusive to require case-by-case determinations of justifications for warrantless searches.

An example of this case-by-case approach arose in *Mitchell v. Wisconsin* (2019), which was decided after Justices Scalia and Kennedy had been replaced by Trump appointees Gorsuch and Kavanaugh. A five-member majority decided that when a suspected drunk driver is unconscious and incapable of submitting to a breathalyzer, then an involuntary blood draw is almost always permissible under the exigent-circumstances exception to the exclusionary rule. The majority opinion distinguished this case from *McNeely* because of the driver's lack of consciousness. Thus, the decision did not overrule *McNeely*. Yet, it raised the possibility that the court may reconsider *McNeely* in a future case as the numerically dominant conservative wing increases its assertiveness. As with other issues for which Thomas asserts a specific prescriptive viewpoint, he may end up gathering the support of a sufficient number of like-minded justices to reduce barriers to the imposition of involuntary blood alcohol testing on drivers.

Warrantless Searches Incident to a Lawful Arrest

Police officers may search a person being arrested or areas around that person in order to protect officer safety and ensure that evidence will not be destroyed. In the *Birchfield* case, the concern was the destruction of evidence as blood alcohol content dissipates during the time it would take to seek a search warrant for a breathalyzer test. Searches that were labeled as "incident to a lawful arrest" were also examined by the Roberts Court in two important liberal rulings, *Riley v. California* (2014) and *Arizona v. Gant*.

The Supreme Court ruled in *Riley* that warrantless cell phone data searches cannot be conducted as part of a search incident to a lawful arrest. Much like other cases dealing with new technologies, the *Riley* decision helped to explain the reach of the contemporary Fourth Amendment. Police stopped Riley for a traffic violation and arrested him for having a suspended license. Police impounded his vehicle and conducted a war-rantless inventory search, consistent with prior Supreme Court decisions about warrantless searches of impounded vehicles. The search led to the discovery that he was in possession of a concealed weapon. During the traffic stop, police seized and reviewed information on his cell phone. Photographs and text messages on the cell phone indicated that Riley was involved in gang activity and showed him with a vehicle involved in a shooting, thus leading to additional criminal charges. Riley argued that the police did not have a legal justification to view the contents of his cell phone at the scene of the arrest, and thus the warrantless search violated his Fourth Amendment rights.

Writing for the court, Chief Justice Roberts's unanimous majority opinion supported Riley's position. According to Roberts, warrantless searches must be based on one of the recognized exceptions to the warrant requirement. Although searches incident to a valid arrest are permissible, such searches are justified only for limited areas, including the clothing and immediate area around the arrestee, because those areas implicate officer safety and the preservation of evidence. Those were the two per-missible justifications for limited searches incident to arrest as established in the Warren Court's seminal precedent, *Chimel v. California* (1969). The reasonableness of these searches does not depend on the probability of finding weapons or evidence. Instead, officers may in all circumstances search the immediate vicinity that is legitimately within a person's reach to detect potential weapons and to find evidence that may be destroyed by the arrestee. With respect to the latter justification, one key issue is whether the arrestee is in a position to destroy evidence at the scene of the arrest.

Chief Justice Roberts noted that cell phones contain significant private information that is entitled to substantial Fourth Amendment protection. After arrestees' phones are securely in the possession of police, as was the case here, defendants are not capable of destroying evidence contained in the cell phone or using a blade or other weapon concealed inside the cell phone. Thus, there is no justification for immediately searching data on cell phones seized by police at the scene of the valid arrest. At that point, officers have the time and opportunity to seek a warrant if they can pre-sent evidence constituting probable cause to a judge in order to justify a warrant for the search of data contained in the cell phone.

The decision was significant not only for its protection of cell phones' contents but also because of its sweeping language protecting information stored as data. As Chief Justice Roberts noted in the majority opinion, "Cellphones differ in both a quantitative and qualitative sense from other objects that might be kept on an arrestee's person. The term 'cellphone' itself is misleading shorthand; many of these devices are in fact minicomputers that happen to have the capacity to be used as telephones. They could just as easily be called cameras, video players, rolodexes, calendars, tape recorders, libraries, diaries, albums, televisions, maps, or newspapers. . . . Even the most basic cellphones that sell for less than $20 might hold photographs, picture messages, text messages, Internet browsing history, a calendar, a thousand-entry phone book, and so on."[16]

This liberal decision on behalf of a gang member implicated in a murder surprised some commentators in light of the Roberts Court majority's generally conservative tendency to expand police authority. However, Linda Greenhouse of the *New York Times* and Yale Law School saw the decision as reflecting a special situation in which the justices, who often seem removed from the experiences of their fellow citizens and the practical impacts of their own decisions, could empathize with others in American society. According to Greenhouse, "The ability to put oneself in someone else's shoes [is] so often missing from the Supreme Court's criminal law decisions but perhaps on display here. . . . The justices are walking in their own shoes. The ringing cellphone could be theirs—or ours."[17]

In *Arizona v. Gant*, another important and unexpected liberal decision, the court limited the use of the "incident to a valid arrest" justification for warrantless searches of vehicles. As noted previously, searches incident to a lawful arrest must be predicated on a need to protect officer safety or preserve evidence. Prior to *Gant*, however, officers frequently searched vehicles incident to arrests without fear that evidence would be excluded, even if neither of these justifications existed. As one analyst noted, "The legal justifications that permit warrantless searches incident to arrest generally, concerns for officer safety and preservation of evidence, had been utterly abandoned by the Court in the automobile context. This police entitlement led to invasions of privacy against persons guilty of no more than mere traffic violations."[18]

Gant was arrested for driving without a license, handcuffed, and placed in the back of a police car. Acting under the presumed authority of the incident to a lawful arrest doctrine, police searched Gant's car and found cocaine. Gant sought to have the cocaine excluded from evidence for being the product of an improper search. Writing for the majority,

Justice Stevens found that the search violated Gant's Fourth Amendment rights. Stevens noted that while the court extended the incident to a valid arrest exception to car searches in *New York v. Belton* (1981), these types of searches must be limited to areas to which the arrested suspect potentially has access. In this case, because Gant had been handcuffed and secured in the patrol vehicle, there was neither danger to officers from the arrestee nor any possibility that evidence would be destroyed by the arrestee. Thus, the underlying rational for searches incident to a valid arrest did not exist, thereby making the search of Gant's vehicle unconstitutional. The case was important because it limited police discretionary authority to conduct car searches.[19]

Justice Stevens's majority opinion aligned an interesting combination of justices as conservatives Scalia and Thomas joined with Stevens and fellow liberals Ginsburg and Souter to form a five-member majority. Justice Breyer crossed ideological lines and wrote the dissent, arguing that the court should respect the precedent established in *Belton*. Justice Alito, joined by Roberts and Kennedy, also dissented by claiming that the majority had made law enforcement officers' jobs more difficult by refusing to uphold the prior rule allowing car searches under most arrest circumstances.

The case of *Bailey v. United States* (2013) involved a parallel issue of searches incident to the execution of a warrant. As noted in the description of *Riley*, one reason that searches incident to a lawful arrest are permissible is to ensure officer safety. Following from this justification, the Supreme Court generally permitted police to detain individuals during the execution of a search warrant and conduct a frisk search of those individuals. In the *Bailey* case, police were watching a residence and preparing to execute a valid search warrant when Bailey drove away from the apartment that was about to be searched. Police followed him for a mile, stopped him, and conducted a frisk search of his outer clothing. The search resulted in the seizure of keys, including one to a residence where a gun and drugs were found. Bailey eventually sought to have the initial search of his person labeled as improper under the Fourth Amendment. He argued that his seizure was invalid because he was not in the immediate vicinity of the apartment targeted for search. The Roberts Court majority agreed. Justice Kennedy's majority opinion found the search to be unlawful because the officers were not concerned about their safety or the potential destruction of evidence in the apartment when the search was conducted incident to Bailey's arrest. The majority thus limited the area that can be searched and the persons who can be properly seized during the execution of a valid search warrant. Interestingly, as in several other Fourth Amendment cases, Justice Breyer, who had a moderately liberal voting record, argued the conservative position favoring broad police authority in a dissent that was joined by Justices Alito and Thomas.

Other Significant Warrantless Search Cases

One of the most important developments in modern criminal justice is the use of DNA testing to identify criminal suspects. Pursuant to a Maryland statute, police officials took warrantless cheek-swab DNA samples from people arrested for certain serious offenses. In *Maryland v. King* (2013), Justice Breyer provided the decisive vote for a five-member conservative majority that endorsed the authority of law enforcement officials to conduct such warrantless searches. The majority opinion was written by Justice Kennedy, who said that taking the warrantless DNA sample was permissible as part of the process to definitively confirm the suspect's identity. Justice Scalia parted company with his usual voting allies and joined the liberal dissenters, as he did for several other Fourth Amendment decisions.

Justice Kennedy noted that the Maryland state law authorizing DNA collection from arrested subjects was narrow in its application. While it did allow the blanket collection of DNA samples from those arrested, it did so only for those arrested for crimes "of violence" and burglary. It also limited analysis of the DNA until after arraignment and until the courts determined that probable cause existed to support the initial arrest. Finally, Kennedy noted that state law said that the DNA sample would be destroyed if the case was dropped at any stage of the criminal proceedings, including a reversal of conviction or a pardon. Thus, Kennedy argued that the state law's requirements limited the potential for abuse. Moreover, Kennedy argued that the use of DNA for the purposes of confirming a suspect's identity served a legitimate state interest. Comparing the collection of DNA samples to fingerprinting, Kennedy added that both were merely methods for identifying suspects. He argued that running DNA samples through national databases was no different from using fingerprint databases.[20]

Justice Scalia wrote a scathing dissent and took the unusual step of reading his dissent aloud from the bench, a mechanism employed by justices only a few times each year to emphasize the intensity of their disagreement with the majority's decision. Justices Sotomayor, Ginsburg, and Kagan joined Scalia's dissent. According to the dissent, other warrantless searches, such as those justified by concerns for officer safety or exigent circumstances, are permissible because law enforcement officials have a non-investigative purpose for conducting those searches. Yet in this case, rather than merely being for identification purposes, Scalia saw the purpose of the search as aiding investigative efforts. With respect to the purported identification purposes of the DNA sample, Scalia noted that by the time of arraignment, the suspect has presumably already been identified using identification documents, fingerprints, photographs, and witness statements. A DNA sample, which takes time to process in a laboratory, would not help with identification. Instead, the DNA sample, when run through a database, would be used to find out what unsolved crimes a person may have committed. Its actual purpose was to compare the sample against preserved and recorded samples from unsolved cases. To the dissenters, this predictable use of DNA evidence for an investigative purpose therefore made the warrantless collection of such samples unlawful searches.

What if a DNA sample taken under the authority of Maryland's law remained in a database because of a clerical error, even though charges against the individual were dropped? The sample would remain available for criminal investigations, and, presumably, its use would not trigger the exclusionary rule if it produced evidence against an individual, despite the state law's requirement that such samples be erased from the database. The Roberts Court majority previously held in *Herring v. United States* that the exclusion of evidence was not required when improper warrantless searches by police were based on erroneous information placed in databases through clerical errors. In the *King* case, Justice Scalia asserted in his final caustic comment in the dissenting opinion that solving crimes should not be treated as a higher value than Fourth Amendment constitutional rights. According to Scalia,

> Today's judgment will, to be sure, have the beneficial effect of solving more crimes; then again, so would the taking of DNA samples from anyone who flies on an airplane (surely the Transportation Security Administration needs to know the "identity" of the flying public), applies for a driver's license, or attends a public school. . . . But I doubt that the proud men who wrote the charter of our liberties would have been so eager to open their mouths for royal inspection. I therefore dissent and hope that today's incursion upon the Fourth Amendment . . . will someday be repudiated.[21]

The legality of warrantless strip searches for law enforcement purposes, including safety and security, was addressed by the Roberts Court in *Florence v. Board of Chosen Freeholders* (2012). The case will be discussed in the chapter 8 coverage of rights in corrections contexts. A narrow majority gave blanket approval to conduct strip searches on any arrestee, no matter how minor the charge that brought the individual into a jail. The case concerned a man subjected to strip searches and visual body cavity inspections at two different jails after being arrested based on an erroneous database record concerning an unpaid fine. The combination of the *King* and *Florence* decisions narrowed the protections provided by the Fourth Amendment for those who are arrested yet still presumptively innocent as they await processing of their cases. As one commentator observed, these decisions are very impactful in light of estimates that nearly one-third of Americans will be arrested by age twenty-three.[22]

In a different warrantless search context, *Safford Unified School District v. Redding* (2009) examined public school officials' authority to strip-search a thirteen-year-old middle school student based on nothing more than a tip from a fellow student. School officials were falsely told that Redding possessed prescription-strength ibuprofen and had provided these pills to another student. The assistant principal summoned Redding to the office, where she denied ownership of the pills possessed by the other student. After no pills were found in her backpack, she was required to remove most of her clothing and then shake out her underwear in the presence of female staff members. No pills were found.

In an 8–1 liberal ruling, the majority opinion by Justice Souter agreed with Redding that her constitutional rights had been violated. Justice Thomas was the lone dissenter on this issue. With respect to a second issue in the case, a 7–2 majority ruled that she could not sue the school officials for violating her Fourth Amendment right because of qualified immunity. Qualified immunity is a legal concept that protects officials from liability if judges conclude that the officials could not have known that their actions violated constitutional rights at the time the actions were taken.

In the majority opinion, Justice Souter found the search of Redding's belongings to be reasonable but that sufficient cause did not exist to subject Redding to the very intrusive visual strip search of her body. Souter did not say that schools could never conduct strip searches. Instead, he asserted that school officials must have a stronger justification than a tip from a student about possession of pain medications before subjecting a student to such a search.

The justices' statements and questions during oral arguments did not suggest that Redding's claim would prevail. During oral arguments, many of the justices seemed to find little fault with the school's actions. Several male justices emphasized the need for school officials to protect students from drugs. They also minimized the nature of the intrusion experienced by the student. One justice implied that it was not intrusive because all students must remove their clothes in the locker room every day before gym class. The nature of the justices' questioning and comments clearly concerned Justice Ginsburg, who repeatedly advocated recognition of the harmful humiliation experienced by the girl who was strip-searched.[23] Before the case outcome was announced, Justice Ginsburg gently criticized her colleagues in a media interview by saying, "The other Court members have never been a 13-year-old girl. . . . It's a very sensitive age for a girl. I didn't think that my colleagues, some of them, quite understood."[24] It is unknown whether Ginsburg's arguments presented during the justices' private discussion of the case changed any other justices' minds. However, the case outcome and the size of the liberal majority were surprising in light of the skeptical comments made by male justices during oral arguments.

The Roberts Court endorsed warrantless "stop and frisk" searches of certain car passengers in *Arizona v. Johnson* (2009). The "stop and frisk" exception allows officers to "pat down" an individual stopped by police based on reasonable suspicion in order to ensure the person does not have any weapons that could endanger the officer or the public.[25] In the case, officers stopped a car in which Johnson was a passenger. Based on Johnson's behavior, officers asked him to leave the car to be questioned. Before questioning, Johnson was subjected to a pat-down search, and officers found a gun. Johnson argued the search was unconstitutional, but the Roberts Court unanimously disagreed, holding that reasonable concern for officer safety justified the frisk search. As chapter 8 will discuss in greater detail, an additional expansion of "stop and frisk" authority was endorsed in *Samson v. California* (2006) concerning the suspicionless search of a parolee who had been released into the community.

Exclusionary Rule

One of the most important developments of the Roberts Court era's Fourth Amendment jurisprudence was the diminution of the exclusionary rule's applicability. Analysts noted that the elimination of the exclusionary rule was a long-standing goal of Chief Justice Roberts. As a lawyer, he was active in attempting to significantly reduce the scope of the rule's protections.[26] While serving on the legal staff for the Reagan administration, Roberts worked on a plan, as he put it in a memo, to "amend or abolish the exclusionary rule."[27] As chief justice of the United States, Roberts may be close to achieving this goal, especially with the formation of a conservative supermajority after the addition of President Trump's three appointees.

The Roberts Court created a new exception to the use of the exclusionary rule in its conservative decision in *Hudson v. Michigan*. The court, which divided along its usual ideological lines, created an exception to the exclusionary rule for "knock-and-announce" violations when executing a warrant. Police with a valid search warrant entered Hudson's home within seconds of announcing their presence and without providing sufficient time for Hudson to respond. Writing for a narrow five-member majority, Justice Scalia's opinion found the exclusionary rule to be inapplicable in this circumstance. Scalia noted that not all search activities that violate legal requirements necessitate the exclusion of evidence discovered in the search. Scalia considered whether the social costs of excluding the evidence are less than the deterrent value for preventing police errors and misconduct. The case provided a strong indication early in the Roberts Court era that the court was poised to reduce the applicability of the exclusionary rule, a move the majority advanced in *Herring v. United States*.

Herring was a conservative decision determined by a closely divided vote. In the case, Herring was arrested and searched when a database erroneously indicated there was a warrant for his arrest. The search resulted in the discovery of drugs and a gun. The court majority found that evidence improperly obtained as a result of police errors in maintaining information in a database need not be subject to the exclusionary rule. As one observer noted, Roberts's "majority opinion established for the first time that unlawful police conduct should not require the suppression of evidence if all that was involved was isolated carelessness. That was a significant step in itself. More important yet, it suggested that the exclusionary rule itself might be at risk."[28]

In an opinion written by Chief Justice Roberts, the majority found that although a Fourth Amendment violation existed, exclusion of evidence was not required. In Roberts's view, when the exclusion of evidence was likely to act as a deterrent to future police misconduct and was worth the social cost of the exclusion, the court should consider the suppression of evidence. However, if the police simply engaged in a careless error, suppression was too extreme as a remedy for the acknowledged rights violation. Roberts concluded that the officers engaged in nothing more than a good-faith mistake and acted reasonably given that error. Chief Justice Roberts and the conservative majority concluded that the police officers did not do anything wrong because they relied in good faith on the erroneous record in a police database. This approach permits Fourth Amendment violations to go unremedied because the focus is on police officers' knowledge or intentions rather than on the issue of whether an individual experienced the violation of a Fourth Amendment constitutional protection.[29] By contrast, during the Warren Court era, the majority of justices did not easily forgive police errors and were much more concerned about remedying rights violations. The Warren Court appeared to analyze cases by asking, "Were any rights violated?" The Roberts Court, however, seemed to focus on the narrow question, "Did the police really do anything wrong?" The latter question can lead to rights violations remaining unremedied when police make errors from carelessness or good-faith reliance on erroneous database records.

On behalf of the four liberal dissenters, Justice Ginsburg strongly disagreed with the majority's reasoning and conclusions. Ginsburg argued that while it was true that the exclusionary rule was intended to deter future police behavior, the rule was also necessary to ensure that the government does not benefit from its own unlawful behavior. She contended that accurate recordkeeping was vital for law enforcement and the criminal justice system. Thus, the use of the exclusionary rule to encourage diligence in recordkeeping was essential because faulty recordkeeping threatens individual liberty.

The Roberts Court further limited the reach of the exclusionary rule in *Heien v. North Carolina* (2014). The majority ruled that evidence gathered from a reasonable mistake by a police officer need not be excluded from use by the prosecution. Heien's vehicle was stopped because his car had only one working brake light. The officer conducting the stop was under the mistaken impression that North Carolina required two working brake lights, and therefore he believed that the traffic stop was justified by a violation of vehicle safety laws. The officer was wrong, however, because North Carolina law required only one brake light to be operational. Thus, the initial stop of the car was unjustified. During the vehicle stop, the officer requested and obtained consent to search and subsequently discovered a small amount of cocaine in a duffel bag.

Writing for the majority, Chief Justice Roberts concluded that the Constitution did not require that the evidence in this case be subject to the exclusionary rule. In his view, the Fourth Amendment requires only that officers act in a reasonable manner. Although the officer was mistaken in his understanding of the law, his actions were a reasonable extension of that initial mistake, and thus a stop based on this faulty knowledge was also reasonable. The case effectively expanded the number of situations in which evidence need not be excluded. After *Heien*, these situations included those in which police officers are ignorant about the details of laws that they are responsible for enforcing.

A further diminution of the exclusionary rule occurred in *Utah v. Streiff* (2016). Police received an anonymous tip about drug activity at a house. While observing the house, an officer saw Streiff leave the house and walk to a convenience store. The officer stopped Streiff and asked for his identification. When checking the identification in a police database, the officer discovered an outstanding arrest warrant for Streiff based on a traffic violation. The officer arrested Streiff, conducted a search incident to a lawful arrest, and discovered illegal drugs that provided the basis for a felony prosecution. The Utah Supreme Court ruled that the evidence should be excluded because there was no legal basis for the officer to stop Streiff and request his identification. Thus, an improper stop led to the discovery of the arrest warrant. However, in a 5–3 decision written by Justice Thomas, the Roberts Court majority declared that the discovery of the warrant attenuated the connection between the unlawful stop and the discovery of the evidence. In other words, the discovery of the warrant was an intervening event that uncoupled the unlawful stop from the acquisition of the evidence and thereby made the evidence admissible in court.

The three most liberal justices, Ginsburg, Kagan, and Sotomayor, objected to this expansion of police authority and the broader opportunities to use evidence whose discovery began with an unlawful stop in violation of the Fourth Amendment. As described by Justice Sotomayor:

> The Court today holds that the discovery of a warrant for an unpaid parking ticket will forgive a police officer's violation of your Fourth Amendment rights. Do not be soothed by the opinion's technical language: This case allows the police to stop you on the street, demand your

identification, and check it for outstanding traffic warrants—even if you are doing nothing wrong. If the officer discovers a warrant for a fine you forgot to pay, courts will now excuse his illegal stop and will admit into evidence anything he happens to find by searching you after arresting you on the warrant.[30]

Impact of the Justices Appointed by President Trump

Because the Supreme Court typically decides several Fourth Amendment cases each year, it will be possible to watch on a year-by-year basis to see whether the establishment of the Roberts Court's conservative supermajority will lead to decisions that differ from those in preceding years. In the 2021 and 2022 Supreme Court terms, the terms in which the three Trump-appointed justices first sat together on the court, the initial Fourth Amendment decisions did not indicate that the justices were aggressively seeking to alter precedents.

Some of the Fourth Amendment decisions by the newly constituted Roberts Court continued to protect constitutional rights. The court's decision in *Caniglia v. Strom* (2021) produced a unanimous liberal outcome. Consistent with prior Roberts Court decisions, the justices emphasized the strength of Fourth Amendment protections for the home. The ruling identified a Fourth Amendment violation when officers without a warrant entered a home and seized firearms owned by man who had just been transported to a hospital for a psychiatric evaluation.

Similarly, in *Lange v. California* (2021), the court emphasized the protection of a home from unjustified intrusion by police. A police officer used the patrol vehicle's overhead lights to instruct a driver to stop along a roadway. The driver, playing loud music and honking his horn, failed to stop. He drove up the nearby driveway to his home and parked the car in the garage. The officer followed the individual into the garage, where the individual failed the sobriety test administered by the officer. The officer justified the warrantless entry into the garage under the "exigent circumstances" exception because the officer was in "hot pursuit" of the individual for the misdemeanor offense of failing to comply with a police signal. The Roberts Court rejected the claim that "hot pursuit" entries into homes are necessarily justified for every offense. In a 7–2 decision, the majority opinion by Justice Kagan said that the pursuit of suspected misdemeanants for minor offenses justifies warrantless entry into a home only if there is some other exigent circumstance present, such as danger to the officer, a risk the individual will escape, or a risk that evidence will be destroyed. Only Chief Justice Roberts and Justice Alito argued in dissent that a warrantless entry is justified by an individual's flight from an officer without regard to the seriousness of the offense that the officer believes the individual committed.

Despite these affirmations of Fourth Amendment protections, there were signs that justices on the Roberts Court advocated reductions, not only in the definition of Fourth Amendment rights but also in the remedies applied for Fourth Amendment violations. In *Lange*, for example, Justice Thomas, joined by Justice Kavanaugh, agreed with the majority that the entry was improper. However, in a concurring opinion, these justices expressed the view that even if officers improperly enter a home while pursuing a misdemeanant, the exclusionary rule should not apply. Instead, the individual whose Fourth Amendment rights were violated by the entry must look to other kinds of legal actions, such as civil lawsuits against the officer, to seek a remedy for the rights violation.

As indicated by the discussion in this chapter, commentators believe that Chief Justice Roberts, as demonstrated by his majority opinion in *Herring*, is interested in severely restricting the application of the exclusionary rule. Justice Thomas expressed similar ideas in his concurring opinions in *Collins* and *Lange*, with Justice Kavanaugh joining Thomas's opinion in the context of hot pursuits. Justice Alito disagreed with the majority opinions in both *Collins* and *Lange*, so he would have admitted the evidence by declaring that both searches were valid. Are these clues that a critical mass of justices is developing that could further reduce the exclusionary rule or expand police authority to conduct searches? In light of the advancement of conservative outcomes through alteration and invalidation of precedents for other legal issues, it will not be surprising if that turns out to be the case for Fourth Amendment issues.

The other avenue for reducing the effective protection of Fourth Amendment and other constitutional rights is through limiting individuals' ability to file civil lawsuits seeking compensation for rights violations. In the Fourth Amendment context, such lawsuits are likely to concern unlawful searches as well as excessive uses of force by police, which are violations of the right against "unreasonable seizures." For example, in *Safford Unified School District v. Redding*, concerning the unjustified strip search of the middle-school girl by school officials, the Roberts Court recognized a Fourth Amendment rights violation. However, seven justices precluded a remedial lawsuit by using the concept of qualified immunity to protect school officials from liability. In a later case, the six justices constituting the new conservative supermajority ruled that an individual could not file a civil lawsuit against a US Border Patrol agent who, he alleged, forcibly pushed him against a vehicle and then threw him to the ground (*Egbert v. Boule*, 2022). The plaintiff had sought to pursue an excessive force claim under the Fourth Amendment protection against "unreasonable seizures."

Because the Supreme Court created a cause of action for constitutional rights lawsuits against federal officials in *Bivens v. Six Unknown Named Agents of the Federal Bureau of Narcotics* (1971), the opportunity exists to use civil litigation to vindicate alleged constitutional rights violations by FBI agents and other federal officers. Such civil rights lawsuits against state and local officials are pursued under a federal statute enacted by Congress and codified in Title 42, Section 1983 of the US Code. The lawsuits against federal officials are commonly called "Bivens actions," and the lawsuits against state and local officials are referred to as "1983 lawsuits." Yet, Justices Thomas and Gorsuch explicitly assert that the Roberts Court should eliminate all opportunities for "Bivens actions" against federal officials. They argue that only Congress, not the Supreme Court, possesses the power to authorize such legal actions, as Congress did in enacting the statute containing Section 1983 concerning alleged rights violations by state and local officials.

In *Hernandez v. Mesa* (2020), a 5–4 decision prior to the replacement of Justice Ginsburg by Trump appointee Justice Barrett, the majority barred a Bivens action lawsuit by the parents of a Mexican teenager who was shot and killed by a US Border Patrol officer who fired his weapon across the border into Mexico. In a concurring opinion, Thomas, joined by Gorsuch, clearly stated a desire to end the availability of Bivens actions. In *Egbert*, Thomas's majority opinion was again critical of the court's creation of a cause of action in the *Bivens case*, and Gorsuch used a concurring opinion to explicitly advocate its demise.

Can Thomas and Gorsuch get the additional votes they need to eliminate constitutional rights lawsuits against federal officials based on the *Bivens case*? Whether or not this proves to be true, the inclination to shrink rather than expand opportunities for constitutional rights lawsuits seems evident among the justices in the conservative supermajority. In the Fifth

Amendment context, the six-justice majority ruled that individuals could not file lawsuits against state and local criminal justice officials when Miranda rights are violated (*Vega v. Tekoh*, 2022). If that decision is an indicator of the chosen path of the Roberts Court majority, no one should be surprised to see remedies for other constitutional rights violations reduced or foreclosed.

Cases concerning reduced applications of the exclusionary rule and limitations on rights-vindicating lawsuits against criminal justice officials tend to divide the Roberts Court justices along ideological lines. Obviously, these developments are of deep concern to the liberals who are watching the effective shrinkage of rights that exist only in theory but not in reality if there are no applicable remedies for violations. As expressed in a dissenting opinion by Justice Sotomayor on behalf of Justices Breyer and Kagan in *Egbert v. Boule*, "This Court's precedents recognize that suits for damages play a critical role in deterring unconstitutional conduct by federal law enforcement officers and in ensuring that those whose constitutional rights have been violated receive meaningful redress. The Court's decision today ignores our repeated recognition of the importance of *Bivens* actions, particularly in the Fourth Amendment search-and-seizure context, and closes the door to *Bivens* suits by many who will suffer serious constitutional violations at the hands of federal agents."[31]

Conclusion

The Roberts Court, while issuing several significant liberal decisions, generally continued a four-decade trend of narrowing the protections provided by the Fourth Amendment. Like decisions from prior conservative-leaning eras under Chief Justices Burger and Rehnquist, the Roberts Court's decisions weakened the exclusionary rule and otherwise increased police authority at the expense of strong, clear protections for individuals. At the same time, the Roberts Court majority was open to recognizing and protecting Fourth Amendment rights, depending on the context of the issue, especially with respect to protecting people's homes and guarding against privacy threats involving cell phones and other aspects of technology.

For example, the Roberts Court's protective decision in *Riley v. California* concerning police officers' warrantless examination of a motorist's cell phone challenged commentators to evaluate why a liberal Fourth Amendment decision in that context would emerge from a conservative court. Longtime Supreme Court correspondent for the *New York Times* Linda Greenhouse did not see this decision as consistent with the logic and reasoning of other Roberts Court cases concerning rights in criminal justice. She opined that the Roberts Court majority was more protective because they could envision themselves in this situation experiencing this intrusion on their privacy. Her commentary, "The Supreme Court Justices Have Cellphones, Too," could plausibly be applied as a speculative explanation for the Roberts Court's other protective decisions.[32] In particular, the justices may empathize with people affected by warrantless GPS monitoring of vehicles' movements (*United States v. Jones*) and governments' acquisition of data about an individual's whereabouts produced by cell phone towers (*Carpenter v. United States*). These are forms of modern device–assisted surveillance that could be applied to affluent people without the existence of reasonable suspicion of wrongdoing. Similarly, there may be greater understanding of the violation of reasonable expectations of privacy when police officers invade people's homes and the curtilage of homes, as in the warrantless front porch entry of a trained dog (*Florida v. Jardines*), a "hot pursuit" entry based on a traffic misdemeanor (*Lange v. California*), and the inspection of a tarp-covered vehicle in a driveway (*Collins v. Virginia*).

Another unexpected liberal decision was issued in the case of *Rodriguez v. United States* (2015). In a 6–3 decision written by Justice Ginsburg, the court declared that a police officer violated the Fourth Amendment by requiring a driver to wait at the scene of a completed traffic stop in order to give another officer time to arrive with a drug-sniffing dog. Justice Ginsburg stated that a seizure at a traffic stop is unreasonable if it extends beyond the time required to complete the traffic stop's purpose of issuing a citation. The dissenters in the case were Justices Thomas, Alito, and Kennedy. Was this another case in which Greenhouse's speculative observation might apply? Certainly, Supreme Court justices and their family members could be stopped by police for traffic violations. Indeed, Justice Scalia received a ticket in 2011 for following too closely while driving and rear-ending another vehicle as he drove to the court in morning rush-hour traffic. If he had been held at the scene, he might have missed oral arguments in a major sex discrimination case scheduled for presentation at ten o'clock that morning.[33] In joining the court's four most liberal justices (Ginsburg, Breyer, Sotomayor, and Kagan), did typically conservative justices Roberts and Scalia empathize with the inconvenience imposed if police officers were granted broad discretionary authority to hold stopped drivers indefinitely at the scene of a traffic violation?

There is little reason to anticipate that the Roberts Court, with its altered composition during its post-2020 natural court period, will step back from protective concerns about technological surveillance and intrusions into homes. Instead, commentators will be watching closely for changes affecting other aspects of the Fourth Amendment, such as the preservation of the exclusionary rule, the reduction in lawsuit-driven remedies, and the application of law enforcement authority in other search contexts.

5. MIRANDA WARNINGS AND RIGHT TO COUNSEL

The Warren Court established new requirements for police questioning of suspects in *Miranda v. Arizona* (1966). The controversial decision created an entitlement for suspects in custody to receive warnings about their right to remain silent and their right to have an attorney present during questioning. The rule sought to prevent police from pressuring people to confess and thereby protected the Fifth Amendment privilege against compelled self-incrimination. Coerced confessions not only violate the Fifth Amendment principle but also adversely affect the justice system by increasing the risk that an innocent person will be punished while the person who actually committed a crime will remain free to harm the community. Miranda warnings also provide a link between the Fifth and Sixth Amendments by creating the entitlement to representation by counsel at an early stage in the process for people drawn into the system as criminal suspects.

The Sixth Amendment right to counsel protects both the defendant's right to a fair trial and the integrity of the adversarial system of justice. These objectives include the opportunity for both parties to present their case and test opposing arguments before an impartial judge or jury. The defense attorney is also a key figure in the criminal justice process who seeks to protect constitutional rights. As Justice Stevens said in *United States v. Cronic* (1984), "Of all the rights that an accused person has, the right to be represented by counsel is by far the most pervasive, for it affects his ability to assert any other rights he may have."[1] Prior to the Roberts Court era, Supreme Court decisions defined and expanded the meaning of the right to counsel, especially with respect to suspects and defendants who could not afford to hire their own attorneys. Decisions from the mid-twentieth century onward created the foundation for the Roberts Court's actions in refining the entitlement to and role of defense counsel in criminal cases.

The Origins of Miranda Rights

In *Miranda v. Arizona*, a rape suspect in police custody was questioned by officers who emerged from the interrogation room with his confession. In a narrow 5–4 decision, Chief Justice Warren described the risks of physical and psychological coercion that can occur during police questioning. Based on risks that he recognized as a former prosecutor, his majority opinion declared that suspects are entitled to the presence of attorneys during questioning in order to protect the Fifth Amendment privilege against compelled self-incrimination. The majority opinion required police officers to inform suspects in custody of certain rights, especially the right to have an attorney present and the right to remain silent, before undertaking questioning of those suspects. The Supreme Court also applied the exclusionary rule to Miranda violations in order to deter improper questioning and prevent prosecutors from using evidence obtained in violation of a suspect's constitutional rights.

The *Miranda* decision and the Warren Court itself became lightning rods in national politics. Richard Nixon criticized the decision during his 1968 presidential campaign as one that would increase crime by "handcuffing police." US Senator Strom Thurmond and other critics of the Warren Court used judicial confirmation hearings to rail against *Miranda* and other rights-expanding rulings.[2] Critics of the Warren Court's strengthening of rights for suspects and defendants portrayed the court as "soft on crime." In Congress, these critics succeeded in passing a statute in 1968 that was designed to overrule *Miranda*'s applicability in federal criminal cases. The law sought to make voluntary confessions generally admissible in federal court. The statute also declared that voluntariness could be shown in several ways, even if interrogators failed to inform a suspect of the rights described by Warren's majority opinion in *Miranda*.

For three decades, the statute remained unused as federal prosecutors continued to treat Miranda warnings as a requirement. In 1999, a US court of appeals concluded that the 1968 law supplanted *Miranda* and ruled that a voluntary incriminating statement could be used as evidence at the trial of a suspect who had not been properly informed of Miranda rights. By a 7–2 vote, the Rehnquist Court not only rejected that interpretation but also declared that the *Miranda* decision had announced a rule required by the Constitution rather than merely a Supreme Court–created policy (*Dickerson v. United States*, 2000). According to Chief Justice Rehnquist's majority opinion, the Miranda rule was beyond the authority of Congress to overrule through legislation.

The *Dickerson* decision surprised many observers given that decisions by both the Burger Court and Rehnquist Court weakened the Miranda warning's effectiveness. One important example of the weakening of Miranda warnings was evident in *Duckworth v. Eagan* (1989), a Rehnquist Court era decision that permitted police to change the wording of the required warnings. Wording changes carry an attendant risk that suspects might not clearly understand the rights to which they are entitled. Earlier examples from the Burger Court era included the creation of exceptions to the exclusionary rule as it applied to Miranda violations. The ruling in *New York v. Quarles* (1984) permitted police to use evidence obtained in violation of *Miranda* whenever a purportedly urgent "public safety" situation led police to ask questions of an arrestee without providing the required warnings. Similarly, Miranda violations were excused if police could claim under the "inevitable discovery" rule that they would have found the evidence anyway despite, in fact, obtaining the evidence through improper questioning (*Nix v. Williams*, 1984).

Over the first terms of the Roberts Court, several leading experts criticized the court for its conservative judicial activism in undervaluing precedents affecting *Miranda*-related issues.[3] Constitutional law scholar Erwin Chemerinsky, for example, asserted that restricting defendants' right to counsel and weakening self-incrimination protections were among the most important changes in criminal procedure during the Roberts Court's first few terms.[4] Other critics charged that the court majority had rejected the fundamental underpinnings of *Miranda*,[5] and thereby contributed to *Miranda*'s "death by a thousand cuts," even without overturning the famous precedent.[6]

Miranda Warnings in the Roberts Court Era

The Roberts Court majority continued the weakening of Miranda warnings that began in the Burger and Rehnquist Court eras. For example, in *Florida v. Powell* (2010), the Roberts Court majority upheld warnings given by Tampa police that read as follows: "You have the right to talk to a lawyer *before* answering any of our questions . . . [and] the right to use any of these rights at any time you want during this interview" (emphasis added).[7] To critics, such wording did not clearly convey the original message of Chief Justice Warren's *Miranda* opinion that guaranteed an entitlement to the presence of counsel during the entirety of questioning. The Florida Supreme Court concluded that the language was confusing and inadequate for communicating that the suspect had the right to counsel throughout an interrogation. Despite conceding the Tampa "warnings were not the *clearest possible* formulation of *Miranda*'s right-to-counsel advisement" (emphasis in original), a majority on the Roberts Court concluded that the wording adequately conveyed the elements required by *Miranda*.[8]

Critics of decisions that endorse deviations from the original wording of Miranda warnings, including dissenters on the Roberts Court, contend that the court endorsed potentially confusing warnings.[9] Moreover, critics claim that these altered warnings cannot be reconciled with the *Miranda* decision's stated intention to reduce the coercive atmosphere of custodial interrogations by clearly informing suspects of their rights. Arguably, clarity is necessary to ensure that any waiver of rights is made knowingly and voluntarily. Even calm, well-educated individuals may struggle to comprehend fully their Miranda rights if given a convoluted set of warnings. An understandably nervous person who is about to be questioned by police could easily feel overwhelmed and unable to fully understand the altered Miranda warnings. Professor Yale Kamisar, the scholar known as the "father of Miranda warnings" because of his extensive research and advocacy on rights protection during custodial interrogations, concluded that the adoption of confusing language can be seen as logical only if the purpose is to provide "police certain advantages not provided by the standard warnings."[10]

With respect to a different aspect of Miranda warnings, the Roberts Court imposed the responsibility on suspects to be clear in their communications with police. In a 5–4 decision in *Berghuis v. Thompkins* (2010), the court's conservative wing effectively narrowed the scope of Miranda protections. The majority ruled that a suspect's silence—even if over a prolonged period—is not sufficient to invoke the right to remain silent. Instead, Chief Justice Roberts and Justices Alito, Thomas, Scalia, and Kennedy declared that suspects must explicitly state they are invoking the right to remain silent in order to end police questioning in respect of that right. Police arrested Thompkins for a fatal shooting. He was informed of his Miranda rights, but he refused to sign a form acknowledging that he understood these warnings. During nearly three hours of interrogation, Thompkins gave only an occasional brief response to questions such as whether he was comfortable during questioning. Near the end of the lengthy interrogation, however, an officer asked Thompkins whether he prayed for forgiveness for shooting the victim, and Thompkins answered "yes." The statement was used at trial, a jury found him guilty, and he was sentenced to life in prison.

The Roberts Court majority held that the assertion of a Fifth Amendment right to remain silent must be unambiguous. Lengthy silence does not meet this requirement, and police reasonably could interpret the statement regarding praying for forgiveness to be an implicit waiver of that right. In part, the decision was analogous to a Rehnquist Court ruling that an unambiguous request for an attorney was necessary in order to assert the Miranda right to counsel during interrogations (*Davis v. United States*, 1994).

In her first major dissenting opinion on the Supreme Court, Justice Sotomayor sharply criticized the majority's reasoning that "turns *Miranda* upside down" and "bodes poorly for the fundamental principles that *Miranda* protects."[11] Justice Sotomayor stressed that the majority ignored precedents that had placed a substantial burden on the government to demonstrate that a suspect waived a particular right when that waiver was not communicated explicitly. Judicial commentators and scholars echoed Sotomayor's assessment, characterizing *Berghuis* as "an alarming break with the philosophy of *Miranda*"[12] because it had the effect of "expressly heightening the standard necessary for suspects to invoke the right to remain silent . . . [while] implicitly lowering the standard necessary to establish waiver [of that right]."[13]

Berghuis v. Thompkins represented one of the Roberts Court's most significant reinterpretations of the spirit of *Miranda*. Accepting a statement made after lengthy silence to be an implicit waiver of the right to remain silent is difficult to square with *Miranda*'s strong language that any waiver must be made voluntarily, knowingly, and intelligently.[14] Combined with rulings involving modified Miranda warnings, *Berghuis* signaled a marked shift in the relative burden borne by police. Police are permitted to provide ambiguous Miranda warnings, while suspects are required to unambiguously state their desire to exercise their rights.

The Roberts Court decided a different right-to-remain-silent issue in *Salinas v. Texas* (2013). The conservative majority again placed the burden on the individual to indicate clearly the desire to exercise the constitutional right to remain silent. Unlike the suspect in *Berghuis*, however, Salinas was not in custody and had not been given Miranda warnings. He voluntarily met with police officers and answered several questions but then remained silent when asked whether ballistic evidence from the scene of a murder would match his firearm. Prosecutors referenced that silence in their case in chief as a sign of his guilt. Subsequently, a jury convicted him. The Roberts Court found that this did not violate Salinas's protections against self-incrimination because he failed to invoke this right clearly when the officer asked the question.

Though *Salinas* was not a *Miranda* case, it remains instructive. A suspect being questioned might not know whether he or she is "in custody" or whether that custody is a key element to trigger Miranda warnings. Even those with a basic awareness of "taking the Fifth" are unlikely to realize that their silence can potentially be used against them when being interviewed by the police.

The Roberts Court addressed the special problem of police questioning juvenile suspects in *J. D. B. v. North Carolina* (2011). A police investigator, a uniformed officer, and school officials questioned a thirteen-year-old student in a closed room at the student's school. They suspected the boy was involved in two neighborhood break-ins. Before questioning began, the juvenile was not provided with Miranda warnings, not informed he could contact his legal guardian, and not told he was free to leave the room. He eventually confessed. Justice Sotomayor's majority opinion concluded that when a suspect's juvenile status is known or objectively apparent, it is an appropriate factor to use in evaluating custody for Miranda purposes. There must be consideration of the fact that children may not be able to assess accurately their ability to refuse to answer questions or to leave the site of questioning. Adults are presumed to know that they can get up and leave if they are not under arrest or otherwise detained by police. Teens are unlikely to possess the same knowledge. A suspect's youth is not necessarily decisive, but "children cannot be viewed simply as miniature adults."[15] Juveniles may be entitled to Miranda warnings in some situations in which police would not be required to provide warnings to adults. Sotomayor's narrow majority was formed because Kennedy joined the four more liberal justices to provide broader Miranda protections for juveniles than for adults.

The Burger Court had ruled in *Edwards v. Arizona* (1981) that police officers must stop questioning when a detained suspect requests an attorney. Moreover, officers also cannot resume questioning until the suspect has met with a lawyer or freely chooses to reinitiate interactions with police.

Years later, in *Maryland v. Shatzer* (2010), the Roberts Court addressed whether *Edwards* prohibits police from resuming questioning when there is a break between the suspect's invocation of his right to counsel during an initial interrogation and the later initiation of the second interrogation. Shatzer was in prison serving a sentence for a separate crime when he was questioned by police about a sex offense. The officer properly stopped the interview when Shatzer invoked his rights under *Miranda* and refused to answer questions without an attorney. The officer soon closed the investigation for lack of evidence. Two and a half years later, another detective reopened the case. Armed with new information, the detective interviewed Shatzer, who was still incarcerated. Shatzer did not mention that he had invoked his right to counsel in this matter years earlier. He subsequently made incriminating statements during the second interview.

A unanimous Roberts Court held that the second round of questioning did not violate Shatzer's rights or require exclusion of his confession under *Edwards*. The court justified the use of the second interview because there was a sufficiently lengthy break in custodial questioning after Shatzer requested counsel during the first interview. Although Shatzer remained imprisoned throughout the process, the court determined that being released into the general prison population after being questioned the first time was a break in "custody" for purposes of the *Miranda* and *Edwards* requirements.

Writing for the court, Justice Scalia established a "14-day rule" in which a two-week period constituted a sufficient break in custodial interrogations for questioning to resume after a suspect invokes the right to counsel in a prior interrogation. The suspect retains the opportunity to assert the right to counsel again in the second or subsequent interrogations. Justice Scalia reasoned that a two-week period "provides plenty of time for the suspect to get reacclimated to his normal life, to consult with friends and counsel, and to shake off any residual coercive effects of his prior custody."[16]

In an opinion concurring in judgment, Justice Stevens agreed that the assertion of the right to counsel during questioning is not eternal. However, he questioned the creation of a time-based rule using an arbitrary fourteen-day break between questioning efforts by authorities. In addition, commentators who were otherwise supportive of the outcome in circumstances of a break exceeding two years found it disconcerting that Scalia equated incarceration in a prison's general population with "normal life" and being "free from custody."[17]

Constitutional Rights and Defense Attorneys in Criminal Cases

A unanimous Warren Court in *Gideon v. Wainwright* (1963) held that the Sixth Amendment right to counsel is a fundamental legal entitlement in both state and federal criminal cases. As such, the protection applied to all indigent defendants who faced serious criminal charges and thereby imposed on states the affirmative obligation to provide attorneys for those who could not afford to hire their own. Within a decade of the *Gideon* decision, the Burger Court extended the right to court-appointed counsel for indigent defendants to all cases ending in the incarceration of the defendant, regardless of whether the charge was classified as a felony or a misdemeanor (*Argersinger v. Hamlin*, 1972).

During the Roberts Court era, the generally conservative Justice Kennedy wielded significant influence by sitting in the ideological middle of a divided court. With respect to the right to counsel, however, he was not the only conservative on the Roberts Court to cast decisive votes upholding individuals' Sixth Amendment claims. For example, Justice Scalia joined members of the court's liberal bloc in *United States v. Gonzalez-Lopez* (2006). In this case from early in the Roberts Court era, the defendant's family hired one defense attorney, while the defendant himself hired a different attorney. The two lawyers briefly worked together before the trial judge dismissed the defendant's counsel of choice for a violation of a court rule. Gonzalez-Lopez was eventually convicted of conspiracy to distribute marijuana.

Justice Scalia's majority opinion declared that the Sixth Amendment protects the defendant's right to counsel of choice. The selection of an attorney can affect nearly every aspect of the trial process, including plea bargaining, jury selection, and the choice of legal tactics and strategies to be pursued. Scalia and the other justices in the majority concluded that the choice of counsel is so fundamental to the accused's defense that the denial of a defendant's preferred representative without compelling justification warranted reversal of the conviction. By contrast, the dissenting members of the court's conservative wing argued that the Sixth Amendment guarantees a certain quality of legal representation but not the choice of who provides that representation.

During the Burger Court era, the court acknowledged the constitutional right to represent oneself in a criminal trial (*Faretta v. California*, 1975).

This decision confirmed the defendant's entitlement to make a specific choice concerning the right to counsel. The Roberts Court narrowed that ruling by allowing the state to appoint counsel against a defendant's wishes when the defendant suffered from mental illness. Such appointments do not violate the Sixth Amendment when the defendant is competent to stand trial yet not sufficiently competent to present a defense without the benefit of professional representation (*Indiana v. Edwards*, 2008).

The Roberts Court examined the defendant's control over the presentation of a defense in *McCoy v. Louisiana* (2018). During McCoy's trial on multiple murder charges, his attorney made a strategic decision to tell the jury that McCoy committed the murders. The attorney then sought to convince the jury to impose a prison sentence rather than the death penalty based on McCoy's mental state. Meanwhile, McCoy insisted he was innocent and objected vociferously to his attorney's actions. Ultimately, he was convicted and sentenced to death. Justice Kennedy wrote the court's opinion on behalf of a six-member majority declaring that McCoy was entitled to a new trial. Justice Kennedy said the attorney's actions violated the defendant's right to make fundamental choices about his own defense. The decision highlighted the roles of dissenters Thomas, Alito, and Gorsuch as the justices most likely to disagree with rulings that supported right-to-counsel protections for criminal defendants.

The Sixth Amendment's words do not specify that indigent defendants are entitled to appointed counsel, let alone identify the point at which courts must assign an attorney to those unable to hire one. These are matters that have been defined through judicial decisions. In *Rothgery v. Gillespie County* (2008), for example, officers mistakenly arrested Rothgery on a firearms possession charge. They brought him to a probable-cause hearing, during which a judge informed him of the charge and set bail. Rothgery made several unsuccessful requests for court-appointed counsel. The county contended that the pretrial hearing did not trigger the right to counsel because prosecutors were not yet involved in the case. A nearly unanimous Roberts Court disagreed. The court ruled that the right to counsel attaches at the beginning of adversarial judicial proceedings when a defendant is apprised of the charge and his or her liberty is restricted. The entitlement to counsel at this point in the criminal justice process is not dependent on the presence of prosecutors. Justice Thomas, who consistently demonstrated his willingness to express unique viewpoints, filed the only dissent. He asserted that Rothgery's hearing did not mark the beginning of a criminal "prosecution" under the original meaning of the Sixth Amendment.[18]

With respect to the right to counsel, the clearest departure from established precedents during the first decade of the Roberts Court occurred in *Montejo v. Louisiana* (2009). In its decision, a divided court made it easier for police and prosecutors to question suspects in custody despite the absence of defense counsel. Montejo was arrested in connection with a murder, given Miranda warnings, and questioned. At a preliminary hearing, a judge ordered the appointment of a defense attorney to represent Montejo. Montejo did not expressly request, accept, or reject the appointment of counsel. Later that day at the jail, he was read his Miranda rights again, and he agreed to a request from officers to join them on a trip to locate the murder weapon. After interacting with officers during the trip outside the jail, Montejo wrote an incriminating letter apologizing to the victim's widow. Upon returning to jail, Montejo met his court-appointed attorney for the first time. The letter was admitted into evidence at trial. Montejo was convicted and sentenced to death.

On behalf of the court's five most conservative members, Justice Scalia's majority opinion overturned the Burger Court decision in *Michigan v. Jackson* (1986). *Jackson* prohibited the questioning of an already-represented defendant unless the accused first communicated with law enforcement officers on his or her own. The Burger Court ruled in *Jackson* that if police initiate and obtain a waiver of the right to counsel from a represented defendant, then that waiver is invalid. In *Montejo*, by contrast, Scalia concluded that the purpose of the *Jackson* rule was not to protect a Sixth Amendment right to counsel but rather a defendant's Fifth Amendment protection against being compelled by police to confess.[19] Thus, represented defendants can waive their right to counsel without counsel being present, provided such waivers are made intelligently and voluntarily after being given Miranda warnings.

Justice Stevens wrote a dissenting opinion joined by fellow liberals Souter, Ginsburg, and Breyer. Stevens was the most prolific dissenter in the history of the Supreme Court, writing more than seven hundred dissenting opinions,[20] yet he chose to read oral dissents from the bench in fewer than two dozen cases over his thirty-five-year career as an associate justice.[21] The *Montejo* decision was among the few in which he felt moved to read his dissent as a means to highlight the intensity of his opposition to the majority's ruling. Justice Stevens asserted that "the rule announced in *Jackson* protects a fundamental right that the Court now dishonors."[22] Stevens, who had written the majority opinion in the *Jackson* decision, criticized the standard adopted by the *Montejo* majority for waiving the Sixth Amendment right to counsel during custodial interrogations. He saw the majority's approach as insufficiently protective and likely to confuse defendants.

Ineffective Assistance of Counsel

Beginning in the final decades of the twentieth century, many of the Supreme Court's right-to-counsel cases examined issues regarding the right to effective assistance of counsel. These cases considered whether inadequacies in a defense attorney's decisions and conduct deprived the client of effective representation. Although ineffective assistance of counsel claims now represent a significant proportion of challenges to criminal convictions in the United States, only a small percentage of these claims succeed in gaining new trials for defendants.[23] Precedents set during the Burger Court era, especially *Strickland v. Washington* (1984) and *United States v. Cronic*, made it very difficult for defendants to prove that their Sixth Amendment right to counsel had been violated by ineffective assistance of counsel. Claimants cannot merely show that errors were made by a defense attorney. They must show that the errors were outside of the boundaries of reasonable performance by an attorney and likely affected the outcome of the case. Yet, judges appear very reluctant to second-guess actions by defense attorneys. For example, if attorneys make strategic decisions during trials, such as declining to raise all possible objections to statements by prosecutors for fear of appearing disruptive in the eyes of the jurors, then judges are not likely to regard these strategic decisions as demonstrating ineffective assistance of counsel. Judges prefer to give attorneys discretionary flexibility without insisting that all possible objections should be raised.

The Roberts Court decided its first significant ineffective assistance of counsel case in *Schriro v. Landrigan* (2007). At sentencing for a capital offense, Landrigan's lawyer attempted to present mitigating evidence in the form of testimony from the client's birth mother and ex-wife. However, these witnesses acquiesced to Landrigan's request that they not testify. Landrigan later interrupted his attorney when she tried to present to the judge what the content of the witnesses' testimony would have included. When asked whether he had anything to say, Landrigan stated, "I think if you want to give me the death penalty, just bring it on. I'm ready for it."[24] The jury obliged and sentenced him to death. Landrigan appealed and claimed his attorney should have investigated other sources of mitigating evidence.

The Roberts Court split along a familiar dividing line, with the five most conservative justices upholding the lower court's denial of Landrigan's request for an evidentiary hearing. The narrow majority determined that Landrigan's request to forgo the presentation of mitigating testimony from two witnesses could be interpreted as referring to all mitigating evidence and that additional sources were unlikely to add substantially to the record. The majority added that the court had never required that a defendant's decision to forgo the introduction of mitigating evidence must be an informed choice.

The other four justices believed that the record indicated that Landrigan's desire to block mitigating evidence was specific to testimony from family members. The defendant's behavior should have prompted defense counsel to investigate other sources of mitigating evidence that her client would agree to have presented, including medical evidence indicating that Landrigan suffered from a serious brain disorder. The dissenters noted several areas of law in which the court required waivers be made knowingly, and they saw no reason why that standard should not apply with respect to mitigating evidence in capital cases.[25]

The Roberts Court's most important decisions concerning ineffective assistance of counsel examined and clarified defense attorneys' obligations in the plea bargaining process. For example, one case involved a defense attorney's advice to plead "no contest" to felony murder and the attorney's attendant failure to seek the exclusion of evidence obtained in a confession (*Premo v. Moore*, 2011). The attorney was motivated by a desire to avoid placing the defendant at risk of a death sentence when providing the advice to plead "no contest" to a lesser charge. The Supreme Court concluded that the convicted individual failed to show that these actions by the defense attorney were unreasonable errors under *Strickland*.

In *Padilla v. Kentucky* (2010), the Roberts Court considered whether defense attorneys provide ineffective assistance of counsel when they base a plea recommendation on their own inaccurate knowledge about the consequences of their clients' guilty pleas. Padilla moved to the United States from Honduras in his youth and served in the US military during the Vietnam War. By the time of his Supreme Court case, Padilla had been a legal permanent resident of the United States for more than four decades. He was working as a truck driver when he was arrested in Kentucky for transporting a large amount of marijuana. Although the law mandated the deportation of noncitizens for a conviction on this charge, his attorney advised him to accept a plea offer and incorrectly told him that he need not worry about the conviction affecting his immigration status. Facing deportation after pleading guilty, Padilla appealed on the grounds of ineffective assistance of counsel. Kentucky, like most jurisdictions at the time, required only that attorneys advise their clients of consequences such as fines and incarceration that are directly part of the penalty imposed for a particular offense. They were not required to advise clients about collateral civil consequences such as loss of voting rights or deportation.[26] As a result, the state denied Padilla the opportunity to withdraw his guilty plea.

Writing for the majority, Justice Stevens noted that while deportation is not a criminal sanction, the court recognized both civil immigration law's long history of being entangled with criminal proceedings and the reality that deportation is a severe "penalty."[27] The majority rebuffed the prosecution's argument that a defense attorney's advice concerning eligibility for deportation was beyond the Sixth Amendment's reach because the amendment is focused on representation for criminal matters. The majority ruled that the defense attorney's performance fell below expected standards and left it for the lower courts to determine whether Padilla satisfied *Strickland*'s second prong of demonstrating that the error prejudiced the outcome of the case. When deportation is an inevitable consequence of conviction, counsel must convey that information to the defendant in a clear manner.[28] In dissent, Justices Scalia and Thomas argued that constitutional protections apply only to advice related to defending the client against the criminal charge and not to collateral outcomes such as deportation.

Three years later, the court ruled that the defense attorney's obligation to inform criminal defendants of deportation risks from guilty pleas does not apply retroactively. The majority determined that *Padilla* announced a "new rule," and the court's doctrines limit the applicability of most new rules in federal habeas proceedings to those individuals whose convictions were not final when the rule was announced (*Chaidez v. United States*, 2013). Thus, Padilla benefited from the court's decision about the defense attorney's obligations during plea bargaining in his case, but other defendants who had previously faced the same situation were not entitled to new proceedings. Nevertheless, the importance of *Padilla* should not be underestimated, especially given the adoption of particularly aggressive detention and deportation policies by presidential administrations in the twenty-first century. In addition, *Padilla* signaled the court's increasing recognition of the role of plea negotiations in a system in which only a small percentage of convictions result from trials rather than pleas.

The Roberts Court revisited the issue in *Lee v. United States* (2017). In this case, a thirty-five-year permanent resident of the United States repeatedly asked his attorney whether he could be deported to South Korea if he entered a guilty plea to drug charges. The attorney erroneously reassured him that he would not face deportation. When the defendant subsequently raised the *Padilla* issue upon learning the truth, the government claimed that he could not demonstrate that the outcome of the case was affected because he was so obviously guilty that he was certain to be convicted at trial. In a majority opinion written by Chief Justice Roberts, a six-member majority ruled that Lee had met his burden by showing that he would not have entered a guilty plea if his defense attorney had given him accurate information about deportation consequences. In dissent, Justice Thomas reiterated his position in *Padilla* that defense attorneys are not required to provide accurate information about deportation risks when advising their clients about guilty pleas.

Justice Kennedy wrote majority opinions for the Roberts Court in two related cases concerning ineffective assistance of counsel during plea bargaining. In *Missouri v. Frye* (2012), the attorney failed to inform his client about a pair of favorable plea offers from the prosecutor. The offers expired, and the defendant pleaded guilty without a deal in place. This resulted in a three-year sentence, compared with the three-month sentence proposed in an expired offer that was unknown to him. In *Lafler v. Cooper* (2012), the defendant rejected the prosecutor's plea bargain offer due to faulty advice from the defense attorney. The attorney misunderstood the elements that the prosecution was required to prove for assault with intent to murder and said that the prosecution would not be able to convict him on this charge at trial. As a result, he turned down the plea bargain offer and was subsequently convicted of this serious charge at trial. He received a sentence with a range averaging seventeen years longer than the sentence range offered in the plea deal that he turned down.

The same five-member majority in each case held not only that ineffective assistance of counsel likely caused less favorable outcomes for the defendants but also that plea bargaining was a "critical stage" in criminal proceedings for which defense counsel's role is essential. Justice Kennedy drew upon precedent to find that Sixth Amendment protections apply to plea negotiations. Noting that guilty pleas account for more than 90 percent of convictions in the United States, Kennedy declared that "the right to adequate assistance of counsel cannot be defined or enforced without taking account of the central role plea bargaining plays in securing convictions and determining sentences."[29]

The court's four dissenting conservative justices balked at what they characterized as constitutionalizing the plea negotiation process. Thus, they anticipated a new flood of appeals and other post-conviction claims raising issues disconnected from the right to a fair trial described in the Sixth Amendment. Justice Scalia, for example, saw counsel's error in *Frye* as depriving the defendant "only of the opportunity to accept a plea deal to which he had no entitlement in the first place."[30] To the dissenters, the defense attorney did not violate any substantive or procedural Sixth Amendment right by failing to inform the client about a plea bargain offer.

Other cases raised additional issues concerning post-conviction representation. In *Maples v. Thomas* (2012), two attorneys from a prestigious New York law firm represented Maples on a pro bono basis during the post-conviction phase of his case. During that phase, however, both attorneys left their law firm to start new jobs. They failed to inform Maples and failed to notify the court of their withdrawal as counsel of record. The New York law firm did not designate other attorneys to take over the case. In addition, the law firm's mailroom returned unopened an important notification from the Alabama court, and the court failed to take any additional action to inform Maples about impending deadlines. As a result, Maples missed filing deadlines in his post-conviction proceedings. Determining that Maples was unaware of the abandonment and thus had no reason to believe he lacked representation, the Roberts Court majority held that he was not responsible for failing to file a timely petition. The majority ruled that the defense attorneys had severed the principal-agent relationship by essentially abandoning the client and missing a filing deadline. Thus, their failings could not be attributed to or imposed as a burden upon the client. Justices Scalia and Thomas were the only dissenters.

In *Garza v. Idaho* (2019), the defendant repeatedly asked his attorney to file a notice of appeal after he had entered a guilty plea. The attorney failed to do so because Garza had signed a waiver of appeals as part of his plea agreement. However, a six-member majority of the Roberts Court, including conservatives Roberts and Kavanaugh, decided that the attorney's failure constituted ineffective assistance of counsel because Garza retained a right to appeal for issues outside of the scope of the waiver in his plea agreement. Thus, the Roberts Court's decision strengthened a specific protection despite the overall conservative voting records of the majority of justices serving in 2019.

Conclusion

The Roberts Court weakened the right to counsel and Miranda protections in some circumstances. However, the court acted to strengthen the protections against ineffective assistance of counsel in plea bargaining and post-conviction proceedings. One could argue that the majority engaged in conservative judicial activism with respect to its treatment of certain precedents. The bare majority in *Montejo*, for example, went out of its way to overturn precedent and alter the existing high standard for waiving the right to counsel. This was a step that neither party to the case initially requested. During oral arguments in *Montejo*, Justice Alito suggested that the court consider using the case to overturn *Michigan v. Jackson*, something not briefed or argued by the parties in the case. This suggestion led the court to make an unusual directive in the case: Each side was told to submit post-argument written briefs addressing the issue of whether the court should overrule Justice Stevens's rights-protective majority opinion in *Jackson*.[31] Thus, the subsequent ruling that expanded police authority to question already-represented suspects in custody reflected an unusually proactive effort by the conservative majority to reconsider the decision in *Jackson*. Normally, the Supreme Court is expected to limit its focus to issues raised by the parties in the case.

Other Roberts Court rulings weakened protections for individuals by altering the criteria for invoking and waiving counsel-related rights. Despite the weakening of rights in certain cases, nearly half of the Roberts Court's nonunanimous *Miranda* and right-to-counsel rulings ended in rights-affirming decisions. In particular, the Roberts Court's decisions moved right-to-counsel doctrine in a protective direction with respect to cases examining ineffective assistance of counsel outside of the trial context, specifically with respect to plea bargaining and post-conviction proceedings.

A regular theme in right-to-counsel cases concerned the practical implications of the Roberts Court's decisions. For example, the reality that far more convictions result from guilty pleas than from trials partly motivated the court to recognize plea bargaining as a "critical stage" imposing obligations on the role of defense counsel. On the other hand, opinions that opposed the expansion of protections often expressed fears that doing so would flood the courts with claims from those seeking a remedy for ineffective assistance of counsel in various stages of the criminal justice process. As one prominent analyst of the Supreme Court wrote, "In a perfect world, there would be no conflict between ensuring a just result in every case and administering a sprawling justice system that must attend to values like efficiency and finality. In the real world . . . those interests often collide."[32]

The ultimate effects of the Roberts Court's decisions on the role of counsel are still being assessed. The *Padilla* decision, for example, presumably forced criminal defense attorneys and trial judges to become more knowledgeable about the risks of deportation for noncitizen criminal defendants. Plea bargaining advice is often not documented, but the court's new requirements for defense attorneys created an incentive for them to adopt the practice of putting such advice on the record in pretrial proceedings.[33] Trial judges may face new responsibilities for ensuring that defendants understand the consequences of guilty pleas, especially with respect to noncitizen defendants. The Roberts Court's decisions, for example, led the Virginia Supreme Court to instruct trial judges to warn noncitizen defendants about the impact a conviction could have on their immigration status.[34]

The Roberts Court's changed composition after the addition of three Trump appointees will likely change the balance of viewpoints in future cases on Miranda rights and the right to counsel. Analysts will watch to see if any justices assume Justice Kennedy's dominant role in the middle of the court, a position from which he cast decisive votes with both liberal and conservative majorities. He voted with the majority in twenty-six of the twenty-seven right-to-counsel and Miranda cases decided in his career during the Roberts Court era. After the arrival of the three Trump appointees, Chief Justice Roberts and Justice Kavanaugh were perceived to be the conservative justices most likely to join the three remaining liberals in specific decisions. In the new era of a conservative supermajority, it will require two conservative justices to join the liberals for Justice Kennedy's role to be recreated and thereby produce close votes in favor of liberal positions on Fifth and Sixth Amendment counsel issues.

There were indications that the representation of criminal defendants could be reconsidered in ways that shrink the protective coverage of constitutional rights. For example, Justice Thomas, joined by Trump appointee Justice Gorsuch, made the assertive suggestion in a dissenting opinion in *Garza v. Idaho* that the court should consider significantly altering Sixth Amendment jurisprudence. Specifically, these justices advocated applying originalist interpretations to eliminate any guarantee of effective representation by criminal defense attorneys. It appears that these justices would elevate the state's interest in achieving "finality" in cases over the defendant's interest in effective representation and the attainment of a correct result. As Justice Thomas said:

> Our precedents seek to use the Sixth Amendment right to counsel to achieve an end it is not designed to guarantee. The right to counsel is not an assurance of an error-free trial or even a reliable result. It ensures fairness in a single respect: permitting the accused to employ the services of an attorney. The structural protections provided in the Sixth Amendment certainly seek to promote reliable criminal proceedings, but there is no substantive right to a particular level of reliability. In assuming otherwise, our ever-growing right-to-counsel precedents directly conflict with the government's legitimate interest in the finality of criminal judgments.[35]

In addition, Thomas's originalist analysis in his dissent emphasized that the framers and ratifiers of the Sixth Amendment did not intend for government-financed attorneys to be provided to indigent criminal defendants. As Thomas observed, "The Sixth Amendment appears to have been understood at the time of ratification as a rejection of the English common-law rule that prohibited counsel, not as a guarantee of government-funded counsel."[36] He added that the Supreme Court's earlier decisions in cases that expanded the provision of counsel to indigent defendants failed "to square the expansive rights [the court] recognized with the original meaning of the 'right . . . to have the Assistance of Counsel.'"[37]

After issuing this dissenting opinion in 2019, Justices Thomas and Gorsuch were joined on the court by another avowedly originalist colleague: Justice Barrett. If the two *Garza* dissenters can gain support for their position from Barrett and then add only two of the three other strongly conservative justices (Roberts, Kavanaugh, and Alito), they could dramatically rewrite the nature of the Sixth Amendment right to counsel.

Certainly, individual states would continue providing attorneys for indigent defendants under their own state constitution and laws. But there would be grave risks that indigent defense might no longer be universal across the country and that there would be little opportunity for oversight and corrective action if federal courts could no longer examine claims of ineffective assistance of counsel.

A clearer indication of doctrinal change was evident in the 2022 Roberts Court decision in *Vega v. Tekoh* (2022). A nursing assistant was questioned at his place of employment by a sheriff's deputy concerning an accusation that the nursing assistant had sexually assaulted a medical center patient. The suspect was questioned at length without being given Miranda warnings and eventually wrote a letter of apology for touching the alleged victim. The incriminating results from the interrogation were used against the nursing assistant in a criminal prosecution. A jury subsequently acquitted the defendant of all charges. Afterward, the defendant filed a civil lawsuit against the deputy under the federal statute that authorizes lawsuits against state and local officials for violating constitutional rights. The legal issue that reached the Roberts Court was whether a violation of Miranda rules should be considered a violation of the Fifth Amendment and therefore susceptible to a constitutional rights lawsuit.

In a 6–3 decision dividing the court along ideological lines, a majority opinion by Justice Alito announced that a violation of Miranda rules does not constitute a violation of constitutional rights under the Fifth Amendment. Justice Alito's reasoning characterized Miranda warnings as judge-created rules useful for but separate from the protection of the Fifth Amendment rights concerning compelled self-incrimination. Thus, a remedy for Miranda violations was eliminated, and, more ominously in the eyes of commentators, the majority opinion's language cast doubt on the validity of the court's authority to create rules such as Miranda warnings and require police to follow such rules. As one commentator complained, "[Justice Alito] couldn't be much clearer: He and his conservative colleagues think *Miranda* and *Dickerson* are wrong but aren't yet willing to spend the political capital necessary to overrule them."[38]

Are the dissenting opinion in *Garza* and the majority opinion in *Vega* harbingers of significant changes in the Roberts Court's right to counsel and self-incrimination jurisprudence? These opinions seek to steer the Roberts Court more quickly and boldly in the direction of diminishing these constitutional rights. Obviously, the subsequent terms of the Roberts Court will reveal whether the trend toward gradual diminution of these rights will be replaced by abrupt changes that dramatically restrict Fifth and Sixth Amendment protections related to legal representation. With respect to these issues, the Roberts Court era could produce a drastic rewriting of the Warren Court's protective initiatives that originated in *Miranda v. Arizona* and *Gideon v. Wainwright.*

6. TRIAL RIGHTS

Defendants' trial rights figured prominently in cases on the Roberts Court docket. Legal, social, and technological changes can generate the need for reconsideration and clarification of certain trial rights. For example, the Equal Protection Clause of the Fourteenth Amendment, ratified more than seven decades after the Bill of Rights, brought to the court claims of racial discrimination in jury selection and sentencing processes as society's views about racial equality evolved. Issues concerning these matters continue to arise in contemporary cases. In another example, the Sixth Amendment's Confrontation Clause requires the opportunity for cross-examination of accusers and adverse witnesses, but who should be on the witness stand when DNA test results and other scientific evidence are presented to a jury? Thus, trial rights issues considered by the Roberts Court included matters that continue to persist and evolve as well as matters, such as aspects of scientific evidence, that simply did not exist during prior court eras.

Confrontation Clause

The precise historical meaning of the Sixth Amendment's guarantee that "in all criminal prosecutions, the accused shall enjoy the right . . . to be confronted with the witnesses against him" is unclear. According to Justice Thomas, a key devotee of an originalist approach to interpretation, "There is virtually no evidence of what the drafters of the Confrontation Clause intended it to mean."[1] For many constitutional provisions, the originalist justices on the Roberts Court express great confidence that they know what the framers and ratifiers of an amendment intended. As described in chapter 3, their approach to interpreting the Second Amendment displays the originalist justices' confident agreement about the amendment's meaning. With respect to the Confrontation Clause, however, the originalist justices must struggle with defining how the right applies in various trial contexts. In general, legal scholars view the Confrontation Clause's purpose as providing the opportunity to test the accuracy of testimonial evidence by subjecting it to vigorous cross-examination as jurors and judges evaluate witness credibility and the substance of the testimony.[2]

Just prior to the start of the Roberts Court era, Justice Scalia authored the court's decision in *Crawford v. Washington* (2004) declaring that the Confrontation Clause bars testimonial statements of a witness not appearing at trial unless the witness is unavailable to testify. Previously, Supreme Court doctrine permitted the presentation of evidence without cross-examination when the evidence was regarded as sufficiently credible.[3] Emphasizing an adversarial focus, Scalia wrote that the Confrontation Clause "commands, not that evidence be reliable, but that reliability be assessed in a particular manner: by testing in the crucible of cross-examination."[4] He further asserted that "dispensing with confrontation because testimony is obviously reliable is akin to dispensing with a jury trial because a defendant is obviously guilty."[5]

Justice Scalia was a consistent member of the court's conservative wing that generally sided with police and prosecutors. Thus, those unfamiliar with Scalia's Confrontation Clause jurisprudence might be surprised by his *Crawford* opinion and his support for a strong constitutional right to confrontation for criminal defendants. His originalist interpretive approach and understanding of early American practices led him to see few exceptions to the right to contest adverse testimony in court. Thus, as one professor put it, conservative Scalia "moonlighted as the Court's most ardent defender of the Sixth Amendment right to confront accusing witnesses."[6]

The issue of what evidence is "testimonial" confronted the justices in a pair of cases decided together early in the Roberts Court era, with the court's decisions focused on the "primary purpose" of eliciting the statements. Writing for a unanimous court in *Davis v. Washington* (2006), Scalia found the statements by a caller to the 911 operator identifying her alleged assailant were not testimonial, and thus the admission of the 911 transcript did not violate the Confrontation Clause. The primary purpose of the 911 operator's questions was to resolve a present emergency rather than to gather evidence. However, in the companion case of *Hammon v. Indiana* (2006), the court held that Confrontation Clause rights were violated when statements to police from a suspected domestic abuse victim were admitted at trial without the victim testifying against the defendant. Justice Scalia emphasized that the *Hammon* statements qualified as testimonial because they were elicited during an investigation of a suspected past crime. When police officers arrived at the home to investigate a complaint, the alleged victim told her story about a past event. Justice Thomas was the lone dissenter in *Hammon*, maintaining that the circumstances of the exchange with police were not sufficiently formalized to constitute testimony and, therefore, the Confrontation Clause should not apply. Formality of circumstances was the key for Thomas. He used the term "formal," or a version of it, eighteen times in his brief opinion in *Hammon* and often reiterated this argument in other cases.

Justice Scalia broke with the majority in *Michigan v. Bryant* (2011) when it determined that the primary purpose of an exchange between police and a dying murder victim was to enable an ongoing emergency response. In the majority's view, this made the victim's statements identifying his killer non-testimonial and admissible without being tested through cross-examination in court under the Confrontation Clause. The majority reasoned that police officers were motivated by a need to respond to an emergency involving an unknown threat to others rather than primarily to investigate a crime.

Justice Scalia ridiculed the majority's depiction as "so transparently false that profession to believe it demeans this institution."[7] His harsh dissent criticized the court for establishing a sweeping exception to the Confrontation Clause. To Scalia, it was obvious that the officers' purpose in questioning a dying victim was investigative, and they clearly sought to acquire evidence. In addition, the victim wanted his words to lead to his assailant's capture and conviction. In a separate dissenting opinion that largely agreed with Scalia, Ginsburg added that while the statements were testimonial, she would be interested in considering the additional question of whether a dying declaration exception applied to permit admission of this evidence without cross-examination.[8] The rules of evidence used in trials traditionally treat declarations made by individuals when they are dying as highly reliable and truthful. Ginsburg wanted the court to consider the implication of this traditional evidence rule for Confrontation Clause rights.

Witness unavailability can arise from other circumstances such as the incompetence of the declarant as a source of reliable testimony. In 2015, the Roberts Court decided a case in which a preschool teacher noticed injuries on a three-year-old student (*Ohio v. Clark*, 2015). In response to the teacher's questions, the young boy indicated that his mother's boyfriend caused the injuries. After the teacher reported the information to a child abuse hotline, the boyfriend was arrested. The trial judge found the young boy incompetent to testify because of his age. Yet, the judge admitted into evidence the child's statements to the teacher. A unanimous Roberts Court held that the admission of the statements did not violate rights under the Confrontation Clause despite the absence of the child from the witness stand. The circumstances here suggested the primary purpose of the teacher's questions was likely the protection of the child, not to gather evidence.

While agreeing with the direction of the outcome, Scalia authored a critical concurrence that challenged the majority's reasoning and motives. Thus, the court's unanimity on the case outcome did not indicate consensus on the reasoning. Justice Scalia suggested the majority sought to dilute the impact of the *Crawford* decision. In Scalia's view, the majority's approach would open the door to a potentially broad range of exceptions to the Confrontation Clause.

Laboratory analyses of blood, fiber, DNA, and other evidence can carry substantial weight in criminal cases and often play a decisive role in determining a guilty verdict. For example, one study found that approximately 90 percent of homicide cases involve forensic evidence submitted to crime laboratories for testing.[9] Unfortunately, revelations about shocking misconduct emerged at scientific testing facilities in several states. For example, a state drug laboratory closed in Boston after a chemist was criminally charged for mishandling and misrepresenting test results in dozens of criminal cases. The individual was later convicted and sentenced to prison for fraudulently producing evidence that caused wrongful convictions. Fears remained that this lab employee may have exaggerated evidence, faked results, forged signatures, and mixed samples in thousands of cases, potentially tainting an unknown number of convictions.[10] In another example, authorities in New York began reviewing more than eight hundred rape cases after an internal review found that a technician may have mishandled DNA evidence.[11] An assistant public defender in Minnesota complained about a lab run by a police sergeant with no scientific credentials where employees relied on Wikipedia as a technical reference. According to the attorney, "These people didn't know what they were doing. . . . And yet they came into court every day and acted as if they did" when testifying about scientific evidence used to prove people's guilt.[12]

The emerging scandals in crime labs around the country provided the backdrop for the Roberts Court's examination of court testimony by forensic scientists and lab technicians. The court handed down three important Confrontation Clause decisions involving laboratory results in the first decade under Chief Justice Roberts. In *Melendez-Diaz v. Massachusetts* (2009), Scalia wrote for a narrow majority holding that a state forensic lab report prepared for criminal prosecution is testimonial evidence. Therefore, such reports are subject to Confrontation Clause requirements for in-person witness testimony and cross-examination. At trial, the prosecution introduced drug analysis certificates prepared by analysts that identified the evidence samples as cocaine. The analysts were not called to testify in person. The court rejected several assertions by the state including that confrontation protections were unnecessary given the neutrality and reliability of such testing results. In dissent, Chief Justice Roberts and Justices Kennedy, Alito, and Breyer criticized the majority for dismissing long-standing rules permitting scientific analysis to be presented as courtroom evidence without requiring analysts to testify from the witness stand about the underlying laboratory testing.

Two years later, the Roberts Court reaffirmed *Melendez-Diaz* by holding in *Bullcoming v. New Mexico* (2011) that the demands of the Confrontation Clause are not satisfied when a supervisor or other surrogate testifies about lab results from tests that he or she did not personally perform or observe. Writing for the five-member majority, Justice Ginsburg concluded, "The accused's right is to be confronted with the analyst who made the certification, unless that analyst is unavailable at trial, and the accused had an opportunity, pretrial, to cross-examine that particular scientist."[13]

The *Bullcoming* decision did not address whether the substance of forensic test results could be brought into evidence through the testimony of an expert witness. In *Williams v. Illinois* (2012), the court said it could. Williams was convicted in a rape trial in which a forensic specialist at the state police crime lab testified that a DNA profile produced by an outside laboratory matched a profile in the state DNA database identified as belonging to Williams. The profile from the outside lab was produced using blood samples and vaginal swabs that were part of the sexual assault kit prepared when the victim was taken to the hospital. At that point, Williams was not a suspect in the rape. The database profile was generated from a blood sample taken from the petitioner after he was arrested on unrelated charges. The defense objected to the expert witness's testimony about tests conducted by the outside lab, which the witness had not performed or observed. According to the defense, such expert testimony violated the Confrontation Clause.

A plurality opinion by Justice Alito held that the expert witness's statements about the results from the outside lab were not offered for their accuracy and did not violate the defendant's rights under the Confrontation Clause. Instead, according to Alito, those statements were presented for explaining the assumptions on which the expert based her opinion. Essentially, she offered an expert opinion that was subject to cross-examination, based on underlying information from the lab profile that would not have been admissible if introduced directly.

The fifth vote rejecting the Confrontation Clause claim was cast by Thomas, who provided his own concurring opinion rather than joining Alito's opinion. Thomas wrote that while he agreed with the plurality's judgment about admitting the testimony, "I reach this conclusion, however, solely because . . . [the results] lacked the requisite formality and solemnity to be considered 'testimonial' for purposes of the Confrontation Clause."[14] Thomas routinely, and usually briefly, expressed his disapproval of the "primary purpose" approach in earlier cases and advocated an emphasis on the formality and solemnity of the circumstances in which the statements were made.[15] Until *Williams*, this distinction emphasized solely by Thomas had little importance in determining case outcomes.

The dissenting opinion by Justice Kagan was joined by Justices Scalia, Ginsburg, and Sotomayor. Kagan described a different case in which a critical mistake involving the same outside lab was revealed only during cross-examination. She then detailed how the expert witness testimony here was functionally identical to the testimony that the *Bullcoming* decision judged to be a violation of the Confrontation Clause.

Justice Scalia adopted a liberal, pro-defendant position in the three laboratory test cases. By contrast, Justice Breyer generally sided with conservative viewpoints in divided Confrontation Clause cases decided by the Roberts Court despite having been part of the majority in the pivotal *Crawford* decision in 2004. Thus, Confrontation Clause cases stand out among those affecting criminal justice processes by dividing the justices in ways that deviated from the expected liberal-conservative splits that were characteristic of many contentious issues decided during the first fifteen years of the Roberts Court era.

The pre–Roberts Court *Crawford* decision in 2004 anchored Confrontation Clause jurisprudence for the first decade of the Roberts era in a way that reduced potential exceptions to the right to confront adverse witnesses with cross-examination during trials. Over time, several developments raised uncertainty about the Roberts Court's potential future direction in interpreting Confrontation Clause rights.[16] These developments included the *Williams* decision permitting testimony about testing that the expert witness had not conducted or observed; the deaths of Confrontation Clause defenders Scalia and Ginsburg; Thomas's unique way of defining testimonial statements; and the addition of three new Trump appointees who significantly shifted the ideological balance on the court at the end of 2020.

Because the first Confrontation Clause case decided by the newly constituted court generated a strong consensus among the justices, it shed little light on how future cases might split the court or lead to changes in legal doctrine. In *Hemphill v. New York* (2022), eight justices agreed that a defendant's rights were violated by the admission of a transcript containing statements from a separate individual's guilty plea proceeding. This individual was not available to provide testimony or be subject to cross-examination because he was outside the country during Hemphill's trial. Only Justice Thomas dissented, relying on procedural grounds because he claimed Hemphill had not properly raised the Confrontation Clause issue in prior state court proceedings.

The Prosecution, Exculpatory Evidence, and Brady Challenges

Although American trial processes employ the adversarial model, as noted in one Supreme Court opinion (*United States v. Bagley*, 1985), "The Court has recognized . . . that the prosecutor's role transcends that of an adversary: he 'is the representative not of an ordinary party to a controversy, but of a sovereignty . . . whose interest . . . in a criminal prosecution is not that it shall win a case, but that justice shall be done.'"[17] This understanding of the government's role in criminal cases has important implications in defining a fair trial. For example, with this perspective in mind, the Warren Court ruled in *Brady v. Maryland* (1963) that due process requires the prosecution to disclose to the defense materially exculpatory evidence in the government's possession. The resulting "Brady rule" applies to evidence favorable to the accused by tending to demonstrate the accused's innocence or weakening the credibility of an opposing witness. Sharing this information in pretrial discovery lessens the likelihood of a miscarriage of justice. As Justice Douglas wrote for the Warren Court in *Brady*, "Society wins not only when the guilty are convicted but when criminal trials are fair; our system of the administration of justice suffers when any accused is treated unfairly."[18]

Cases arose from the actions of the district attorney's office in New Orleans, which had a long history of alleged and demonstrated misconduct, including committing Brady violations.[19] The Innocence Project found that the district attorney's office withheld exculpatory evidence in nine of thirty-six death penalty convictions under a single prosecutor.[20] In *Smith v. Cain* (2012), the prosecution withheld notes from an investigating detective indicating that the only witness purportedly linking the defendant to a shooting could not actually identify the murderer. At trial, a different statement from the eyewitness identifying the defendant as the shooter was entered into evidence. In a short opinion written by Chief Justice Roberts, the court found that the state wrongly rejected the petitioner's Brady claim. According to Roberts, there was a reasonable probability that the case outcome would have been different had the undisclosed witness statement been presented at trial. Justice Thomas was the lone dissenter.

The Roberts Court justices split sharply when considering a large monetary judgment against the New Orleans district attorney for a Brady violation that led to a wrongful conviction. The wrongly accused defendant served eighteen years in prison, including fourteen years on death row. In *Connick v. Thompson* (2011), Thompson had been arrested for murder. Victims of an unsolved robbery identified Thompson as the robber after seeing his picture in connection with the homicide arrest. The district attorney's office went forward with the robbery trial first and in so doing failed to disclose a lab report showing that Thompson's blood sample did not match blood from the perpetrator found at that crime scene. Convicted on robbery charges, Thompson then faced a capital murder trial during which he chose not to testify because the prosecution would have used the robbery conviction to impeach his testimony. A codefendant testified that he saw Thompson commit the murder, and Thompson was convicted and sentenced to death. Years later and a mere month before his execution date, a lab report on the blood evidence was discovered in court records by an investigator for Thompson's attorneys. A lower court vacated the convictions, and the robbery charge was dropped. He was retried on the murder charge and found not guilty.

Thompson filed a lawsuit seeking monetary damages for rights violations under a federal civil rights statute. The case included shocking evidence that an assistant prosecutor had removed evidence from the evidence room and never returned it in order to hide the fact that Thompson's blood did not match the blood on the item of evidence. That assistant prosecutor later confessed to another assistant prosecutor that he had stolen the exculpatory evidence, yet neither assistant prosecutor informed the defense about the exculpatory evidence. Ultimately, the jury in the civil lawsuit found the district attorney liable for failing to train his prosecutors regarding Brady obligations and awarded Thompson $14 million in damages—$1 million for each year on death row.

Writing for the five most conservative justices, Thomas's opinion invalidated the jury award and held that a district attorney cannot be held liable for failing to train assistant prosecutors based on a single Brady violation allegedly arising from the deficient training. The plaintiff needed to demonstrate that the prosecutor was deliberately indifferent to the need to train prosecutors and that the lack of training caused the specific Brady violation. This "deliberate indifference" standard with respect to Brady violations required that patterns of similar violations by the district attorney's office be ignored.

Thompson based much of his argument on an example given in the earlier case *City of Canton v. Harris* (1989) in which the Rehnquist Court noted that failure-to-train liability might attach from a single rights-violating incident if the need for training was obvious. The Roberts Court majority in *Thompson* rejected this analogy. In addition, Thomas assumed that assistant prosecutors had received training about the Brady rule in law school so that the district attorney's office was not entirely responsible for the assistant prosecutors' education and knowledge about this important rule.[21]

Writing for dissenting justices from the court's liberal wing, Ginsburg's strong objections to the majority's conclusions led her to read her dissent from the bench. Justice Ginsburg asserted that the *City of Canton v. Harris* example applied to the New Orleans case, that the majority ignored the district attorney's history of prosecutorial misconduct, and that the district attorney, despite being aware of the need to so do, failed to ensure assistant prosecutors in his office understood their *Brady rule* obligations. Ginsburg noted that the district attorney's "cavalier approach to his staff's knowledge and observation of *Brady* requirements contributed to a culture of inattention to *Brady* in Orleans Parish" and to multiple *Brady* violations in other cases.[22]

Criticism of the court's decision came from numerous commentators. A leading legal commentator, for example, wrote that "[because a] *Brady* violation . . . causes suppression of evidence beyond the defendant's capacity to ferret out . . . [and] may result in the conviction of an innocent defendant, it is unconscionable not to impose reasonable controls impelling prosecutors to bring the information to light."[23] Another expert warned that given the *Connick* decision, "the outlook for future litigants in this area can best be described as grim."[24] One commentator concluded that the Roberts Court "missed the opportunity to ensure that municipalities would more vigilantly . . . guard against constitutional violations."[25]

Another lawsuit arising from a *Brady* violation unified the justices as the unanimous Roberts Court rejected the claim of a formerly imprisoned individual who sued supervisory prosecutors for failure to train employees and manage documents (*Van de Camp v. Goldstein*, 2009). Prosecutors failed to disclose that the jailhouse informant who testified against the defendant had received benefits for his testimony. Clearly, this could have proven valuable for challenging the reliability of the state's witness at trial. The court held the failure of the prosecutor's office to ensure that all assistant prosecutors knew of the arrangement with the informant constituted a critical error. However, the justices ruled that the supervisory prosecutors were entitled to absolute immunity from civil lawsuits for this failure. Drawing on precedent rooted in common law, the court emphasized that without prosecutorial immunity, the fear of litigation might jeopardize the ability of prosecutors to exercise the discretion and independent judgment required of the position. Similarly broad immunity is provided to several other government officials, such as judges and legislators, while acting within the scope of their official duties.

Jury Selection

By the end of the American Revolution, widespread public support existed for the right to trial by jury as "the bulwark of liberty" in the newly established states.[26] Indeed, the right to a jury trial was specifically protected in initial state constitutions.[27] Its importance was also highlighted by its status as the rare right for individuals mentioned in the original Constitution's Article III and not merely added belatedly in the Sixth Amendment with the other rights in the Bill of Rights.

Scholars note the adverse effects that discrimination during jury selection can have on defendants' fates and the perceived legitimacy of jury verdicts.[28] The prosecution and defense may exercise a set number of peremptory challenges to exclude members of the jury pool without providing reasons for those discretionary decisions. The use of peremptory challenges during jury selection raises special risks of discrimination.[29] Historically, prosecutors used their discretionary, unexplained exclusions from the jury pool to engage in racial discrimination, especially by constructing all-white juries to judge Black defendants after Black potential jurors were systematically excluded. Ostensibly, the purpose of questioning and excluding specific potential jurors is to help empanel an impartial jury by excluding potentially biased jurors. In fact, attorneys may use challenges to exclude potential jurors with the goal of constructing a jury that will be biased in favor of their side's evidence and arguments.

In *Batson v. Kentucky* (1986), the Burger Court recognized that the peremptory challenge plays a time-honored role in the trial process. Defendants are not constitutionally guaranteed that the jury will include members of their own race, yet the court said that the Fourteenth Amendment's Equal Protection Clause should prohibit the prosecutor from excluding potential jurors on account of race. The *Batson* decision established procedures for contesting the prosecution's use of discretionary peremptory challenges that exclude prospective jurors when such exclusions raise the inference of a racially discriminatory purpose. In what became known as a "Batson challenge," the defense attorney can claim that the prosecutor appears to be excluding potential jurors based on their race. Then the burden shifts to the prosecutor to provide the judge with an acceptable, race-neutral reason for dismissing those individuals through the discretionary use of peremptory challenges. The *Batson* decision focused on discrimination by prosecutors, but subsequent decisions by the Supreme Court expanded the prohibition on racial discrimination to the application of peremptory challenges by criminal defense attorneys (*Georgia v. McCollum*, 1992) and attorneys in civil cases (*Edmonson v. Leesville Concrete*, 1991). The court also prohibited discriminatory challenges in jury selection based on the gender of potential jurors (*J. E. B. v. Alabama ex rel. T. B.*, 1994). In the final months of the Rehnquist Court, the justices strengthened *Batson* by striking down two state laws that narrowly interpreted a defendant's right to challenge the prosecutor's use of peremptory challenges in jury selection (*Miller-El v. Dretke*, 2005; *Johnson v. California*, 2005b).

In subsequent cases, questions about the dismissal of prospective jurors split the Roberts Court justices in varying ways. For example, a seven-member majority in *Snyder v. Louisiana* (2008) extended the pro-defendant rulings handed down late in the Rehnquist Court era. After an initial paring down of the jury pool, five Black members remained among the thirty-six potential jurors in a capital case against a Black man charged with stabbing his estranged wife and killing the man she was dating. Through peremptory challenges, the prosecutor removed all five Black potential jurors, including a college student. The prosecution's race-neutral rationale for dismissing the student included concern that his academic obligations might encourage him to shorten the deliberation process. For example, he might vote on a lesser charge so he could return quickly to his studies and other responsibilities. The trial judge accepted this reason, and the state supreme court twice rejected Snyder's Batson claim, thereby upholding his conviction and death sentence. This trial of a Black defendant by an all-white jury garnered added attention because the prosecutor made several pretrial statements comparing the case to the controversial O. J. Simpson murder trial. At sentencing, the prosecutor returned to the theme, telling the jury that Simpson "got away with it."[30]

The Roberts Court reversed the state court and determined that the trial judge erred by accepting an implausible explanation. The majority found the explanation impermissible, in part, because white jurors were not dismissed despite having conflicting obligations that seemed at least as serious as those affecting the excluded Black college student. Having ruled that this discriminatory misuse of a peremptory challenge alone was sufficient to overturn the conviction, the court did not address the exclusion of other Black potential jurors or the prosecutor's potentially inflammatory comments about the O. J. Simpson case. Notably, *Snyder* is the only liberal, nonunanimous criminal justice decision authored by Justice Alito during the first ten terms of the Roberts Court. The two dissenters, Thomas and Scalia, repeated their frequent call for the court to show greater deference to decisions by trial court judges.[31]

The Roberts Court was less inclined to overturn a conviction when the trial judge's error involved seating a juror that the defense had tried to exclude. Michael Rivera's defense counsel attempted to use a peremptory challenge to remove a Black woman from the jury pool. The trial judge disallowed the exclusion without specifying the reason for suspecting discriminatory intent, and the woman eventually became the foreperson of the jury that convicted Rivera. The Illinois Supreme Court considered the trial judge's later explanation that he suspected gender discrimination in the attempt to exclude her. The state court justices viewed the trial judge's conclusion as unpersuasive and insufficient under existing law. While the state court determined that the defense should have been able to dismiss the prospective juror through a peremptory challenge, it also found the trial judge's error to be harmless and thus upheld Rivera's conviction and eighty-five-year sentence for murder.

The Roberts Court unanimously determined that the Illinois Supreme Court properly exercised its power to make such determinations, acknowledging that there is no constitutional right to peremptory challenges (*Rivera v. Illinois*, 2009). Thus, the mistaken denial of such a challenge, by itself, does not violate the Constitution. Rivera did not demonstrate that the error jeopardized his right to a fair and impartial trial. If the denial is the product of a trial judge's good-faith mistake and if the seated jurors are qualified and unbiased, there is no substantive error, and the Due Process Clause does not require the automatic reversal of a conviction. In these situations, states may determine for themselves which errors require a new trial and which errors are harmless in their own court proceedings.

The unanimity of the *Rivera* decision could be misperceived to suggest a consensus on basic issues regarding peremptory challenges. Such a consensus does not, in fact, exist on the Roberts Court or among lower court judges and legal commentators. For example, Justice Thomas was the lone dissenter in a later case involving particularly obvious efforts by the prosecution to remove Black jurors (*Foster v. Chatman*, 2016). He also advocated overturning *Batson* altogether in another case (*Flowers v. Mississippi*, 2019). For him, *Batson* provides a "windfall to a convicted criminal" who has not actually been injured.[32] Justice Thomas echoed positions previously asserted by Scalia and Rehnquist. Indeed, in his dissent from the original *Batson* decision in 1986, Rehnquist argued that even the purposeful exclusion of members from a particular racial group through peremptory challenges would not violate the Equal Protection Clause.[33] In contrast to these interpretations, judges and scholars cite the persistence of racially motivated discrimination in jury selection as a reason to either abolish peremptory challenges or adopt a modified selection process ensuring greater representation in the jury box from members of historically excluded demographic groups.[34] *Batson*-related cases concerning peremptory challenges will likely continue given the current lack of support within the Roberts Court for Thomas's call to overturn *Batson*.

The Roberts Court considered a removal for cause in *Uttecht v. Brown* (2007). Unlike peremptory challenges—which are unexplained, discretionary decisions by attorneys—challenges for cause arise when lawyers claim to identify a reason that a specific juror could not be properly impartial in making decisions. In *Uttecht*, jury selection was a lengthy process with several potential jurors dismissed for cause in the trial of Cal Brown, who was charged with carjacking, rape, and murder. Brown was convicted, and he appealed on the grounds that the trial judge improperly excluded potential jurors. A federal appeals court agreed with Brown's argument regarding one excluded juror. Thus, the appeals court ruled that the error violated Supreme Court precedents and thereby violated Brown's Sixth and Fourteenth Amendment rights.

The Roberts Court split along ideological lines with a narrow majority reversing the federal appeals court and finding that the trial judge acted properly in excluding the potential juror. Writing for members of the court's conservative wing, Justice Kennedy summarized precedents that emphasized the need to balance two interests: (1) a defendant's "right to an impartial jury drawn from a *venire* that has not been tilted in favor of capital punishment by selective prosecutorial challenges for cause," and (2) the state's "interest in having jurors who are able to apply capital punishment within the framework state law prescribes."[35] According to Kennedy, the trial judge possessed the ability to assess the prospective juror's demeanor and responses during jury selection questioning. Thus, the judge should be given considerable deference in making the decision on whether an individual is insufficiently capable of imposing the death penalty. In this instance, the trial judge believed the prospective juror could not overcome his dislike of capital punishment, and the Roberts Court majority upheld the removal from the jury pool.

In a dissenting opinion joined by Ginsburg, Souter, and Breyer, Justice Stevens charged that the majority mischaracterized the excluded potential juror's responses to questions. Stevens saw nothing in the record to substantiate the claim that the juror was "substantially impaired" in his ability to follow a court's death penalty instructions. According to Stevens, the Supreme Court should not blindly accept a state court's conclusion that departs from precedent.[36] Justice Breyer's brief, separate dissent added that the majority "read too much into too little" and ignored much of the relevant record of the questioning of potential jurors in this case.[37]

Jury Decisions

For many years, the states of Oregon and Louisiana authorized juries in criminal cases to find defendants guilty based on split majority votes, such as votes of 10–2 or 9–3. This practice deviated from the usual American tradition of requiring unanimity for findings of guilt beyond a reasonable doubt. The Burger Court endorsed these states' split-vote guilty verdicts in *Apodaca v. Oregon* (1972).

In 2018, the voters of Louisiana ended the practice of split-vote verdicts by approving a ballot issue requiring unanimity for felony convictions in all subsequent trials. Later, by a 6–3 vote in *Ramos v. Louisiana* (2020), the Roberts Court ruled that criminal juries must have unanimous agreement to convict defendants. As Justice Gorsuch noted in the majority opinion, the 10–2 vote that led to the murder conviction and life sentence for Ramos would have led to a mistrial in forty-eight of the fifty states. The majority opinion also emphasized the racial bigotry that motivated the original initiation of nonunanimous verdicts in both states. In the late nineteenth century, Louisiana sought to nullify the participation of Black jurors during its imposition of a rigidly discriminatory society after the end of Reconstruction. If there were no more than three Black jurors, the white jurors could just ignore them and convict Black defendants by a 9–3 vote. Similarly, the roots of nonunanimous jury rules in Oregon coincided with the rise of the Ku Klux Klan in the early twentieth century and efforts to limit the civic participation and power of minority demographic groups.[38]

The dissenting opinion by Justice Alito, and joined by Chief Justice Roberts and Justice Kagan, emphasized the importance of established case precedent and the risk that courts would be flooded with appeals from imprisoned people in Oregon and Louisiana who had been convicted by nonunanimous verdicts. The following year, after the creation of a conservative supermajority with the confirmation of Trump-appointee Justice Barrett, the court divided along conservative-liberal lines in a 6–3 ruling declaring that the *Ramos* decision did not apply retroactively for federal habeas corpus cases (*Edwards v. Vannoy*, 2021). This decision blocked the potential post-conviction challenges that the dissenters in *Ramos* so feared.

People in Oregon and Louisiana previously convicted by nonunanimous verdicts were forced to rely on state remedies, if any were available, to enforce the *Ramos* principle. In 2022, the Oregon legislature considered a proposal to create an opportunity to appeal for three hundred people seeking to use the *Ramos* principle to have their nonunanimous convictions reconsidered. However, the legislative proposal did not receive a final vote.[39] Subsequently, the Oregon Supreme Court decided in 2022 that the *Ramos* unanimity requirement applied retroactively in Oregon cases, thus permitting individuals previously convicted by nonunanimous verdicts to challenge their convictions (*Watkins v. Ackley*, 2022). By contrast, also in 2022, the Louisiana Supreme Court declined to permit retroactive application of the *Ramos* principle,[40] thereby denying the opportunity to appeal for fifteen hundred imprisoned people convicted in that state by juries' split votes.[41] Many of these individuals remain imprisoned in Louisiana.

In *Pena-Rodriguez v. Colorado* (2017), two jurors approached the defense attorney after a trial and reported that a fellow juror made racially stereotyped comments about the defendant who was convicted of the crime. Comments made by jurors during deliberations typically cannot be examined to challenge a verdict. With the judge's approval, the defense attorney obtained affidavits from the two jurors describing the anti-Latinx comments made by the juror in question. The judge agreed that the comments demonstrated bias but declined to order a new trial because of the traditional rule against challenging jurors' statements made during deliberations.

The case was heard by the Roberts Court during the period when there were only eight justices after the death of Justice Scalia. By a 5–3 vote, the court said that remarks by a juror indicating racial bias or hostility toward a specific defendant provide a justification for overriding the traditional deference to juror deliberations. Thus, the court said the trial judge should consider whether the comments deprived the defendant of a fair jury trial. This was a case in which Justice Kennedy provided the pivotal vote and wrote the majority opinion while the court's three solidly conservative justices, Roberts, Alito, and Thomas, dissented. It is very unusual for jurors' deliberations to be examined after the verdict has been delivered. However, Kennedy's majority opinion demonstrated that for this Roberts Court majority, the prevention of racial discrimination was more important than preservation of the traditional rule. It remains to be seen whether this priority will be evident in subsequent cases decided after President Trump's appointment of three new conservative justices.

Sentencing and Juries as Finders of Fact

Twice in 1986 the Burger Court stated that the Constitution does not require juries to make sentencing determinations. In the majority opinion in *McMillan v. Pennsylvania* (1986), then Associate Justice Rehnquist wrote, "There is no Sixth Amendment right to jury sentencing, even where the sentence turns on specific findings of fact."[42] Similarly, Justice Byron White wrote for the majority in *Cabana v. Bullock* (1986), "The decision whether a particular punishment . . . is appropriate in any given case is not one that we have ever required to be made by a jury."[43] Although the court did not base its determination on an extensive historical analysis, the limited research and documentation available on the topic suggested that juries played a relatively minor role in sentencing at the time of the eighteenth-century adoption of the Bill of Rights.[44]

Nineteenth-century practices in many states entrusted juries with an active role in the criminal sentencing phase of their justice processes. Ironically, liberal reforms in the twentieth century advocating indeterminate sentencing and a treatment model of sentencing helped swing the pendulum back and pull power away from juries. Judges, parole boards, and other decision-makers were presumed to possess expertise and be better able to consider the complex factors involved for determining the nature and length of sentences on a case-by-case basis. Subsequent disenchantment with the rehabilitation approach to punishment and the rise of mandated sentencing schemes altered sentencing power once more—this time, placing sentence-defining authority primarily in legislatures and sentencing commissions.[45]

Mandatory sentencing laws raised significant questions concerning what was an "element" of a criminal offense that must be proven for conviction and what was simply a sentencing "factor" for increasing or reducing sentences. For example, the charge might be illegal possession of a prohibited drug, but the amount or type of drug could set the mandatory sentence at very different levels. This element requires a determination of objectively recognizable facts. Judges often rely on factors such as the defendant's remorse to determine a specific sentence. These matters are subjective determinations. Yet, defendants have the right under the Sixth Amendment and Due Process Clause to be informed of all elements of the charges they face and to have those elements proven to a jury beyond a

reasonable doubt.[46] In the preceding example, do the amount and nature
of the drug serve as sentencing factors or as elements of the crime that
must be proven to a jury? Mandatory sentencing schemes increasingly
generated such questions for the Supreme Court to answer.

Cases involving the role of juries as fact finders in sentencing sharply
divided justices on both the Rehnquist and Roberts Courts.[47] The alignment of justices in 5–4 decisions on this issue differed from those in other
criminal justice cases decided by a single vote. In the minimally winning
coalitions for other issues, case outcomes were often determined either
by the five justices on the court's conservative wing or by the defection of
one conservative justice to produce a liberal result. In cases on the role of
juries as fact finders, however, not one of the five-justice majorities was
produced by the decision of a lone swing voter who crossed philosophical
lines as Justice Kennedy did for other issues. Instead, there were unusual
combinations of liberal and conservative justices defining the jury's role.

The first unusual lineup of justices on this issue emerged in the landmark decision in *Apprendi v. New Jersey* (2000). The case concerned the
determination of aggravating circumstances to enhance sentences. A
divided Rehnquist Court held that any fact increasing a defendant's sentence beyond the statutory maximum was an "element" of the criminal
offense. Such elements of an offense must be proven to a jury beyond a
reasonable doubt rather than determined later by a judge alone using a
lower preponderance-of-evidence threshold. Justices Scalia and Thomas
joined liberals Stevens, Ginsburg, and Souter in requiring that facts used
in sentencing be determined by juries. Justice Breyer's dissent placed him
alongside Chief Justice Rehnquist and Justices O'Connor and Kennedy in
opposing this reduction in judges' sentencing power.

After Apprendi pleaded guilty to firearms-related charges, the trial judge
concluded by a preponderance of evidence that the crimes were racially
motivated and sentenced Apprendi to a term longer than the maximum
incarceration allowed for the underlying firearms conviction alone. In a
lengthy opinion written by Justice Stevens, the court ruled that the state
law providing trial judges with such discretion violated the defendant's
constitutional rights. The majority emphasized how requiring a jury's
findings beyond a reasonable doubt served as an important procedural
safeguard against biases that can improperly affect sentencing determinations. In its final terms, the Rehnquist Court extended the *Apprendi* rule
in a trio of key rulings challenging other state and federal laws that gave

judges authority to enhance sentences based on their own determinations of aggravating circumstances (*Ring v. Arizona*, 2002; *Blakely v. Washington*, 2004; *United States v. Booker*, 2005). Justices Scalia and Thomas provided critical votes supporting the jury's essential role in each of these cases.

In the Roberts Court era, a five-justice majority formed when Justice Thomas joined the court's liberals. This majority continued to emphasize the importance of jury fact-finding in *Alleyne v. United States* (2013). The majority ruled that because mandatory minimum sentences increase the penalty for an offense, any fact that increases the mandatory minimum is an "element" of the crime that must be submitted to the jury and not merely identified by the judge. In this instance, the jury found the defendant guilty of illegally "using" a firearm—a crime compelling a mandatory minimum sentence of five years. The judge, however, determined during sentencing that the defendant "brandished" the firearm, which increased the mandatory minimum sentence to seven years. Justice Thomas wrote the court's opinion holding that this type of judicial discretion violated Alleyne's right to a jury trial.

Alleyne was the only criminal justice case decided during the first decade of the Roberts Court era in which Thomas provided the lone swing vote to create a liberal majority. Justice Thomas's liberal criminal justice positions typically coincided with Scalia's, as evidenced by most of the *Apprendi*-issue cases. In *Alleyne*, however, Scalia distinguished between juries' and judges' authority with respect to mandatory maximum and mandatory minimum sentences. Thus, Scalia joined Chief Justice Roberts's dissent from Thomas's opinion for the court.

A different five-member majority in *Oregon v. Ice* (2009) chose not to extend *Apprendi*'s reach. The majority ruled that the Sixth Amendment does not prohibit states from allowing judges to make fact-finding determinations necessary to impose consecutive rather than concurrent sentences when the defendant is convicted of more than one offense. For the majority, Justice Ginsburg's opinion argued that respect for state sovereignty and the long history of granting judges the authority to decide how a defendant serves multiple sentences justified the decision in this case. Compared with other jury-as-fact-finder cases that tended to produce atypical alignments of justices, *Ice* split the court in a truly unique way. The case is the only one of the nearly one hundred criminal justice decisions handed down during this natural court period in which Roberts, Scalia, Thomas, and Souter dissented from a majority consisting of Stevens, Ginsburg, Breyer, Kennedy, and Alito.

The arrival of President Trump's three appointees to the court raised questions about how, despite predictions concerning their likely conservatism, they may affect cases addressing issues that did not divide the justices along usual liberal-conservative lines. The role of the jury in sentencing stood out as an issue that mixed the justices in unusual ways. In the first decision on this issue after the confirmation of Trump appointee Gorsuch, he showed that he, too, would address these issues in ways that could place him in the company of liberal colleagues, depending on the circumstances presented in the case. In *United States v. Haymond* (2019), a judge imposed a new mandatory minimum sentence on a defendant who downloaded child pornography while on supervised release following imprisonment on child pornography charges. Gorsuch wrote the opinion for the five-member majority, joined by the liberal justices Ginsburg, Sotomayor, Kagan, and Breyer, finding that the judge's actions violated the individual's Sixth Amendment right to trial by jury. The decision may have served notice that Gorsuch would take an even broader view of the jury's role in sentencing than fellow conservatives Thomas and Roberts, who had supported the jury's role in certain prior cases.

A decision in 2022 provided a preview of potential splits within the conservative supermajority with respect to sentencing issues. In *Concepion v. United States* (2022), the dispute concerned the applicability of the First Step Act that authorized sentence reductions for those convicted of federal crack cocaine offenses who had been treated more severely than individuals convicted of powder cocaine offenses. The five-justice majority that supported the individual's claim of eligibility for a sentence reduction saw conservatives Thomas and Gorsuch join the liberal justices Sotomayor, Kagan, and Breyer. The dissenters in the case were Roberts, Kavanaugh, Alito, and Barrett. Although this case concerned a statutory issue, it raised the intriguing possibility that sentencing issues may continue to be a realm in which certain conservative justices part company with their usual allies.

Double Jeopardy

The Supreme Court concluded more than a century ago that, at a minimum, the Double Jeopardy Clause prohibits further prosecution of a defendant formally acquitted for the same offense in a previous trial (*United States v. Ball*, 1896). Allowing a prosecutor to repeatedly try such a case until a desired outcome is reached presents an "unacceptably high risk that the Government, with its vastly superior resources, might wear down the defendant so that 'even though innocent he may be found guilty.'"[48] In a decision handed down on the final day of the Warren Court era, the court determined that the protection against double jeopardy was so fundamental to the American scheme of justice as to warrant its incorporation into the Fourteenth Amendment's Due Process Clause for application to state court proceedings (*Benton v. Maryland*, 1969).[49]

In *Evans v. Michigan* (2013), the Roberts Court confronted the issue of whether double jeopardy bars retrial when a defendant was acquitted due to a trial judge's error and before the case was given to the jury. When the prosecution rested its arson case against Evans, the defense moved for a directed verdict of acquittal on the mistaken theory that conviction for the offense under state law required the prosecution to prove the defendant burned a building that was not a dwelling. The judge mistakenly accepted this erroneous interpretation of state law, ruled against the prosecution, and acquitted the defendant because the prosecution had not proved that element of the crime. State appellate courts reversed the trial court decision. The state appellate courts' decisions held that the Double Jeopardy Clause did not bar a retrial when the initial trial did not resolve any factual element of the case and, instead, ended in a directed verdict based solely on the government's failure to prove an element that was not actually part of the offense's statutory definition. The Roberts Court recognized that "there is no question the trial court's ruling was wrong . . . [and] predicated upon a clear misunderstanding of what facts the State needed to prove under state law."[50] However, the court held that the constitutional double jeopardy protection precluded a retrial after an acquittal based on a trial judge's erroneous decision. Justice Alito was the lone dissenter.

In *Blueford v. Arkansas* (2012), by contrast, the petitioner's capital trial reached the jury deliberation stage. The jury was instructed to consider sequentially the charge of capital murder followed by evaluation of the lesser included offenses of first-degree murder, manslaughter, and negligent homicide. Jurors were to deliberate on the next most serious charge only if they unanimously voted to acquit on the more serious charge or charges. After a few hours of deliberation, the jury foreperson informed the judge that the jurors were unanimously against conviction on capital murder and first-degree murder, were split on manslaughter, and had not voted on negligent homicide, presumably because they were not unanimous on the manslaughter charge. The judge denied Blueford's request for a partial verdict reflecting the jury's acquittal vote on the capital and first-degree murder charges and directed the jury to continue deliberating. A half hour later, the foreperson reported that the jury still had not reached a verdict, and the judge declared a mistrial without first asking again for the vote count on individual charges. When the state sought to retry Blueford, he moved unsuccessfully to dismiss the two most serious charges on double jeopardy grounds, noting that the jury voted unanimously in his favor on those counts. The state supreme court upheld the denial of his motion.[51]

Writing for a six-member majority, Chief Justice Roberts held that retrial would not violate the defendant's protection against double jeopardy. Roberts concluded that the foreperson's report of unanimity among the jurors on the top two counts neither constituted a formal judgment of acquittal nor served as a final resolution on any of the elements of the charged offenses. Nothing in the jury instructions, according to Roberts, prevented any juror during the thirty-one minutes of added deliberation from reconsidering his or her position reflected in that earlier vote count. Thus, the absence of a formal acquittal meant double jeopardy was not implicated by the state's decision to retry Blueford.[52]

Justices Ginsburg, Sotomayor and Kagan were the three dissenters. Justice Sotomayor criticized the majority's portrayal of the jury's vote on the two most serious charges. She maintained that the jury's adherence to instructions not to consider lesser charges unless it reached a unanimous finding of not guilty on the more serious offense and the announcement of the vote in open court represented an acquittal for double jeopardy purposes.[53]

The trial judge in each of these double jeopardy cases made a critical mistake. In *Evans*, the Roberts Court protected the defendant's right against double jeopardy when it was the failure of the judge to properly consider elements of the charge that would have led to a retrial. The majority in *Blueford*, however, chose instead to protect the trial judge's mistake of failing to secure an official final vote. It was a choice many analysts saw as overly rigid and improperly emphasizing the form of a jury's decision more than its substance.[54]

The foregoing cases illustrate the technical nature and complexity of double jeopardy jurisprudence. There is no agreed-upon rule for double jeopardy, especially given the variety of circumstances in which double jeopardy claims are raised. *Currier v. Virginia* (2018) illuminated the complexity and lack of consensus among the justices after the arrival of the first Trump appointee, Justice Gorsuch. Currier was charged with burglary, larceny, and unlawful possession of a firearm by a convicted felon. The prosecutor and judge agreed to the defense attorney's request to separate the unlawful possession charge from the other two charges and hold a second trial solely on that charge. The defense attorney feared that evidence about Currier's prior conviction concerning the third charge would bias the jury's consideration of the first two charges. In the first trial, Currier was acquitted of both charges and then sought to bar the second proceeding on a double jeopardy claim due to the overlapping evidence for the three charges.

In a 5–4 decision, with a majority opinion written by Gorsuch, the Roberts Court rejected the double jeopardy claim and permitted Virginia to proceed with prosecution on the possession charge. In essence, because Currier had sought to have the possession charge tried separately, he consented to surrender any double jeopardy claim in these circumstances. Justice Kennedy provided the decisive fifth vote for the majority. The four most liberal justices, Ginsburg, Breyer, Kagan, and Sotomayor, dissented. The deep division among the justices reinforced the lack of consensus on the meaning of the Double Jeopardy Clause's protections in various trial circumstances.

In *Gamble v. United States* (2019), the court considered the issue of whether the protection against double jeopardy was violated by a subsequent federal prosecution on the same charge for which a state criminal proceeding had already been finalized. Prior cases had established a dual sovereignty doctrine that permitted subsequent prosecutions arising from the same circumstances because state and federal criminal laws are statutes of separate jurisdictions and therefore the later prosecutions technically did not concern the same offense. Thus, for example, if police officers were acquitted of state criminal charges in cases involving allegations of excessive use of force, including shooting deaths, federal officials often examined the cases for potential prosecution under federal civil rights statutes.[55]

Gamble entered a guilty plea to violating Alabama's law criminalizing the possession of a firearm by individuals with prior felony convictions. Nine years of his ten-year sentence were suspended, so he faced the prospect of serving one year in prison. Federal prosecutors apparently believed this punishment was too lenient, so they charged him under the parallel federal statute. He entered a guilty plea while reserving his right to raise a double jeopardy claim and was sentenced to three years in federal prison. He asked the Roberts Court to overturn the dual sovereignty doctrine and rule that his federal prosecution was barred by the Fifth Amendment protection against double jeopardy.

In a strong display of consensus concerning this specific aspect of double jeopardy jurisprudence, seven justices, including liberals Breyer, Sotomayor, and Kagan, joined the majority opinion authored by Alito that rejected Gamble's claim. The other justices in the majority were Roberts, Thomas, and Kavanaugh. Their endorsement of the dual sovereignty doctrine was challenged in separate dissenting opinions by Justices Ginsburg and Gorsuch. The opinion by Gorsuch was notable for its strong language asserting that originalist interpretation should lead to rejection of the dual sovereignty doctrine. Justice Gorsuch wrote, "A free society does not allow its government to try the same individual for the same crime until it's happy with the result. Unfortunately, the Court today endorses a colossal exception to this ancient rule against double jeopardy. . . . This 'separate sovereigns exception' to the bar against double jeopardy finds no meaningful support in the text of the Constitution, its original public meaning, structure, or history. Instead, the Constitution promises all Americans that they will never suffer double jeopardy. I would enforce that guarantee."[56]

Justice Thomas wrote a separate concurring opinion to explain specifically why he concluded an originalist analysis did not support the view expressed in Gorsuch's dissent. The competing conceptions of originalism's application to the Fifth Amendment protection against double jeopardy served as a reminder that advocates of originalism regularly disagree with each other about their understanding and interpretation of history. Despite their confident assertions about history's guidance concerning certain issues, such as Second Amendment gun rights, originalist justices regularly reveal the uncertainty, disagreements, and viewpoint-driven nature of their conclusions that purport to rely on history.

Justice Gorsuch dissented again, joined by Justices Sotomayor and Kagan, in *Denezpi v. United States* (2022). The six-member majority, in an opinion written by Justice Barrett, denied a double jeopardy claim when the federal government prosecuted a Code of Federal Regulations offense on a Native American reservation. Subsequently, the federal government prosecuted the individual again under the federal Major Crimes Act for actions in the same incident. Gorsuch noted that Native Americans have been uniquely subject to these double prosecutions under federal regulations and federal criminal statutes since the creation of the Court of Indian Offenses in the 1890s for Native American territories in which tribal courts have not been established.

Conclusion

Because of their number and doctrinal complexity, trial rights in the Fifth and Sixth Amendments regularly raise challenging issues for the Supreme Court. The Roberts Court made its mark on these issues through such clarifying decisions as establishing the principle requiring juror unanimity for guilty verdicts (*Ramos v. Louisiana*) and reconfirming the dual sovereignty rule that permits separate state and federal prosecutions for the same offense without violating double jeopardy (*Gamble v. United States*). The decision in *Connick v. Thompson* providing immunity from lawsuits for prosecutors, even in circumstances of overt Brady violations and a wrongful conviction that sent a man to death row for many years, dampened any hopes that the court might recognize a need for greater accountability for justice system officials.

Trial rights cases provided many examples of the Roberts Court divided into its liberal and conservative wings. However, there were also examples of individual conservative justices taking rights-protective stances on specific issues. Justice Scalia stood out for his liberal opinions on Confrontation Clause issues. Justice Gorsuch wrote rights-protective opinions on double jeopardy and the jury's fact-finding role in the sentencing process, with the latter issue also drawing support from Justices Thomas and Scalia, depending on the specific facts of the case. Yet, many of these decisions were determined by close votes. Thus, it is unclear what this will mean for new decisions on these issues in the aftermath of the Roberts Court's period of rapid compositional change with new four justices, including Biden appointee Justice Jackson, joining the court since 2017.

7. SENTENCING AND RIGHTS IN CORRECTIONS

Issues concerning sentencing and punishment pose especially profound questions about the nation's commitment to aspirational ideals and constitutional rights. It is often said that "liberty" is the premier value underlying the Constitution, but how should that concept affect decisions about whether and how we deprive people of their freedom as punishment for a crime? Questions about punishment in the United States, unlike in other industrialized democracies, also raise issues about the government extinguishing people's lives through capital punishment. Under the Constitution, what are the circumstances, standards, and procedures that should guide decisions about the ultimate punishment? In addition, there are continuing questions about whether and how constitutional rights provide protections for people in prisons and jails. From the 1970s onward, the changing composition of the Supreme Court over the course of the Burger, Rehnquist, and Roberts Court eras has led to decisions that have generally limited post-sentencing rights protections for people undergoing criminal punishment. On the issue of sentencing decisions, by contrast, the court continued to produce rights-expanding decisions through the first years of the Roberts Court era.

In *Trop v. Dulles* (1958), the seminal case providing the definition of the Eighth Amendment's Cruel and Unusual Punishments Clause, Chief Justice Warren declared that the meaning of the clause must be defined using the "evolving standards of decency that mark the progress of a maturing society."[1] As justices who employed originalist approaches to interpretation joined the court, this articulation of a flexible, changing standard for assessing "cruel and unusual punishments" became controversial. It clashed directly with originalist justices' view of a static meaning for "cruel and unusual punishments" defined by the punishment practices in 1791. Yet, the *Trop* standard remained as the guiding precedent during the Roberts Court era. Under the *Trop* standard, when justices evaluate cruel and unusual punishment claims, they are supposed to ask themselves if current societal standards permit the challenged punishments.

The Roberts Court produced Eighth Amendment decisions with important impacts concerning sentences for juvenile lawbreakers, various aspects of capital punishment, and the expanded applicability of the Excessive Fines Clause. Just as in the Rehnquist Court era, Justice Kennedy was especially influential in many of the court's most important Eighth Amendment cases.[2] He was the justice most likely to cast the deciding vote in cases considering the constitutionality of specific punishments for the first ten years of the Roberts Court era. During the Rehnquist Court era, for example, Kennedy provided a crucial liberal vote in Eighth Amendment cases, including *Roper v. Simmons* (2005), concerning the application of capital punishment for murders committed while under the age of eighteen, and *Atkins v. Virginia* (2002), which forbade the imposition of the death penalty on developmentally disabled individuals. In the Roberts Court era, Kennedy cast similarly decisive liberal votes favoring individuals' rights claims in *Kennedy v. Louisiana* (2008), which prohibited capital punishment for the rape of a child, and *Panetti v. Quarterman* (2007), which limited imposing the death penalty on individuals suffering from mental illness. Thus, the Eighth Amendment was an issue area that created a context for a single justice sitting in the middle of a divided court to wield notable influence over case outcomes and doctrinal development.

Sentencing Juveniles

In his Rehnquist era majority opinion barring the imposition of capital punishment for teens who commit murders prior to age eighteen, Justice Kennedy emphasized the emerging scientific research analyzing juveniles' still-developing brains and their inability to fully understand the consequences of their actions (*Roper v. Simmons*). Consistent with this understanding of the limited culpability of juveniles, Kennedy wrote the liberal majority opinion in another important case concerning juveniles in the Roberts Court era. In *Graham v. Florida* (2010), the court ruled by a 6–3 vote that the punishment of life imprisonment without possibility of parole cannot be imposed on juveniles for non-homicide offenses. Chief Justice Roberts concurred in the result of this Cruel and Unusual Punishments Clause decision. *Graham* was a landmark ruling because, in addition to its liberal outcome, the court created another categorical rule limiting sentences for juveniles convicted of serious crimes.[3]

This example of a new categorical rule illustrated Justice Kennedy's willingness to break from the long-standing court practice of evaluating all noncapital sentencing issues on a case-by-case basis.[4] Indeed, although Chief Justice Roberts agreed that Graham's sentence was unconstitutionally excessive, he disagreed with Kennedy's creation of a categorical rule. In his concurring opinion, Roberts preferred that the court examine Graham's individual crime while leaving open the possibility of life-without-parole sentences for other juveniles whose crimes were more "heinous."

In this case, Graham participated in a home invasion thirty-four days before his eighteenth birthday. He was on probation for other crimes at the time of the home invasion. Graham committed two home invasions in one day, and during the second one, one of Graham's accomplices was shot. Graham was eventually caught, and police found three guns in his car. Graham was found guilty of a probation violation as well as home invasion. As a result, under Florida law, he was sentenced to life without the possibility of parole. Graham's life sentence could be reduced only by the governor.

Graham appealed and argued that the sentence violated the Eighth Amendment's prohibition on cruel and unusual punishments. Justice Kennedy agreed and started his majority opinion by quoting the *Trop v. Dulles* standard emphasizing the "evolving standards of decency that mark the progress of a maturing society."[5] His opinion concluded that although a majority of states and the federal government allow the sentence of life without the possibility of parole for juveniles committing non-homicide crimes, the sentence was seldom imposed. Only 129 juveniles in the entire nation received that sentence. Out of these 129 individuals, 77 were sentenced in Florida, suggesting it was rarely used outside of Florida. Indeed, the 52 juveniles who received this sentence outside of Florida were spread out over ten states. The infrequent actual imposition of the sentence indicated to Kennedy and the justices in the majority that a contemporary national consensus did not exist justifying its use.

Justice Kennedy cited other reasons for prohibiting this sentence for juveniles. He found that juveniles' reduced capability to understand consequences, due to their still-developing brains, should be taken into consideration for sentencing. Further, Kennedy argued that non-homicide crimes do not deserve the most severe punishments, especially for juveniles. Life without possibility of parole is especially harsh when applied to juveniles because, based on life expectancy, they will presumably be imprisoned longer than an adult sentenced to the same punishment. In the aftermath of the *Graham* decision, states were required to impose sentences that gave juveniles a meaningful opportunity to petition for parole, although there need not be any guarantee of parole release.

Justice Thomas, writing in dissent for Justices Scalia and Alito, argued that the determination of the appropriateness of any punishment should be left to the elected branches of government. Thomas also noted that, because the categorical prohibition approach had previously been used only in death penalty cases, the court did not have any precedent for using it here. Thus, in Thomas's view, the court should not have done so. In addition, as an originalist, Thomas criticized the use of the flexible *Trop* standard for evaluating cruel and unusual punishment claims. As Thomas noted, "The text of the Constitution is silent regarding the permissibility of this sentencing practice, and although it would not have offended the standards that prevailed at the founding, the Court insists that the standards of American society have evolved such that the Constitution now requires its prohibition. The news of this evolution will, I think, come as a surprise to the American people."[6]

The concurring opinion by Justice Stevens responded directly to the Thomas dissent and furthered their ongoing debate on originalism. His opinion reiterated support for the *Trop* standard and noted that it had been applied consistently since 1958. Stevens also made a sharp comment about the implications of Thomas's originalist perspective. In Stevens's view, the Thomas approach would permit punishments deemed unconscionable by American society: "While Justice Thomas would apparently not rule out a death sentence for a $50 theft by a 7-year-old, . . . the Court wisely rejects his static approach to the law. Standards of decency have evolved since 1980. They will never stop doing so."[7]

The Roberts Court also expanded sentencing protections for juveniles in *Miller v. Alabama* (2012). In *Miller,* the court held that states cannot impose *mandatory* sentences of life without possibility of parole for juveniles convicted of homicide crimes. These sentencing schemes are impermissible under the Eighth Amendment because they do not take into consideration the culpability of the juvenile lawbreaker and do not adequately provide for individualized consideration of cases, including mitigating circumstances. At the age of fourteen, Miller, along with a friend, beat a man with a baseball bat and set fire to the man's trailer. The victim died from the beating and exposure to smoke from the fire.

Miller was charged as an adult and, pursuant to Alabama law, was given a mandatory sentence of life without possibility of parole. There was no provision in the law for a less severe sentence.

Consistent with the rulings in *Roper* and *Graham*, Justice Kagan wrote for a narrow five-person majority, including a pivotal liberal vote by Justice Kennedy. She declared the mandatory life sentence to be unconstitutional. Kagan reiterated the theme that juveniles are less culpable than adults and that the Eighth Amendment requires this fact to be taken into consideration. The *Miller* decision did not hold that juveniles committing homicides cannot be sentenced to life without possibility of parole. However, it specified that they cannot be given this sentence under a mandatory sentencing scheme. Citing Justice Kennedy's opinions in *Roper* and *Graham*, Kagan noted that juveniles have been recognized by the court to be "constitutionally different" from adults for the purposes of sentencing.[8] Mandatory sentencing schemes, however, prevent mitigating circumstances about the juveniles' upbringing and personal problems from being given appropriate weight.

Chief Justice Roberts viewed this case differently from *Graham* and therefore dissented from the majority opinion. His dissent was joined by Scalia, Alito, and Thomas. Roberts argued that the mandatory sentencing scheme does not violate *Trop*'s "evolving standards of decency" analysis that was used to limit the imposition of severe sentences on juveniles in both *Roper* and *Graham*. Specifically, Roberts found that there was no national consensus against mandatory life-without-parole punishments for murder, and therefore Miller's sentence was permissible under the Eighth Amendment.

The *Miller* majority left open the question of what to do about the twenty-five hundred individuals sitting in prison who were previously given a life-without-possibility-of-parole sentence as juveniles. In *Montgomery v. Louisiana* (2016), the court applied the ruling in *Miller* retroactively. At age seventeen, Montgomery killed a police officer in 1963. He was found guilty of the crime and sentenced to life in prison without possibility of parole. Montgomery spent a half century in prison before the Roberts Court issued its *Miller* decision. Following the ruling in *Miller*, Montgomery requested a new sentencing hearing. The court, in a 6–3 decision with Chief Justice Roberts joining the majority, agreed that Montgomery should be afforded the opportunity to argue for release on parole.

Justice Kennedy wrote the majority opinion and asserted that the ruling in *Miller* was a major substantive ruling that must be applied retroactively.

While the decision did not guarantee that everyone convicted as a juvenile would receive a new sentence, it ruled that these individuals must have a meaningful opportunity to be considered for parole. Justice Scalia, joined by Thomas and Alito, dissented and argued that *Miller* did not create a substantive rule that required retroactive application.

In 2021, with three Trump-appointed justices on the bench, the Roberts Court revisited the issue of sentencing juveniles to a lifetime behind bars. In *Jones v. Mississippi* (2021), a then thirty-two-year-old man who had been convicted at age fifteen of murdering his grandfather challenged the mandatory life-without-parole sentence that he received. He relied on the Roberts Court precedents in *Miller* and *Montgomery*. At the judicial proceeding to consider imposition of a new sentence, the judge made a discretionary decision to reimpose the life sentence. Jones argued on appeal that his entitlement to a resentencing hearing included an obligation for the judge to consider evidence and make a finding that Jones was "permanently incorrigible" in order to reimpose a life sentence.[9] The newly constituted six-member conservative supermajority of the Roberts Court rejected the argument.

Justice Kavanaugh wrote the majority opinion. He concluded that the prior precedents still left trial judges with the discretionary authority to reimpose a life sentence without either an evidentiary hearing on "permanent incorrigibility" or even any explanation for the formal continuation of the life sentence. In his concurring opinion, Justice Thomas noted that the majority opinion had effectively "overruled *Montgomery* in substance but not in name."[10] In other words, the entitlement to retrospective application of *Miller* in the form of a resentencing hearing required by *Montgomery* merely obligated the trial judges to go through the motions of having a hearing prior to making their own unexplained discretionary decision. There was no attendant obligation either to consider specific factors or to explain resentencing decisions. Thomas did not make this point in order to object to the results that could be produced by such pretextual hearings. He merely sought to argue that *Montgomery* had been wrongly decided. Thomas argued that the *Miller* precedent should be formally overturned. He saw no basis for treating *Miller* as producing a rule of substance that would require retroactive application and trigger new hearings for those already serving life sentences for murders committed while under age eighteen.

The three dissenters, Justices Sotomayor, Kagan, and Breyer, agreed with Thomas's conclusion that the majority's decision had effectively turned the *Montgomery* ruling into merely a symbolic statement. In an opinion by Justice Sotomayor, the dissenters went even further to declare that the *Jones* decision "guts" both *Miller* and *Montgomery*. In Sotomayor's words, the holding in *Jones* "would come as a shock to the [justices who decided] *Miller* and *Montgomery*" by effectively nullifying "*Miller*'s essential holding that 'a lifetime in prison is a disproportionate sentence for all but the rarest of children.'"[11] The new Roberts Court majority undercut the precedents that treated juveniles differently from adults for purposes of imposing life sentences. It remains to be seen whether the conservative supermajority may reverse precedents such as *Graham* and *Miller* in future decisions now that the dissenters in those cases have been joined by a critical mass of like-minded allies to form a new conservative majority.

Categorical Limitations on the Death Penalty

Beginning in the Burger Court era, the court categorically banned or created significant hurdles for the use of the death penalty in certain circumstances. In these cases, the court typically concluded that either the perpetrator lacked the requisite intent and culpability to be executed or the crime was not sufficiently heinous to justify the death penalty.[12] In *Coker v. Georgia* (1977), for example, the Burger Court held that the rape of an adult was not a crime for which capital punishment could be imposed. After his confirmation to the Rehnquist Court in 1987, Justice Kennedy became a key figure in writing majority opinions and casting decisive votes within the divided court on issues concerning categorical exclusions from capital punishment.[13]

In 2007, with Kennedy writing on behalf of a narrow majority, the Roberts Court ruled in *Panetti v. Quarterman* that death row residents cannot be executed if their condition of mental illness prevents them from understanding the reasons for their death sentence. In so ruling, the Roberts Court majority effectively turned aside an effort to eliminate the Burger Court's precedent set in *Ford v. Wainwright* (1986). In *Ford*, a five-justice liberal majority held that the Eighth Amendment prevented the execution of individuals who are insane at the time of execution, even if they were mentally competent to stand trial at the time of conviction.[14] The decision left open the question about how to identify and define which imprisoned individuals were affected by mental illness conditions that would preclude their execution. The most concrete definition of when a person's mental illness was so severe as to make them ineligible for execution came from

Justice Powell's concurrence in *Ford*. Powell argued that in order for executions to be permissible, "those who are executed must know the fact of their impending execution and the reason for it."[15] Because Powell provided the fifth liberal vote to form the majority and the actual majority opinion by Justice Marshall did not present a definition, Powell's articulation of a definition was used by lower court judges as guidance for determining when executions of mentally ill individuals were permissible.[16]

In the Roberts Court's case, Panetti killed his estranged wife's parents. He also took his wife and daughter hostage before eventually surrendering to the police. Panetti had a long history of mental illness and had been hospitalized for his mental illness, and several witnesses testified that he suffered from delusions. Nevertheless, he was not only deemed competent to stand trial but also allowed to waive his right to counsel and represent himself during the trial. Despite his increasingly erratic and evident mental illness issues, he was convicted of murder and sentenced to death.

After several unsuccessful appeals on procedural grounds, lawyers filed a habeas petition on behalf of Panetti arguing that, under Eighth Amendment requirements from *Ford v. Wainwright*, he lacked the mental competence to be executed due to his mental illness. The lower federal courts denied his request. The federal judge found that the state court did not adequately determine Panetti's mental competency for trial. However, Panetti had not presented enough evidence of mental illness to set aside his death sentence. At the Supreme Court, Justice Kennedy, writing for the five-justice majority, found Panetti's execution to be constitutionally prohibited. According to Kennedy's opinion, those who can neither understand the severity of their crime nor properly comprehend why they are being executed cannot be subject to the death penalty. Thus, Kennedy's opinion held that Panetti must be given a competency hearing in the lower courts to determine whether he qualified for execution.

The *Panetti* decision presented a newly expanded definition of mental illness for Eighth Amendment purposes. According to one analyst, "Justice Kennedy rejected the [*Ford* precedent's] 'awareness' standard. . . . Instead, . . . the proper test is whether the defendant's 'mental illness obstructs a rational understanding of the State's reason for his execution.'"[17] Thus, awareness of the impending execution is not enough. The individual must have a rational understanding of the reasons for the punishment.

The decision broadened the conception of mental illness for Eighth Amendment purposes, thus potentially enabling more individuals to show that their mental condition made them ineligible for the death penalty. Kennedy's opinion questioned the constitutionality of executing those who are less able than typical adults to understand the severity of the crime they have committed. Some commentators argued that this decision paved the way for a future decision declaring a categorical ban against imposing the death penalty on those affected by mental illness at the time of the commission of the murder. However, Kennedy's retirement occurred before the court accepted a case to examine this issue. The newly constituted post-2020 Roberts Court majority seems unlikely to revisit the issue unless the conservative justices wish to reverse *Panetti* and *Ford* and thereby make those with disabling mental illnesses eligible for capital punishment.[18]

In *Moore v. Texas* (2017), the Roberts Court examined the implementation of the Rehnquist Court's landmark decision in *Atkins v. Virginia*, which prohibited imposing the death penalty on individuals with developmental disabilities. Moore, whose attorneys claimed he was developmentally disabled, was nevertheless determined by the Texas Court of Criminal Appeals to be eligible for execution. Using an outdated testing standard, the Texas court did not find Moore's disability sufficient to preclude the imposition of the death penalty. The Roberts Court reversed that decision, 5–3, with Justice Kennedy providing the fifth vote. Writing for the majority, Justice Ginsburg acknowledged that the determination of intellectual capacity under the *Atkins* decision was left up to the states. However, the states' responsibility for implementation of the *Atkins* rule did not mean the states were permitted to use outdated methods to assess developmental disabilities.[19] The decision guided states about what they are forbidden from doing but did not clearly define how to assess the extent of individuals' developmental disabilities in order to determine eligibility for the death penalty.

In *Kennedy v. Louisiana*, Justice Kennedy again cast a decisive liberal vote on a deeply divided court to identify a categorical exclusion from death penalty eligibility. In *Kennedy*, a narrow five-justice majority decided that the rape of a child is a crime for which the death penalty cannot be imposed as the punishment. The decision was controversial, with several commentators criticizing the outcome and the court's reasoning.[20] Meanwhile, others applauded this application of the proportionality principle in Eighth Amendment jurisprudence.[21] Patrick Kennedy was convicted of the rape of his eight-year-old stepdaughter. Although he claimed that two boys from the neighborhood committed the crime, the investigation into Patrick Kennedy's actions raised questions about the story. Three months after the rape, the victim told her mother that Patrick Kennedy had committed the crime. He was found guilty of aggravated rape of a child. Under Louisiana law, the rape of a child under the age of twelve was a capital offense. He was sentenced to death and subsequently appealed his sentence. His attorneys argued that because the Supreme Court had held in *Coker v. Georgia* that the death penalty was an unconstitutionally disproportionate punishment for the rape of an adult, it followed that it was also an unconstitutional punishment for the rape of a child.

Justice Kennedy's majority opinion, joined by the four liberal justices, relied on the *Trop* standard that focused on evolving standards of decency and the punishments acceptable to contemporary society. According to Justice Kennedy, social norms reserve the death penalty for the most heinous crimes, and such crimes do not include offenses that do not result in the death of a victim. Specifically, the majority opinion found that only six states had the death penalty for the rape of a child. In four of those states, capital punishment was permitted only if the defendant had a prior rape conviction. Furthermore, since 1964 no one had been executed for the crime of rape in the United States, regardless of the victim's age. Patrick Kennedy and one other individual in Louisiana were the only people in the entire nation on death row for the rape of a child. Thus, Justice Kennedy's opinion concluded that the use of the death penalty for rape of a child did not satisfy the *Trop* standard and was therefore unconstitutional.

Unlike prior majority opinions by Justice Kennedy limiting the application of the death penalty and life-without-parole sentences for certain categories of lawbreakers, the decision in *Kennedy v. Louisiana* created a limitation based on a proportionality assessment of whether the punishment fit the crime.[22] Although Justice Kennedy supported the removal of certain crimes and categories of individuals from death penalty eligibility, he was less inclined to support liberal positions if the questions involved only methods of execution rather than eligibility for capital punishment.

Sentencing Factors

Most death penalty cases examined by the Supreme Court concern the definition of proper procedures that courts must use in such cases. For example, the court emphasizes that defendants must receive individualized sentencing deliberations that allow a jury to properly evaluate any mitigating circumstances and that provide adequate guidance for jurors deciding what sentence to impose in murder cases. In death penalty cases, juries and judges consider mitigating and aggravating factors. Mitigating factors are those that may make the defendant less deserving of execution than other murder defendants, such as psychological problems or traumatic childhood experiences. Aggravating factors are those that may make a murder defendant more deserving of the death penalty, such as a prior criminal record or a murder committed during the commission of a second crime, typically robbery, kidnapping, or sexual assault. Several cases before the court raised questions about whether the state adequately protected a defendant's constitutional rights during the sentencing phase of the trial, including proper consideration of sentencing factors.[23] These decisions often divided the Roberts Court's liberals and conservatives and, prior to 2018, were generally determined by whichever wing of the court that Justice Kennedy chose to join.

The Roberts Court handed down a conservative decision in *Kansas v. Marsh* (2006) that divided the justices along typical conservative-liberal lines. Kansas's death penalty statute specified that if the jury uses the reasonable doubt standard to find the existence of one or more aggravating factors and does not find any mitigating circumstances that outweigh the aggravating factors, then the death penalty will be automatically imposed. Marsh shot and killed a woman and then burned down a house with her nineteen-month-old daughter still inside. The jury identified aggravating factors, including the heinous nature of the killings, and heard testimony from character witnesses presented by Marsh as mitigating evidence. The jury sentenced him to death under the Kansas statute. Marsh challenged the statute as unconstitutional because, in his view, it favored the imposition of the death penalty when aggravating and mitigating circumstances were deemed equal. Justice Thomas wrote the majority opinion in a 5–4 decision and found no fault with the statute. Thomas concluded that the Kansas law satisfied the requirement that death sentences be rendered only after individualized sentencing factors have been considered. Justice Souter, joined by Stevens, Ginsburg, and Breyer, argued that the law was unconstitutional because it mandated a sentence of death in what Souter called "doubtful" cases. Souter was not calling Marsh's case a "doubtful case. Instead, the dissenters were concerned with how the statute would affect the full range of cases to which it would be applied.

In *Brown v. Sanders* (2006), the Roberts Court issued another conservative 5–4 decision addressing sentencing factors. The majority concluded that even if some aggravating factors, called "special circumstances" under California's law, are later invalidated on appeal, a death sentence can still stand if the other special circumstances found by the jury justify keeping the death sentence in place. In this case, the jury found four special circumstances related to Ronald Sanders's first-degree murder conviction and sentenced Sanders to death. Each of these four special circumstances alone would have made Sanders eligible for the death penalty. These circumstances included such aspects of the crime as the commission of a murder during a robbery and a homicide to silence a potential witness. The California Supreme Court's justices found that two of the special circumstances were invalid, but, because they upheld the remaining special circumstances, they also upheld the death sentence.

The Roberts Court, in an opinion written by Justice Scalia, found no violation of law in the imposition of the death penalty. Justice Scalia concluded that so long as the remaining valid special circumstances were sufficient to support a death sentence, then the jury's mistaken identification of invalid special circumstances was not relevant. In essence, Scalia assumed that initial consideration of an invalid sentencing factor had no impact on the determination of the sentence in a capital case because it was generally independent of the jury's consideration of other factors.[24]

Justice Breyer's dissenting opinion, joined by Justice Ginsburg, argued that the state appellate courts should have determined whether the jury's mistake was indeed "harmless error." In other words, there should have been a specific finding regarding whether the invalid special circumstances contributed to the determination of the sentence. Justice Stevens was harsher in his criticism of the majority's decision. He argued that the court should have overturned the sentence because there was no way to know whether the two subsequently invalidated sentencing factors had contributed in essential ways to the jury's original decision to impose the death penalty.

The Roberts Court addressed the consideration of mitigating circumstances for sentencing decisions in *Ayers v. Belmontes* (2006). The court split 5–4 along the predictable divide between liberal and conservative justices. The five-member conservative majority ruled that juries did not need to be specifically instructed to evaluate forward-looking mitigating circumstances when considering death sentences. Belmontes was convicted of first-degree murder in 1982. During sentencing, his attorney presented evidence that he had become a religious person while at a youth center and that, if given a life sentence, he would continue to live a religious life and help others in the prison system. This evidence, which Belmontes viewed as mitigating the potential severity of the sentence, was corroborated by a chaplain, an assistant chaplain, and others. Despite Belmontes's forward-looking evidence purporting to show that he would lead a productive life and make positive contributions to the rehabilitation of other imprisoned people, the jury sentenced him to death.

Belmontes appealed, arguing that his Eighth and Fourteenth Amendment rights were violated when the judge did not specifically instruct the jury to consider the forward-looking mitigating circumstances concerning Belmontes's religious commitments. Instead, the judge had given only a general instruction inviting the jury to consider circumstances that might provide a basis for mitigation. Belmontes argued that a jury might reasonably, but improperly, believe that the instruction allowed juries only to consider elements of the crime and current characteristics of the defendant, not the possibility of future rehabilitation on the part of the defendant.

Justice Kennedy wrote the majority opinion and found that the instructions given to the jury did not prevent jurors from considering any mitigating circumstances. Kennedy noted that it would be "counterintuitive if a defendant's capacity to redeem himself through good works could not extenuate his offense."[25] Thus, Kennedy presumed it was likely that the jury did, in fact, consider the forward-looking evidence when it sentenced Belmontes to death.

Justice Stevens wrote a dissenting opinion on behalf of the liberal wing of the court. Stevens argued that the language of the state's law on sentencing instructions was so restrictive that juries might not understand that they can consider a person's future potential. Jurors might reasonably believe that the only factors they can consider are those suggesting the crime was less severe than other murders for which the death penalty would be appropriate.

The question of proper jury instructions arose in additional closely divided cases, both decided by a decisive liberal vote from Justice Kennedy. In *Brewer v. Quarterman* (2007) and *Abdul-Kabir v. Quarterman* (2007), the court addressed whether the jury was adequately instructed to consider mitigating circumstances during sentencing. The court interpreted and used the Anti-Terrorism and Effective Death Penalty Act of 1996 to determine whether habeas corpus relief could be granted to the petitioners.[26]

Jalil Abdul-Kabir was convicted of capital murder. During the sentencing phase of the trial, the prosecution presented evidence that Abdul-Kabir remained a threat to society and that he was a sociopath. During the defense's opportunity to present mitigating evidence, Abdul-Kabir's attorneys told the jury about his troubled childhood as well as psychological evidence intended to cast doubt on his culpability. The judge instructed the jury to consider whether Abdul-Kabir acted deliberately to cause another's death and whether he was likely to be violent in the future. The judge did not instruct the jury to consider mitigating circumstances. The jury handed down a death sentence.

In *Brewer v. Quarterman*, in circumstances similar to those in *Abdul-Kabir*, the judge directed the jury to consider whether Brewer had deliberately caused the death of another and whether he posed a future danger to society. Although Brewer presented mitigating circumstances, the jury was not directed to consider that evidence. As in *Abdul-Kabir*, the jury imposed a death sentence.

The Roberts Court overturned both death sentences when Justice Kennedy voted with his liberal colleagues to create a five-justice majority. Justice Stevens concluded that the judges' instructions violated the defendants' constitutional rights. Using the federal Anti-Terrorism and Effective Death Penalty Act, Stevens noted that the federal courts may grant post-appeal habeas corpus relief if the lower courts have followed procedures that "resulted in a decision that was contrary to, or involved an unreasonable application of, clearly established Federal law, as determined by the Supreme Court of the United States."[27] Stevens noted that in *Penry v. Lynaugh* (1989), the Rehnquist Court held that if a defendant introduced mitigating evidence, the jury must be instructed to consider that evidence. According to Stevens, the court reiterated that point in several cases after *Penry*, and thus the rule that juries must be instructed to consider mitigating evidence was well established in the court's precedents. Stevens devoted a considerable portion of the opinion to show that this rule was clearly established.[28] In both *Abdul-Kabir* and *Brewer*, Stevens concluded that the juries may not have placed proper weight on mitigating evidence when the trial judges' jury instructions did not call their attention to this factor.

Nearly a decade later, the court returned to the issue of procedures for death penalty sentencing. The Roberts Court consolidated three cases addressing jury questions in its decision in *Kansas v. Carr* (2016). The Carr brothers were convicted together for a series of capital crimes, and they were jointly sentenced to death. Writing for an eight-justice majority,

Justice Scalia found no fault with the state's sentencing process and thus rejected the claim of a rights violation. Scalia concluded that there was no constitutional requirement mandating separate sentencing hearings for co-defendants. The sentencing of such defendants jointly did not deprive them of the individualized sentencing mandated by the court's precedents. Scalia's opinion also emphasized that jurors did not need to be informed by the judge that there is no requirement that the "beyond-a-reasonable-doubt" standard be used in identifying the existence of mitigating factors. In dissent, Justice Sotomayor argued that the court should not have accepted the case for hearing. By resting on a strong consensus among the Roberts Court justices, this decision differed from the divided results in prior cases regarding capital case procedures and jury instructions.

The key consequence of the cases concerning capital jury instructions was that the Roberts Court did not require trial judges to call sentencing jurors' attention to specific aspects of the available mitigating evidence. This was demonstrated in the lack of guiding instructions on the standard of proof for mitigating evidence (*Kansas v. Carr*) and the forward-looking aspects of mitigating evidence that could show the potential for positive future contributions by the defendant (*Ayers v. Belmontes*).

Execution Procedures

In one of the key cases shaping the Roberts Court's overall impact on the death penalty, the court's plurality opinion in *Baze v. Rees* (2008) upheld the use of lethal injection as a method of execution. The variety of opinions issued by the justices highlighted the existence of differences in viewpoints on capital punishment within the Roberts Court. Although the case did nothing more than uphold Kentucky's method of execution, it led to other challenges to lethal injection protocols and contributed to debates and controversy over the constitutionality of lethal injection.[29]

Baze and Bowling both were sentenced to death after being convicted of double homicides in Kentucky. Kentucky used a standard three-drug combination to carry out lethal injection executions, and while neither defendant challenged their death sentences, both challenged the use of the drug protocol. The first drug was intended to produce a deep state of unconsciousness. It was intended to ensure that the death is painless. The second drug caused paralysis and stopped respiration. Then the final drug caused cardiac arrest. Neither Baze nor Bowling challenged the constitutionality of the protocol when it is administered and functions correctly. However, they both argued that the risk that the first drug would not be administered correctly was too great to allow the protocol to be used because improper administration of the first drug would result in a very painful death.

Chief Justice Roberts's plurality opinion, joined by Alito and Kennedy, found the use of the three-drug protocol consistent with the Eighth Amendment. The opinion concluded that the petitioners did not demonstrate a proven constitutional deficiency in the way Kentucky carried out executions. Roberts noted that at least twenty-nine other states used the same system. He argued that the Eighth Amendment does not require the elimination of all pain and that some risk of pain was an inevitable element in an execution. If a method of execution presented, as Roberts put it, an "objectively intolerable risk of harm," then perhaps the method could be impermissible.[30] Using this standard, rather than the "significant risk of pain" standard urged by Baze and Bowling, these three justices determined that the three-drug protocol used by Kentucky complied with the requirements of the Eighth Amendment's Cruel and Unusual Punishments Clause.

Justice Stevens's opinion concurring in judgment articulated his evolving views on the death penalty. Early in his tenure on the Burger Court, he voted in *Gregg v. Georgia* (1976) to allow states to retain the death penalty so long as juries had proper guidance on its application and an ability to determine that the sentence was appropriate.[31] Stevens would later admit that he regretted that vote, and his concurring opinion in *Baze* showed the full evolution of his views about capital punishment's flaws and questionable constitutionality.[32]

In his lengthy opinion, Stevens expressed significant concern about lethal injection as a method of execution as well as the use of the death penalty generally. Justice Stevens raised doubts about the second drug rather than the first in the three-drug cocktail. Stevens noted that the second drug, pancuronium bromide, is a paralytic agent. Thus, it is possible that the person being executed feels significant pain but cannot move or react in ways that permit outside observers to recognize the severity of the pain. He observed that the considerable risk of pain led Kentucky to prohibit the use of the drug to euthanize animals, yet the state allowed its use on humans for executions. This seeming inconsistency made the use of the drug highly questionable in Stevens's view. In addition, the second drug was not even needed since the third drug caused cardiac arrest. The second drug was intended to prevent the individual subjected to execution from twitching and having muscle spasms. While Roberts's plurality opinion asserted that the second drug provided the condemned individual with a dignified death, Stevens argued that this rationale does not justify potentially allowing significant pain to be rendered invisible to observers by the drug's paralytic effects.

Justice Stevens then turned to a general discussion of the death penalty and identified several reasons to discontinue its use. He argued that the possibility an innocent person will be executed was too significant to tolerate. He also noted that the jury selection process aimed at producing death-qualified juries resulted in overrepresentation of jurors with a pro-conviction bias. Moreover, he observed that the death penalty continued to be a punishment that was applied in a discriminatory manner. Justice Stevens concluded that the death penalty was no longer acceptable under contemporary standards for society.

At the time of the *Baze* decision, Stevens became the fifth justice in Supreme Court history, in addition to departed Justices Brennan, Marshall, Blackmun, and Powell, to announce that he had come to the conclusion that the death penalty itself was unconstitutional.[33] Five years later, two more justices, Breyer and Ginsburg, effectively joined this list through a dissenting opinion in a subsequent lethal injection case, *Glossip v. Gross* (2015). In *Baze*, Stevens noted that because the question at hand in the case was not about the constitutionality of the death penalty and court precedents supported the plurality's opinion, he concurred in the judgment permitting the continued use of lethal injection.

Justice Ginsburg, joined by Justice Souter, filed a dissenting opinion in *Baze*. Ginsburg argued that the risk of pain if the condemned individual was not properly anesthetized was too great to allow the protocol's use to continue without further review. Other states that used lethal injection for executions had safeguards in place to make sure that condemned individuals were rendered unconscious prior to the actual execution. For example, one state had medical staff examine the individual, and another state used ammonia tablets to gauge the individual's responsiveness. However, Kentucky did not do any of these things. Because Kentucky did not have these safeguards in place, further investigation into the execution protocol was needed.

In *Glossip v. Gross* (2015), the Roberts Court revisited the lethal injection issue. Because previously used drugs were not readily available, Oklahoma substituted a different drug, midazolam, for the first drug in the three-drug execution cocktail. European pharmaceutical manufacturers had begun to refuse to sell to American states eight different anesthesia drugs used in executions, thus necessitating the search for replacement drugs that could serve the same purposes. Death row prisoners in Oklahoma claimed that the use of midazolam created an unacceptable risk of severe pain. One Oklahoma execution using the drug appeared to be botched when the supposedly unconscious individual began to move and make sounds after the drug was administered. An investigation of the execution concluded that the reason for the awkward delay during the execution was that the IV needle slipped from his vein, not that the drug was ineffective for its intended purpose.[34]

Justice Alito wrote the court's majority opinion that relied on the decision in *Baze v. Rees* to reject this challenge to a specific lethal injection method. The majority cited the plurality opinion in *Baze* as requiring claimants to identify an available alternative method of execution that entails less risk of pain. Alito said that the petitioners failed to fulfill this requirement that *Baze* established for all method-of-execution challenges under the Eighth Amendment. The majority also accepted the lower court's conclusion that the petitioners had failed to demonstrate that the new drug was very likely to cause needless suffering.

In a dissenting opinion, Justice Breyer, joined by Justice Ginsburg, wrote a lengthy critique of capital punishment presenting evidence concerning wrongful convictions, discrimination, and arbitrariness. Rather than focus on the lethal injection issue in *Glossip*, his opinion served as an extended request for the court to reconsider the constitutionality of the death penalty. At the end of the opinion, he explicitly stated his own view that the death penalty was highly likely to violate the Eighth Amendment. Justices Scalia and Thomas each wrote concurring opinions solely to refute Breyer's opinion and make their own case for the constitutionality of capital punishment. As originalists, their arguments and conclusions were predictable and consistent with their support for capital punishment throughout their careers.

A second dissenting opinion written by Justice Sotomayor on behalf of all four dissenters directly addressed the lethal injection issue in the case. She was sharply critical of the majority's decision and characterized the result as leaving people to potentially experience a form of torture during execution that may be akin to being burned at the stake.[35] She observed that the expert witnesses in the case agreed with the US Food and Drug Administration's disapproval of using midazolam alone for anesthesia during surgery. Therefore, it could not be regarded as a drug that can reliably induce and maintain unconsciousness during an execution.

The 5–4 decision in *Glossip* solidified the court's endorsement of lethal injection as a method of execution. The next challenge to lethal injection executions accepted for hearing by the Roberts Courts was *Bucklew v. Precythe* (2019). The man scheduled for execution asserted that Missouri's lethal injection methods posed the risk that he might choke to death on blood in his throat or otherwise suffer an excruciating death because of his rare medical condition involving tumors in the blood vessels of his neck and brain. He suggested an alternative method of execution relying on nitrogen hypoxia: having him breathe pure nitrogen instead of oxygen, thereby causing death by asphyxiation. In a 5–4 decision that divided the Roberts Court along familiar ideological lines, Justice Gorsuch's majority opinion rejected the claim. According to the majority, the petitioner failed to prove that his suggested alternative would avoid the needless suffering that he speculatively asserted could be produced by Missouri's established execution method.

In the aftermath of Justice Barrett's appointment in 2020 to replace Justice Ginsburg, it will be interesting to see whether the Roberts Court in subsequent cases moves beyond preserving the status quo in capital punishment law. Will the majority instead act to reverse prior decisions that limited the applicability and methods of capital punishment? Could there be a return to the electric chair or gas chamber, two execution methods that were retired based on state court decisions and state officials' anticipation of what the US Supreme Court might decide about these methods? The change in the court's composition raised the possibility that, for example, Justice Thomas might gain support for his argument that the Eighth Amendment is violated only if the execution "is deliberately designed to inflict pain."[36]

The Excessive Fines Clause

During the 1960s, the Warren Court incorporated and applied to state justice systems most of the criminal justice–related provisions of the Bill of Rights. After applying the Sixth Amendment right to trial by jury to the states in *Duncan v. Louisiana* (1968), there were very few provisions of the Bill of Rights that had not yet been applied to protect individuals against actions by state and local officials. The few provisions that applied only against the federal government included the Fifth Amendment entitlement to indictment by a grand jury and the Eighth Amendment's Excessive Bail and Excessive Fines Clauses. During the Burger and Rehnquist Court eras, there were no additional rights incorporated and applied against the states. Forty-two years after the Warren Court's last incorporation decision in *Duncan* in 1968, the Roberts Court incorporated the Second Amendment right to own firearms in *McDonald v. City of Chicago* (2010), a case that challenged Chicago's restrictions on gun ownership. Nearly a decade later, in *Timbs v. Indiana* (2019), the Roberts Court acted again to apply against states and localities one of the few remaining unincorporated rights from the Bill of Rights.

Timbs entered a guilty plea to drug and theft charges. He was sentenced to one year of home detention, five years of probation, and participation in a substance abuse treatment program. He was also required to pay court costs and fees totaling $1,203. At the time of his arrest, the police seized his $41,000 Land Rover SUV that he had purchased with the proceeds of a life insurance policy after the death of his father. Justice system officials refused to return the vehicle and said it was subject to forfeiture because Timbs allegedly used it to transport heroin. He hired an attorney to seek the return of the vehicle because its value was four times that of the maximum fine of $10,000 that could have been imposed on him for his conviction on these charges. Timbs asserted that the forfeiture of a vehicle with a value in excess of the maximum financial punishment for the crime at issue meant that he was subjected to an excessive fine in violation of the Eighth Amendment.

The Roberts Court issued a unanimous decision declaring that the Excessive Fines Clause applies to state justice systems. The majority opinion by Justice Ginsburg announced that the protection provided by that clause was incorporated into the Due Process Clause of the Fourteenth Amendment and henceforth applicable to state criminal justice cases. In her words, "The protection against excessive fines guards against abuses of government's punitive or criminal-law-enforcement authority. This safeguard, we hold, is 'fundamental to our scheme of ordered liberty.'"[37]

The ruling in *Timbs* expanded the protective reach of a specific Eighth Amendment right. Thus, individuals being prosecuted for state crimes now can raise this issue when it is potentially applicable to their cases. However, it is difficult to know how frequently this rights issue will be raised successfully because the Roberts Court did not present a clear test to assess when a fine is constitutionally excessive. After the high court remanded the case to the lower courts for reconsideration, Timbs prevailed in the state court proceedings and finally had the vehicle returned to him seven years after it was originally seized.[38]

Will the Roberts Court incorporate additional rights? The lone remaining unincorporated right that seems eligible for potential application to state justice systems is the Eighth Amendment's Excessive Bail Clause. As with the Excessive Fines Clause, it seems plausible that an extreme outlier case, much like the forfeiture of Timbs's expensive vehicle, could lead to such a decision, especially with the imposition of a very high bail for a lesser, nonviolent offense. If that were to happen, then, as in the *Timbs* case, the decision would likely correct an egregious situation without defining any specific standard for evaluating when bail amounts are "excessive." Other unincorporated rights, such as the Fifth Amendment right to a grand jury indictment and the Seventh Amendment right to a jury trial in civil lawsuits for small amounts of money, would impose such extraordinary expenses on state court systems that both liberal and conservative justices are likely to avoid incorporating these rights.

Rights in the Context of Corrections

The Roberts Court era approached the end of its first decade at an important milestone in the history of defining rights for imprisoned people and pretrial detainees: the fiftieth anniversary of the Supreme Court's June 22, 1964, decision in *Cooper v. Pate.* In *Cooper,* the Warren Court justices approved the use by prisoners of Title 42, Section 1983 of the US Code for pursuing lawsuits in federal courts alleging the violation of constitutional rights by state officials. Prior to the *Cooper* case, there was uncertainty about whether people in prisons and jails were permitted to file Section 1983 lawsuits based on the civil rights statute intended to enable people to sue state and local officials for violating their rights. The *Cooper* decision issued by the Warren Court was a brief declaration that cited only two US courts of appeals decisions as authority. Despite its brevity, it had a major impact thereafter by enabling imprisoned people to challenge practices in correctional institutions that allegedly violated various rights under the Bill of Rights and the Fourteenth Amendment.[39]

Although the Supreme Court's 1964 decision permitted Section 1983 lawsuits against corrections officials, it did not immediately thereafter give definition to constitutional rights in prisons. Thus, for example, on October 26, 1964, the justices declined to hear *Sostre v. McGinnis*, a case filed by Muslim prisoners in New York objecting to a ruling by lower federal courts that state courts and other state officials could determine what religious practices should be available to imprisoned people. Coincidentally, almost exactly fifty years later, on October 7, 2014, the Roberts Court heard oral arguments in *Holt v. Hobbs* (2015), a case concerning a claim by a Muslim prisoner in Arkansas that he possessed a legally protected right to grow a short beard in order to comply with his religious practices and beliefs.[40] Ultimately, the Roberts Court justices unanimously agreed that the prisoner did indeed enjoy the right to grow a short beard as part of his protected freedom to practice his religion inside the prison. Obviously, much had changed in the Supreme Court's decisions concerning prisoners' rights over the fifty-year period from 1964 to 2014. The contemporary Supreme Court accepts very few cases for hearing concerning constitutional rights for imprisoned people. Thus, the Roberts Court's impact on these rights has been limited.

Claims Filed Under Federal Statutes

The preceding example presented a contrast between the Warren Court in 1964 declining to hear an imprisoned person's claim about the free exercise of religion and the *Holt v. Hobbs* case in which the Roberts Court unanimously endorsed a prisoner's right to grow a beard for religious purposes. In one sense, these contrasting examples demonstrate the extent to which the Supreme Court moved over a half century from recognizing scarcely any legal protections for people under correctional supervision to a very different era when certain protections are universally endorsed. It should be noted, however, that the *Holt v. Hobbs* case was not decided under an interpretation of First Amendment religious rights. It was decided under a federal statute, the Religious Land Use and Institutionalized Persons Act (RLUIPA). As such, it created a greater likelihood that those Roberts Court justices who take a very narrow view of constitutional rights in prisons would show deference to Congress by seeking to carry out the underlying purposes of the statute. Congress explicitly intended the RLUIPA to mandate that judges use strict scrutiny rather than deference to corrections officials in deciding free exercise of religion claims in prisons. Under strict scrutiny analysis, corrections officials must present compelling justifications in order to impose limitations on the exercise of religion.

By contrast, if the *Holt* case had been decided as a constitutional claim under the First Amendment's protection for free exercise of religion, the vote might have been different. There would have been a greater likelihood that conservative justices, such as Justices Thomas and Alito, may have shown deference to prison officials' unsubstantiated claims that religious beards grown by prison residents pose security risks.

In more than thirty years on the Supreme Court, Justice Thomas has acknowledged only one constitutional right to which people are entitled while confined to prison: the right of access to the courts. Yet, he appeared to view that right in an extraordinarily limited fashion as merely a right to have a prison mail slot into which prisoners can place petitions to be mailed to a courthouse. Unlike other justices, he did not believe that prison officials are obligated to provide paper, pens, stamps, or envelopes in order to ensure that the right to mail petitions to a courthouse can actually be exercised.[41] He apparently believed the constitutional right of access to the courts is fulfilled even if the mail slot is merely an unavailable, symbolic object for the prison residents who have no money to purchase needed stationery, writing implements, and mailing supplies to give practical effect to the right.

In the *Holt* case, Arkansas officials argued that they had two compelling interests underlying the policy against beards grown for religious purposes. First, they argued that Holt might hide a weapon, drugs, or other contraband in his beard. Second, they argued that Holt might disguise his identity after an escape by shaving his beard and thereby make it difficult for the public to recognize him from his prison photo. In a unanimous majority opinion by Justice Alito, the justices rejected both asserted justifications. The justices questioned how anyone could hide contraband in a half-inch beard. Moreover, they noted that Arkansas did not have hair-length regulations for prisoners, thus demonstrating their tolerance for the risk that prisoners would hide contraband elsewhere on their bodies, such as their scalp. Thus, there was no compelling reason to reject Holt's beard. In addition, other prison residents already had medically necessary beards due to skin conditions, so Holt's short beard would pose no greater risk than the risk that these officials already accepted by overseeing other bearded prisoners. With respect to the second justification, the justices noted that prison officials could easily take two photos of Holt—one before he grew the beard and one afterward. Thus, the purported identification issue could be handled very easily. The RLUIPA requires judges to take a close look at officials' justifications and question those justifications closely. Thus, Arkansas had little hope of succeeding, especially because other prison systems around the country already permitted imprisoned adherents of the Muslim faith to grow short beards without any reports of significant problems.

Similarly, in *Ramirez v. Collier* (2022), a death row prisoner filed an action under RLUIPA claiming that Texas improperly deprived him of religious liberty by denying his request to have his pastor "lay hands" on him and "pray over" him during his execution. By an 8–1 vote, with only Justice Thomas dissenting, the court found in favor of the condemned man because the state did not have a compelling justification to deny his request. The majority opinion was written by Chief Justice Roberts. Thus, with instruction from the statute enacted by Congress about applying strict scrutiny analysis to prison-imposed barriers to free exercise of religion, the liberal and conservative justices demonstrated a strong consensus that often did not exist for other issues.

The most controversial prison case of the Roberts Court era, *Brown v. Plata* (2011), was also decided through a debate among the justices about the meaning of a federal statute. In *Brown*, the debate concerned the limitations of the Prison Litigation Reform Act (PLRA) on judges' remedial authority, as well as a determination of whether prison conditions violated the Eighth Amendment's Cruel and Unusual Punishments Clause. In the case, California was sued for failing to provide adequate medical and mental health treatment inside its prisons. California's prisons held 156,000 prisoners, nearly twice as many as its institutions were designed to hold. In part, this overcrowding stemmed from the expansion of a "three-strikes law" that mandated a sentence of twenty-five years to life for a third felony offense, even if that third offense was nonviolent and the two prior offenses happened many years earlier. As a result, there were news stories about people sentenced to twenty-five years to life for a third offense of stealing a slice of pizza or stealing a dollar's worth of change from a parked car.[42] Given the range of offenses that caused repeat offenders to be sentenced to a quarter-century in prison, California's prisons became overcrowded. The state tried unsuccessfully to build enough prisons to keep pace with the increased flow of people into imprisonment with very lengthy sentences.

With substantial overcrowding, California's most immediate problem was finding ways to house and feed the growing prison population. Thus, the gymnasiums in many prisons became crammed with bunk beds as prisoners were housed in locations never intended for sleeping. At the same time, California failed to add adequate medical and mental health facilities for the large prison population. Eventually, the state prison system resorted to practices that violated humane treatment protocols, such as locking prisoners with mental illnesses in phone booth–sized cages without toilet facilities as they waited for treatment. In addition, there were documented cases of prisoners needlessly dying from lack of medical care for treatable conditions.

A lawsuit over mental health care was filed in 1990. In 1995, the federal judge overseeing the case appointed a special master to supervise the implementation of remedies for Eighth Amendment violations involving deprivations of the right to appropriate care. A separate lawsuit over inadequate medical treatment was filed in 2001. The state conceded that deficiencies in services existed, but it failed to make adequate progress toward fixing the problems. Eventually, the two cases were combined and entered a proceeding under the requirements of the PLRA for considering a possible judicial order to reduce prison populations. The PLRA contained specific provisions to forbid individual federal judges from ordering prisons to reduce their populations. Instead, according to the requirements of the PLRA, any prisoner release order to remedy constitutional violations must be decided by a specially constituted three-judge panel. In the California case, the three-judge panel heard fourteen days of testimony before issuing an order in 2010 that required California to move from nearly 200 percent capacity to 137.5 percent of the system's planned capacity. In effect, the reduction order required California to reduce the prison population by 46,000 incarcerated people.

The Roberts Court heard the case to determine whether the three-judge panel had accurately identified Eighth Amendment violations and properly issued a prison population reduction order under the PLRA, including the required consideration for the public's safety. The court's 5–4 decision upholding the three-judge panel's order was written by Justice Kennedy. The majority opinion reviewed the evidence of suffering and death experienced by prisoners, and, in a very unusual component, the court's published opinion included actual photographs of the overcrowded conditions.

The dissenting opinions argued that the three-judge panel and the Supreme Court majority failed to fulfill the PLRA's requirement that judges issuing a population reduction order "give substantial weight to any adverse impact on public safety."[43] Justice Alito's dissenting opinion raised the frightening image of thousands of dangerous individuals invading society: "The three-judge court ordered the premature release of approximately *46,000 criminals—the equivalent of three Army divisions*" (emphasis in original).[44] He also cited statistics about a wave of violent crimes committed by people released from a correctional institution under a judge's population reduction order in Philadelphia. Justice Alito used this example from his home region to warn that Californians could face the same harms. Justice Scalia's dissenting opinion echoed the same themes but gave extra attention to the argument that judges lack the expertise to make appropriate decisions about how criminal justice institutions should operate. The intense disagreement within the divided Supreme Court, along with the dissenters' claims about the frightening consequences of the population-reduction order, made *Brown v. Plata* the most highly publicized and controversial corrections decision in the first two decades of the Roberts Court era.

As it turned out, the dissenters were wrong in their predictions about the consequences of reducing the California prison population. Instead of releasing scores of people from prison, California adopted a strategy of limiting the number of newly convicted people entering prison. In a prison system as large as California's, numerous people are entering and exiting the system every week. The state used the usual flow of departures, through releases on parole or completion of sentences, to reduce the population. It simultaneously became more restrictive about who would enter prison. Voters had already modified the "three-strikes law" that caused so many problems. Thus, the state no longer imposed the harsh mandatory sentences that contributed to the overcrowding problem in the first place. State officials negotiated an arrangement with counties, called "realignment," to send individuals serving sentences of three years or less into county jails rather than into prisons. The state provided financial support to counties for accepting this new burden. This action greatly reduced the number of people entering the state prison system, although it presented challenges for county jails that typically lacked facilities and programs equivalent to those in prisons.[45]

A study of changes in California's crime rates after implementation of the prison population reduction plan found no notable increase in violent crime, merely an uptick in property crimes, specifically with respect to automobile thefts.[46] Yet, as the authors of the study noted, it was much less expensive for the state in human and financial terms to endure a few more automobile thefts than to hold larger numbers of people under the expensive conditions of imprisonment without adequate access to medical and mental health care.[47]

Other federal statutory issues arose concerning procedural details within the PLRA that required interpretation. These decisions called upon the justices to determine what members of Congress intended by choosing the specific wording for statutes. Thus, unlike constitutional issues, these cases were less likely to reflect the values and policy preferences of the justices. The strong consensus among the justices across the liberal-conservative spectrum on these issues provided evidence of their effort to think about congressional intent rather than their own preferences for interpreting law. For example, in *Ross v. Blake* (2016), a unanimous Roberts Court declared that prisoners' reasonable mistakes in following complaint procedures do not automatically justify an exception to the statutory requirement to go through the prison's entire grievance process before filing a federal lawsuit alleging a rights violation.

Justice O'Connor's Turner Test in Full Bloom

Justice O'Connor's Rehnquist Court era majority opinion in *Turner v. Safley* (1987) established an especially influential judicial test for the applicability of constitutional rights inside prisons. O'Connor's "Turner test" requires judges to go through a four-step evaluation process to determine whether prison policies and practices violate First Amendment rights to expression and association. The first step requires judges to ask whether there is a valid, rational connection between a prison regulation and a legitimate governmental goal. Second, the judge must ask whether there is an alternative means through which the imprisoned individual can exercise the right, such as another way to communicate if a regulation limits a specific form of communication with the outside world. The third step requires consideration of how accommodating the right will affect both residents and staff inside an institution. Will it cause conflict or otherwise have adverse effects within the institution? And, finally, the judge must ask whether there is an alternative, simple way through which the imprisoned individual can be permitted to exercise the claimed right while corrections officials are still able to protect their legitimate objectives. The Rehnquist Court applied the deferential Turner test for many years to deny claims by imprisoned people concerning a variety of rights, including a purported First Amendment right to provide legal assistance for a fellow imprisoned person (*Shaw v. Murphy*, 2001) and a First Amendment right of association to have visits from family members (*Overton v. Bazzetta*, 2003).[48]

In *Turner*, on behalf of four justices who disagreed with O'Connor, Justice Stevens complained that O'Connor's test was "virtually meaningless" and too deferential to prison officials.[49] As Stevens explained, in his view, "application of the standard would seem to permit disregard for inmates' constitutional rights whenever the imagination of the warden produces a plausible security concern."[50] These dissenters believed that it is too easy for judges to accept the existence of a purportedly legitimate goal when they feel obligated to defer to prison officials' claims about threats to security and safety.

The Roberts Court applied the test to reject rights claims by prison residents denied access to newspapers, magazines, and family photographs while assigned to a punitive special housing unit. In *Beard v. Banks* (2006), prison officials claimed that withholding access to these reading materials and photographs protected safety and security because it kept prisoners from using them to start fires or make weapons. The officials also said the deprivation served as an incentive for good behavior with the intention of motivating prisoners to improve their behavior in order to regain access to these materials. In applying the Turner test, Justice Breyer's plurality opinion adopted a deferential posture by accepting the deprivations as a valid, rational means to advance the prison's legitimate security justification. Justice Breyer acknowledged that the prison policy did not pass the second step of the four-part test by providing an alternative means to access materials and that the third and fourth Turner test steps had little to contribute to the analysis of this policy. Breyer declared that the first step in the Turner test mandated the court's approval of the prison policy by deferring to corrections officials' assertions about the risks to safety and security that justified the policy. Under *Turner*, he was supposed to apply all four parts of the test, but he applied only the first step.

In a concurring opinion, Justice Thomas criticized Breyer's application of the Turner test. Thomas had previously praised the test as providing a "unitary, deferential standard for reviewing prisoners' constitutional claims,"[51] as if it applied to all rights issues beyond the First Amendment, including equal protection claims concerning racial segregation.[52] In *Beard*, however, he noted that Breyer's inability to apply all four components of the Turner test demonstrated that the test was flawed. As an alternative, Thomas argued for his unique viewpoint envisioning a near absence of any constitutional protections for people in prison because, as he saw it, prison residents should enjoy only the rights that states decide to grant to them as part of their imprisonment.[53]

The dissenting opinion by Justice Stevens skewered prison officials' purported safety rationale that was deferentially accepted by Justice Breyer's plurality opinion. He noted that the officials' arguments about the risk that newspapers, magazines, and photographs could be used as weapons or tinder for starting fires was exaggerated since these same imprisoned people had other potentially flammable paper products, such as toilet tissue, legal papers, and religious books, remaining in their cells. He also claimed that it was unconscionably dehumanizing to deprive prison residents of family photos without any valid basis for the deprivation.[54]

The Roberts Court's decision in *Beard v. Banks* seemed to confirm the triumph of the deferential approach for most contested constitutional rights claims, even when the issues do not fit neatly within the Turner test's four-part framework. Specific rights claims from prisoners receive greater judicial scrutiny and protection than the limited protective coverage provided by the Turner test, such as equal protection rights against racial discrimination through a Rehnquist Court precedent in *Johnson v. California* (2005a) and free exercise of religion rights through the federal RLUIPA statute. The judicial deference approach emphasized in *Beard* poses a significant impediment to the recognition of any legal protections for prison residents that were not clearly established prior to the Roberts Court era.

The Diminution of Rights in Corrections

A deferential approach to issues that create tension between security and constitutional rights can be seen in the court's decisions about Fourth Amendment rights in correctional contexts. In the Roberts Court case of *Florence v. Board of Chosen Freeholders* (2012), a passenger in a car stopped for a traffic violation was placed under arrest when a computer check erroneously indicated that he was the subject of an outstanding arrest warrant for an unpaid fine. In fact, he had paid the fine two years earlier, but for unknown reasons the warrant remained in a computer database.

At the county jail, the arrestee walked through a metal detector and then was subjected to a strip search and body cavity inspection. He endured the intrusive search process again when he was transferred to a different county jail six days later. The searches included being required to lift his genitals so the officers could see underneath and to squat and cough to see if any drugs or other contraband would be expelled from his anal cavity. He sued county officials claiming there was no justification for such intrusive, humiliating searches being imposed on people arrested for minor offenses. His attorney argued that such searches should be limited to those whose behavior upon arrest or prior criminal record created reasonable suspicion that they may be hiding contraband or weapons on their bodies. At the time of his lawsuit, many people around the country arrested for minor offenses had won lawsuits against county jails for conducting intrusive body searches without a specific basis for reasonable suspicion. Indeed, there were cases in which it appeared that people arrested for minor, nonviolent offenses, such as trespassing while participating in a political protest, had been subjected to humiliating body cavity inspections for the very purpose of embarrassing and punishing them. These cases led various federal courts around the country to reach contradictory conclusions about whether jails could impose strip searches on all arrestees.[55]

The majority opinion, written by Justice Kennedy on behalf of a narrow five-member majority, approved the searches imposed on Florence at the two jails. His emphasis on judicial deference was especially explicit and clear for correctional search cases. Justice Kennedy wrote, "Deference must be given to the officials in charge of the jail unless there is 'substantial evidence' demonstrating their [policy and its justifications are] . . . exaggerated."[56] He concluded that officials in the *Florence* case were appropriately concerned about contraband being smuggled into the jail and that the across-the-board policy of strip searches and body cavity inspections was reasonable. The case did not consider whether the same rule would be needed in jails with the physical facilities to separate those arrested for minor offenses from those detained for serious crimes.

The four dissenters pointed to evidence from studies at other jails that showed only rare circumstances in which those arrested for minor offenses were found to be carrying contraband on or inside their bodies. They protested that the majority opinion could not give any examples of problems having arisen in specific jails from using a policy that relied on individualized suspicion instead of across-the-board searches.[57] Thus, they argued that these exceptionally intrusive and humiliating searches of presumptively innocent arrestees brought to jail for minor offenses should not be permissible without a basis for suspecting that individuals might be smuggling contraband into the jail.

The *Florence* decision was particularly striking because it concerned a man who never should have been arrested in the first place. Yet it took more than a week for the criminal justice system to rectify the computer error and release him. In the meantime, Florence not only had to live in the unhealthy and risk-laden environment of jail, but he also had to endure intrusive strip searches and body cavity inspections. His situation helped to highlight one of the significant consequences of the *Florence* decision: It affected a broad universe of people who could potentially be subjected to intrusive strip searches and body cavity inspections. When there is no outstanding arrest warrant, all it takes is a police officer's discretionary decision to arrest someone, whether guilty or not, for very minor offenses. As a result, the presumptively innocent individual may be subject to an intrusive strip search when booked into the local jail.

In *Samson v. California* (2006), the Roberts Court limited Fourth Amendment protections for people released from prison on parole. Under California law, as a condition of release into the community on parole, former prison residents must agree in writing to be subject to search by law enforcement officers at any time and without the officers having any reason for the search. Given the primacy of liberty as a constitutional value for Americans, along with the understandable human desire to depart from the difficult and dangerous environment of prison, there is reason to debate whether this mandated agreement should be regarded as an uncoerced, voluntary waiver of rights.

A police officer saw Samson walking down the sidewalk with a woman and a child. The officer knew Samson was on parole. Without any articulable basis for suspecting wrongdoing by Samson, the officer decided to conduct a search. A small quantity of illegal drugs was found in a cigarette package in Samson's pocket, thereby leading to an arrest, a criminal charge, conviction at trial, and a new sentence of seven years in prison.[58]

The majority opinion by Justice Thomas declared that Samson did not have a reasonable expectation of privacy and that California's interest in preventing people on parole release from committing new crimes outweighed the individual's interests. Justice Thomas's view was unaffected by evidence that other states manage to combat recidivism and provide parole supervision without authorizing suspicionless, discretionary searches. Justice Thomas indicated that people on parole were protected against abusive treatment by California's prohibition on searches that are "arbitrary, capricious, or harassing."[59] Yet, that purported protection appears to be illusory in practice without a clear way to identify "arbitrary" searches among discretionary searches that lack any articulable basis for suspicion whatsoever.

The three dissenters, led by Justice Stevens, complained that people living in the community under parole supervision should be regarded as having reasonable expectations of privacy. They should not be treated as if their status is no different than that of an imprisoned person. Justice Stevens said that the majority opinion had endorsed "an unprecedented curtailment of liberty."[60]

The Fourth Amendment was not the only topical area for which Roberts Court decisions clarified constitutional rights questions through a restrictive view of legal protections. In *Howes v. Fields* (2012), a man serving a sentence in a county jail was escorted upstairs from his cell to a sheriff's office conference room in the evening. Two armed deputies questioned him about an unsolved child sex abuse case. He was free from handcuffs and other restraints as the deputies told him that he could leave to go back down to the jail. They questioned him through the early hours of the morning during a period estimated to last five to seven hours. Eventually, the man confessed to the crime. He later claimed that he had said several times during the interview that he did not want to talk to the deputies. Throughout the lengthy encounter, he was never informed of his Miranda rights nor told that he was not obligated to talk to the deputies.

In this case, the Roberts Court majority decided that the jailed offender was, in fact, free to leave and therefore not entitled to Miranda rights. The majority opinion by Justice Alito focused on the fact that the man was told that he could leave at any time, notwithstanding the fact that he could not actually leave. When he ended the interview after confessing, he had to wait twenty minutes for a corrections officer to arrive to escort him downstairs to the jail. Thus, he was "free to leave" for Miranda purposes because of the decision available to him to end the interview. However, he was not literally free to leave the conference room on his own. In the majority's view, he was not "in custody" during questioning, the triggering requirement for an entitlement to Miranda warnings. The majority stated this conclusion even though he was being held in a jail and was brought involuntarily to the conference room for questioning by law enforcement officers.

The dissenting opinion by Justice Ginsburg focused on prior precedents in considering whether he was entitled to be informed of his Miranda rights. According to Ginsburg, rather than focus on the concept of being "in custody" for Miranda purposes, the court should have focused on whether he was subjected to "incommunicado interrogation in a police-dominated atmosphere" and whether his freedom of action "was curtailed in a significant way."[61] In comparing the analyses presented in the majority and dissenting opinions, it is difficult to avoid concluding that this clarification of Fifth Amendment rights in the context of corrections constituted a diminution of those rights and an expansion of law enforcement authority.

An Expanded Protection in Jails

The most notable exception to the Roberts Court's pattern of deferring to corrections officials and Congress came in *Kingsley v. Hendrickson* (2015). The case concerned the constitutional rights of people detained in jail prior to trial when they allege improper victimization by corrections officers' excessive use of force. In *Kingsley*, the detainee used a piece of paper to cover the light fixture in his cell. When a jail officer walked past during inspection, the officer ordered him to remove the paper. He refused. Subsequently, four officers arrived at his cell to move him to a different cell. According to the detainee, he did not resist being placed in handcuffs, but one officer placed a knee in his back and, after he used impolite language to tell the officer to stop pressing into his back, the officer slammed his head into a concrete bunk. Then the officer gave him a five-second jolt with an electroshock weapon. The officers claimed that the detainee resisted being handcuffed but admitted that a knee was placed in the individual's back and that an electroshock weapon was used.

Protections against excessive use of force for people detained prior to trial in county jails find their source in the Fourteenth Amendment's Due Process Clause. The Eighth Amendment protection against cruel and unusual punishments protects only imprisoned people who have already been convicted of crimes. Thus, the parallel protection for unconvicted detainees in jails must find its source elsewhere in the Constitution. Historically, many Supreme Court justices use the Due Process Clause as an all-purpose source of rights that they see as existing but not specifically described in the Constitution. In particular, the Due Process Clause explicitly protects people's "liberty," and therefore this protection for liberty has been used as the source for rights to privacy, travel between states, and other fundamental entitlements not otherwise specifically described.[62] This is why the detainee's claim in *Kingsley* was analyzed by interpreting the Due Process Clause. The Roberts Court accepted the case to decide whether the detainee was required to prove the officers' subjective intent, in parallel fashion to Eighth Amendment excessive use-of-force lawsuits in prisons, or whether a different standard applied to Due Process Clause claims.

In a narrow 5–4 decision written by Justice Breyer, the Roberts Court decided that a pretrial detainee only must show proof of objective intent. In other words, a judge or jury can examine evidence about what occurred in order to determine whether the officers' actions were reasonable, without regard to whether the officers actually intended to cause harm. By contrast, in Eighth Amendment cases concerning use of force in prisons, the claimant must prove the subjective intentions of the officials who allegedly used excessive force. Providing proof of what an officer was thinking at any given moment is exceptionally difficult. Just as in *Brown v. Plata*, Justice Kennedy provided the decisive fifth vote in favor of the individual's claim by parting company with the court's four most conservative justices with whom he often voted. As a result, unconvicted people in jails have, in effect, greater possibilities for gaining remedies in use-of-force lawsuits than those available to imprisoned people who have been convicted of crimes. The standard of proof required to establish a rights violation is less specific and demanding under the Due Process Clause because judges and juries can make their own determinations about the reasonableness of a jail officer's action without proof of what the officer was thinking when force was employed.

Conclusion

The first decade of the Roberts Court era produced a significant number of liberal Eighth Amendment–related decisions concerning sentencing. These liberal rulings came in important cases narrowing the categories of individuals and crimes eligible for capital punishment and, in the case of juveniles, life without parole sentences. In these cases, Justice Kennedy cast critical votes and wrote important majority opinions. As a result, Kennedy's position in the middle of a philosophically divided court enabled him to be especially influential for these issues. His influence helped to narrow the application of the death penalty, but he did not push the court toward abolition. For other issues related to the death penalty, such as using lethal injection as a method of execution and various aspects of jury instructions, his votes made clear that he accepted the use of capital punishment.

Because so many cases on these issues were decided by 5–4 votes, observers will watch intently as the Trump-influenced majority on the Roberts Court may seek to reverse liberal decisions previously determined by the now-departed Justice Kennedy's decisive vote. The departing justices in the second decade of the Roberts Court era—Justices Scalia, Ginsburg, Kennedy, and Breyer—were, except for Breyer, all replaced by newcomers whose prior judicial records as appellate judges led to predictions that they would be as conservative as their predecessors or more so on criminal punishment issues.

Indeed, the first signs of change may be evident in the court's decision in *Jones v. Mississippi* that authorized judges to reimpose life sentences on juveniles without presenting evidentiary findings or explanations for their decisions. In that case, the court's three remaining liberals complained in dissent that Justice Kavanaugh's majority opinion seemed to "gut" life-sentenced juveniles' entitlement to reconsideration of their sentences.[63] Similarly, *McKinney v. Arizona* (2020) represented a diminution of a defendant's entitlement to have a citizen jury rather than a judge to evaluate aggravating and mitigating factors that affect the determination of death sentences. Justice Kavanaugh's majority opinion on behalf of the court's conservatives approved a reweighing of aggravating and mitigating factors by a state appellate court when collateral review identified errors in the trial court's processes. Do these decisions indicate that the post-2020 Roberts Court conservative supermajority will move to reduce or erode, if not eliminate, various rights-protective sentencing decisions issued during the first decade of the Roberts Court era? It is certainly possible.

In the realm of rights for imprisoned people, the Roberts Court cannot be regarded as having a major impact. In general, the conservative-leaning court clarified the meaning of rights in ways that deferred to criminal justice officials and diminished legal protections for individuals. In so doing, the Roberts Court majority continued the trends that began in the later years of the Burger Court era and continued throughout the Rehnquist Court era. With the exception of the rights-enhancing decision in *Kingsley v. Hendrickson*, the notable Roberts Court decisions that favored claims by pretrial detainees and prisoners occurred when the justices interpreted and applied statutes that were created by Congress, such as the RLUIPA. These decisions were influenced by the justices' understanding of the congressional intent underlying the relevant statutes rather than by their own preferred approaches to constitutional interpretation. With respect to the interpretation of rights from the Constitution, there is the possibility that new decisions by the conservative-dominated post-Trump court may reduce the scope of prisoners' rights now that the longtime critics of prisoners' rights, Justices Thomas and Alito, are surrounded by a thoroughly conservative majority.

8. INCREMENTAL CONSERVATISM
OR ACCELERATED CHANGE?

The Roberts Court continued the path of the Burger and Rehnquist Court eras, with specific case decisions preserving rights amid a general trend of weakening rights and expanding law enforcement authority. President Obama's two appointees, Sotomayor and Kagan, replaced two similarly liberal justices, Stevens and Souter, and thereby initially preserved the nature and strength of the court's four-member liberal wing. By contrast, beginning with President George W. Bush's appointment of Justice Alito in 2006, the Republican nominees to the Roberts Court were either similarly conservative as or more conservative on criminal justice issues than the justices whom they replaced. Thus, judicial scholars' challenge is to assess whether the Roberts Court's impact on criminal justice merely continued the reactive, conservatizing trends of the Burger and Rehnquist Court eras or whether the Roberts Court produced a markedly different and accelerated diminution of criminal justice rights.

New Decision-Makers and Voting Patterns

Every newly appointed justice effectively creates a new and different Supreme Court as justices develop interactions and relationships with a new colleague.[1] Moreover, the retirement or death of a justice may thrust already-serving justices into new roles, such as filling the departing justice's functions. As a result, individual justices may become more assertive in oral arguments, take leadership roles in developing dissenting opinions, or otherwise change their interactions with long-serving colleagues. In many respects, the extent of these changes may depend on how different in either ideology or temperament the newcomer is from the departing justice being replaced.

Each change in the court's composition begins a new "natural court" period in which a specific set of justices serves together. In the nineteen terms in which the Rehnquist Court made decisions from 1986 to 2005, there were only five new justices appointed to the Supreme Court. By contrast, the Roberts Court consisted of eight different natural court periods in its first seventeen years. These new natural court periods were triggered and defined by the arrival of seven new justices in these seventeen years, as well as one natural court period with only eight justices as Republican senators blocked consideration of President Obama's nominee to replace the late Justice Scalia. Subsequently an eighth appointee arrived, Justice Ketanji Brown Jackson, when Justice Breyer retired in 2022. At the end of this period, only Justice Thomas remained from the Rehnquist Court era. As a result, there were multiple points at which newcomers were learning the patterns and practices of Supreme Court decision-making as their senior colleagues sought to discover how to work effectively with and persuade the new justices.

In the view of Justice Stevens, Chief Justice Roberts was a more effective leader of the court than either of his predecessors, Chief Justices Rehnquist and Burger.[2] Stevens appreciated that Roberts was impartial when leading the justices' discussions of cases. Moreover, unlike his predecessors, Roberts permitted more extensive discussions of the merits of cases and the reasoning behind individual justices' stated positions during the conference meetings in which the justices provided their initial votes in each argued case.[3] With respect to substantive decision-making, however, the arrival of Roberts did not change trends in decision-making, because he typically continued Rehnquist's pattern of taking a conservative approach to criminal justice issues. Chief Justice Roberts's voting percentage (66 percent) in support for conservative outcomes in criminal justice cases was lower than that of Chief Justice Rehnquist's lifetime voting percentage (83 percent) in such cases.[4] Yet, Roberts's percentage support for conservative outcomes was similar to his predecessor's record in specific terms during Rehnquist's final years on the court when Rehnquist supported conservative results in 73 percent or less of criminal justice cases.[5] Thus, Roberts is regarded overall as generally providing a continuation of Rehnquist's voting pattern and impact in this issue area.

The first significant change in the court's composition came with Justice O'Connor's replacement by Justice Alito in early 2006. One indicator of the significance of this change was revealed in table 7 concerning "swing votes." This table illustrated the frequency with which consistently conservative justices departed from their usual ideological allies and cast votes that led a divided court to produce liberal outcomes. Over his first seventeen terms on the court, Alito provided only one vote that was decisive in producing a liberal outcome in cases traditionally regarded as concerning criminal justice–related issues in the Supreme Court Judicial Database. The sole case in which Alito's vote was decisive for a liberal outcome concerned a very narrow interpretation of a congressional statute about preservation of documents in criminal cases (*Yates v. United States*, 2015). By contrast, looking only at her final ten terms on the court, Alito's predecessor, Justice O'Connor, provided the "swing vote" to produce liberal outcomes in twelve such divided criminal justice cases.[6] Although generally conservative, O'Connor was only moderately conservative compared to Alito's consistency in favoring arguments to advance the authority of police, prosecutors, and corrections officials. Thus, by filling O'Connor's seat on the court, Alito immediately had the impact of reducing the likelihood of liberal outcomes in divided criminal justice decisions.

Looking solely at evidence from voting records in criminal justice cases, the justices appointed from 2009 through 2018 did not definitively turn the court's voting patterns in a more conservative direction. Justice Sotomayor's voting record was slightly more liberal than that of her predecessor, Justice Souter. Justice Stevens's voting record for criminal justice cases was quite similar to that of his replacement, Justice Kagan. Justice Gorsuch was conservative, yet somewhat less conservative than his predecessor, Justice Scalia, while Justice Kavanaugh was somewhat more conservative as the replacement for Justice Kennedy.

With respect to the latter pair, it appears that Kavanaugh will not replicate and replace Kennedy's extraordinary record as the key swing justice in the largest number of liberal criminal decisions determined by one vote. In part this is due to Kavanaugh's greater consistency in casting conservative votes in criminal justice cases. But it is also due to the contextual change at the court affecting Kavanaugh's impact from his third term onward: the existence of a six-member supermajority formed by Trump's appointment of Justice Barrett in 2020. Thus, even if Kavanaugh joins the court's liberal justices, Kavanaugh's action alone could contribute only to the formation of a four-member minority. By contrast, when Kennedy joined the liberals, that typically determined the outcome of a case because there were four liberals among the court's nine justices during his years on the bench. As a result, Justice Barrett's replacement of liberal Justice Ginsburg in 2020 posed the prospect of producing markedly conservatizing impacts unless and until a conservative justice leaves the court while Democrats control the White House and Senate and thereby determine the selection of a replacement.

Impactful Decisions

By counting and classifying cases and linking those classifications to individual justices' voting records, there is a basis for monitoring the nature of case outcomes, including patterns of consistency and change. Such empirical measures are useful but provide only a rough basis for examining changes in the court's impact on law and society. Many decisions of the Supreme Court have relatively limited applications and affect only specific kinds of cases. Moreover, the effect of specific decisions on future cases may be modest, especially if the court is merely clarifying the meaning of words in a federal statute. These decisions give guidance to prosecutors and judges about such matters as elements of proof for specific criminal charges and the procedural steps in trials and appeals. Their impact on case outcomes and the treatment of individuals by officials in the criminal justice system may, in fact, be quite limited.

For example, in *Shaw v. United States* (2017), a criminal defendant was unsuccessful in convincing the Roberts Court that he should not be convicted of defrauding a bank when he used a stolen account number to steal money from a bank customer. The decision clarified how prosecutors could use the federal criminal statute to prosecute crimes involving thefts using stolen account numbers. However, even if the decision had turned out the other way, it merely would have instructed prosecutors to pursue these cases under other statutes focused on thefts from victimized individuals rather than from banks. It would not have changed the susceptibility to prosecution for individuals who undertake these kinds of thefts. In a counting and classifying system, this decision counted as one conservative decision just like decisions favoring police authority to make discretionary warrantless searches. Yet, the interpretation of the bank fraud statute did not have the same potential impact as the Fourth Amendment rulings that determine how police investigate cases, how criminal evidence can be obtained, and who can be drawn into the criminal justice system. As a result, in evaluating the Roberts Court and criminal justice, it is important to think about the court's impact on people's lives and not just focus on patterns of decision-making that equate decisions of differential importance.

Impactful Effects on an Identifiable Set of People

Although this chapter's discussion of impactful decisions will focus on those with broad effects, it is important to note that certain decisions profoundly impact a limited but clearly defined set of people. For example, Supreme Court decisions can have powerful consequences when the justices determine whether specific rulings will receive retroactive application to people previously convicted of crimes. In *Ramos v. Louisiana* (2020), the Roberts Court decided that jury verdicts to convict people of serious crimes must be unanimous. The decision had limited impact because only two states, Louisiana and Oregon, had permitted nonunanimous guilty verdicts. Moreover, Louisiana had already changed its law prior to the Supreme Court's decision in *Ramos*. Thus, the decision's immediate importance was limited to its effects on criminal trials in Oregon from mid-2020 onward because nonunanimous verdicts could no longer determine defendants' fates.

Yet, the most profound impact of the decision became clear in the Roberts Court's decision the following year declaring that the ruling requiring jury unanimity did not apply retroactively to benefit people in those two states who were previously convicted by nonunanimous verdicts (*Edwards v. Vannoy*, 2021). Following the *Edwards* decision, the Oregon Supreme Court acted the next year to retroactively grant new trials to that state's three hundred imprisoned people who had been convicted by nonunanimous verdicts.[7] However, fifteen hundred people remained in Louisiana's prisons based on prior nonunanimous jury votes.[8] These people were convicted of serious crimes by juries with individual members who did not believe that guilt had been proven beyond a reasonable doubt. In addition, these convictions also generated enhanced sentences when these individuals became classified as habitual offenders under state law. Thus, someone convicted by a nonunanimous jury could later receive a much lengthier prison sentence based on convictions for other crimes—which may also have been decided by nonunanimous verdicts. These were significant, profound, and continuing impacts on identifiable human beings who were treated in a uniquely punitive fashion by one outlier state. In this example, the human consequences of the Roberts Court's rejection of a retroactive application of the *Ramos* ruling were readily apparent for fifteen hundred identifiable people in Louisiana who lived in prison confinement with the knowledge that they experienced an unremedied Sixth Amendment rights violation in their trials. Moreover, they would know that they would not have endured continued imprisonment without possibility of retrial if they had been accused of their crime in any other state.

Another decision with potentially significant, albeit less specifically measurable, continuing consequences for a defined set of individuals was *Brown v. Plata* (2011). The case concerned prison overcrowding and its impact on medical and mental health services for imprisoned people. A narrow majority of justices approved a lower court order requiring a significant reduction in California's prison population. California reduced the flow of new admittees to prison by sending those convicted of lesser offenses to county jails to serve sentences of up to three years. For certain individuals in prison, the changes from this Roberts Court decision reduced, but did not eliminate, the misery of overcrowding and denial of services.[9] For those newly sent to jail instead of prison for sentences up to three years in length, their experiences differed from what they would have faced in prison. Yet, the new experiences still posed challenges due to jails' limited facilities and programs that were designed for relatively short periods of detention, typically ranging from a few hours to a few months.[10] These were significant impacts on detained individuals in California from the *Brown* decision, but not the kind of widespread consequences associated with other criminal justice–related decisions of the Roberts Court.

The Roberts Court's decisions granting reconsideration of sentences for people serving life sentences imposed for crimes that they committed as juveniles had major consequences for those who gained release on parole as a result. By 2023, approximately one thousand juvenile lifers had gained release on parole, a development entirely attributable to the Roberts Court era's decisions making these imprisoned people entitled to new hearings concerning their sentences for serious crimes. Obviously, this was a very significant impact on the lives of these individuals, many of whom had been confined in prison for decades.[11]

Impactful Effects on Legislative Power

One category of decisions producing major consequences concerns the establishment of precedents that either endorse or limit legislatures' authority to define crimes and punishments. Indeed, the Roberts Court's decisions that limit the authority of legislatures to regulate campaign contributions and firearms were the most dramatically impactful of any criminal justice–related decisions. How are these issues impactful? With respect to the first issue, campaign contributions influence the selection and behavior of elected policymakers who define crimes and punishments and direct developments affecting other areas of public policy. With respect to the second issue, the use of guns in crimes affects fear of crime, the number of people arrested, the nature of crimes for which they are charged, and the sentences that they receive. There are also consequences for victimization rates, family trauma, and medical expenses for society.

The entire landscape of American elections changed after the Roberts Court's decisions on First Amendment issues surrounding corporate entities' financial contributions to influence political campaigns and elections. *Citizens United v. Federal Election Commission* (2010) and *McCutcheon v. Federal Election Commission* (2014) declared that corporations have First Amendment expression rights embodied in political contributions. The decisions virtually eliminated political contribution limits for corporations and wealthy individuals. Moreover, the decisions barred spending limits for corporate-funded super PACs so long as they do not coordinate their expenditures with individual candidates' campaigns. These decisions prohibited the criminalization of substantial contributions by wealthy individuals and corporations to certain kinds of PACs. They also enabled these individuals and entities to exert disproportionate influence over elected officials. How significant were these decisions for the flow of money into elections? In 2010, the biggest Republican donor to candidates and political action committees contributed $7.6 million.[12] With barriers to unlimited contributions to PACs removed by the Roberts Court, the biggest Republican donor in 2020 gave $183 million.[13] In the 2024 presidential election, the world's wealthiest individual, Elon Musk, reportedly spent $277 million to elect Donald Trump and support other Republican candidates.[14] There was $338 million spent by outside groups on the 2008 presidential election. After *Citizens United*, that figure rose to over $1 billion in 2012 and grew even higher in subsequent election cycles.[15] Empirical research on elections after *Citizens United* provided evidence that Republicans gained the greatest benefits from ending the limits on spending by outside groups. Moreover, there was evidence of a conservatizing impact on state legislatures, including the possibility that candidates altered their policy positions to align themselves better with well-funded conservative super PACs.[16] These impacts can certainly affect the nature of criminal justice policies developed by legislatures.

With respect to the Second Amendment, the Roberts Court's decisions transformed the definition of individuals' gun-ownership rights and triggered significant litigation to test newly imposed limits on legislatures' authority to regulate firearms. In *District of Columbia v. Heller* (2008), the Roberts Court for the first time in constitutional history interpreted the Second Amendment as protecting an individual's right to own a firearm. Previously, legal scholars and judges generally agreed that the amendment's opening words, "A well regulated Militia, being necessary to the security of a free State," indicated that the amendment's purpose was to prevent the federal government from disarming state militias.

After the arrival of President Trump's appointees on the court, the new conservative supermajority issued the decision in *New York State Rifle & Pistol Association v. Bruen* (2022) that made it easier to gain licenses to carry firearms in states that previously imposed the most significant restrictions. The decision in *Bruen* quickly demonstrated that legal rules established in Supreme Court decisions provide only one aspect of judicial impact on legislative authority and society in general. The court's reasoning in a decision can instruct lower court judges on how to decide whether legislatures have exceeded their authority in subsequent cases. Thus, these instructions on how to decide certain categories of cases can have widespread and dramatic consequences, as occurred in lower court cases challenging various regulatory gun laws in the aftermath of *Bruen*.

In the *Bruen* decision, lower court judges were directed to approve gun laws only if there was a historical analogy among laws in existence at the time of the Second Amendment's ratification in 1791 (federal laws) or at the time of the Fourteenth Amendment's ratification in 1868 (state and local laws).[17] Based on the instruction in *Bruen*, lower court judges struck down a variety of gun laws. Most notably, in *United States v. Rahimi* (2023), the US Court of Appeals for the Fifth Circuit struck down the federal law barring people from possessing firearms if they were subject to protection orders for domestic violence. In effect, because lawmakers in 1791 tolerated violence against women within families and did not prevent perpetrators of that violence from possessing guns, twenty-first-century legislatures were not permitted to impose gun restrictions that address the widely recognized problem of intimate partner violence. Although the Supreme Court later reversed this specific decision, the nation's highest court handles too few cases each year to examine all of the decisions being made throughout the country striking down gun safety laws through the use of historical analysis. Thus, other lower court decisions followed the mandated reliance on history to strike down a variety of laws, such as New York's laws preventing civilians from having guns in various locations, such as subways and Times Square.[18]

Even a federal trial judge who was openly critical of the Roberts Court for requiring lower court judges to pretend to be historians felt obligated to prevent a gun-possession prosecution against an individual who served time in prison for manslaughter.[19] Such a law prohibiting gun possession by convicted felons did not exist in 1791, and therefore the judge followed the Roberts Court's instruction to prohibit modern legislatures from imposing gun safety laws based on principles not enunciated in eighteenth-century laws (*United States v. Bullock*, 2023). The sweeping and highly controversial impact of the *Bruen* instruction to lower court judges will undoubtedly lead the Roberts Court to revisit the majority's reasoning in individual cases. However, it remains to be seen whether any recalibration of the *Bruen* reasoning will diminish the federal judiciary's Roberts Court-driven restrictions on legislative efforts to regulate firearms.[20]

The especially intense controversy and criticism that accompanied the Roberts Court's upending of legislatures' gun policy decisions were exacerbated by societal developments immediately prior to and continuing after the *Bruen* decision. During the pandemic era from 2020 to 2022, Americans seemed concerned about the country's political polarization, visible political protests, and perceptions of rising violent crime. These concerns became associated with a nationwide gun buying spree. More than twenty-two million guns were sold in 2020, a figure 64 percent higher than the number of guns purchased in 2019. Eight million purchases were by people who had never owned guns before. At the same time, the number of homicides and suicides rose.[21] By adding to the number of privately owned guns, this flurry of purchases contributed to estimates that there were nearly four hundred million civilian-held guns in the United States.[22] In addition, in each year from 2019 through 2023, the United States reached a total of four hundred mass shootings within the first eight months of the year. By contrast, it took nearly the entire year of 2018 to reach that total.[23] Will the Roberts Court–initiated elimination of gun laws impact the levels of gun purchases, mass shootings, and other gun-safety related developments? It is difficult to anticipate precisely how legal developments will interact with societal trends involving guns as the Roberts Court's actions significantly curtail the authority of legislatures to address gun safety issues.

Campaign spending and guns are among the hotly debated rights issues that stand at the dividing line of polarization between the country's conservatives and liberals. Political conservatives typically support the recognition of constitutional rights for corporations, such as *Citizens United*'s First Amendment right to contribute to and spend money on political campaigns. They also support an interpretation of the Second Amendment that provides gun-owning and gun-carrying rights for individuals. By contrast, political liberals typically argue that constitutional rights are possessed by individual human beings rather than corporate entities and that the first words of the Second Amendment show that the provision should concern arming a "well regulated" state "Militia."

The stark, polarizing divide between these viewpoints was well demonstrated by liberal Justice Stevens's characterization of *Citizens United* and *Heller* as two of the three "very, very bad" case decisions during his thirty-five years on the court.[24] Justice Stevens referred to *Heller* specifically as "unquestionably the most clearly incorrect decision that the Court announced during my tenure on the bench."[25] He described *Citizens United* as "a giant step in the wrong direction."[26] In discussing the impactful nature of these decisions, he saw *Citizens United* as "allow[ing] persons who are not qualified to vote—whether they be corporations or nonresident individuals—to have potentially greater power" to influence election outcomes than eligible voters.[27] With respect to the right to gun ownership established by *Heller*, Stevens complained about the "distort[ion] of intelligent debate about . . . proposed legislation designed to minimize the slaughter caused by the prevalence of guns in private hands."[28] His dismay about the direction of these decisions and their impact on society led him to include them among the six Supreme Court doctrines for which he advocated new constitutional amendments as a means of reversal.[29] The fact that Stevens harshly criticized these decisions, not only in lengthy dissenting opinions that he wrote in each case but also in books that he wrote after his retirement, highlighted the controversial, doctrine-altering, and impactful nature of these decisions.

Impactful Decisions on Constitutional Rights and Officials' Authority

Like its predecessor eras, the Roberts Court era produced many decisions reshaping aspects of constitutional rights through interpretations of the Bill of Rights and the Fourteenth Amendment. Such rulings define the extent of criminal justice officials' legal authority and can thereby produce widespread effects on actions that determine people's experiences and fates. For example, when the Roberts Court approved suspicionless searches of parolees walking down the sidewalk in *Samson v. California* (2006), the ruling clarified the permissibility of searches imposed on people under correctional supervision in the community. Such searches undoubtedly occurred prior to being challenged in this case. However, the ruling officially freed police and parole officers to use their discretion to conduct such suspicionless searches without fear that evidence discovered in these stop-and-frisk searches will be excluded from use in criminal prosecutions. Given that there were nearly nine hundred thousand people under community supervision while on parole in 2020, this decision created broad potential impacts for a significant number of people.[30]

As indicated by table 2, most of the Roberts Court's liberal criminal justice decisions reflected consensus on the court by having two or fewer dissenters, including fifty-two unanimous liberal decisions. Several of the liberal decisions did not necessarily prevent police investigatory actions but merely ensured they followed certain procedural steps, such as obtaining search warrants. For example, *Carpenter v. United States* (2018) barred police from accessing cell phone location records without a warrant. This decision had protective implications for everyone in the United States with a cell phone but did not hinder police from seeking a warrant when they had actual evidence of criminal activity. In *Florida v. Jardines* (2013), the court required a warrant before bringing a drug-sniffing dog on the porch of a house to test for the presence of drugs. In another example, the court clarified that school officials cannot use their own discretion to strip-search students (*Safford Unified School District v. Redding*, 2009).

These decisions were arguably impactful in light of the potential number of people receiving protection from unrestrained warrantless examinations of persons, property, and personal information. The decisions required officials to obtain warrants rather than act instantly based on their own judgments. Yet, the court still left open accessible avenues for conducting searches in cases for which officials can provide a justification. In *Riley v. California* (2014), which barred unfettered discretionary examinations of arrested drivers' cell phones, there are still circumstances in which these devices might be examined quickly if police make claims about "exigent circumstances" justifying a warrantless search. Much the same is true in the case of vehicle searches in conjunction with arrests, as in *Arizona v.*

Gant (2009). Officers merely need to conduct the search and then articulate an after-the-fact justification for concluding there was probable cause to search the vehicle.[31] A parallel situation resulted from *Lange v. California* (2021), in which the Roberts Court unanimously ruled that police cannot automatically make a warrantless entry into a home when pursuing a misdemeanor suspect. Yet, the justices left open the possibility for such entries based on the circumstances of the situation.

These liberal decisions deprived officials of unfettered discretionary authority for certain kinds of searches. However, in the foregoing contexts involving drivers, homeowners, phone data, and students, officials are likely to be able to obtain warrants relatively quickly and easily if they can provide justifications for their suspicions about specific individuals' potential involvement in crime. In critical academic literature, local courts and their judges have been described as "component[s] of the modern police bureaucracy" by frequently acting as facilitators of police action rather than as the rights-protecting barrier between the coercive state and the individual.[32] One aspect of this facilitation process is the issuance of warrants without demanding proper legal justifications to establish probable cause under the Fourth Amendment.[33] Shocking examples arise with disappointing frequency of judges automatically issuing warrants requested by police in circumstances in which more or different evidence should have been demanded. Typically, news media outlets notice these examples only when they are flagrantly frequent or produce tragic outcomes, as in the case of unjustified no-knock warrants,[34] or are clearly contrary to well-established law, such as a search of news reporters' homes and offices.[35] Thus, newly requiring that police take the time to obtain a warrant in specific situations often has little impact on their ability to ultimately undertake a search. The freedom to conduct random "fishing expeditions" for evidence may be curtailed, but police can obtain warrants relatively easily in many jurisdictions because judges often do not impose strict standards in defining "probable cause" to justify a warrant.[36]

Other examples in which the Roberts Court indicated to police officers that they should have sought a warrant concern very specific fact situations with less expansive impacts. The decision in *Collins v. Virginia* (2018), for example, required officers to obtain a warrant before looking under a tarp to see whether a motorcycle parked outside a home was the one that they were seeking. This was a very specific and infrequent fact situation. Moreover, the ruling did not hinder officers' other easy options for identifying the vehicle, such as merely waiting for the driver to come out of the residence and remove the tarp in order to ride the motorcycle.

In contrast to the liberal decisions affecting police authority and constitutional rights, the Roberts Court's conservative decisions opened doors to widespread impacts through the expansion of police authority. For example, two cases clarified Fourth Amendment doctrine in ways that subjected unconvicted arrestees to substantial bodily intrusions. In *Florence v. Board of Chosen Freeholders* (2012), the Roberts Court majority ruled that even those arrested for nonviolent minor offenses whose behavior provides no basis for suspecting that they have hidden contraband within their bodies can be subjected to intrusive strip searches and body cavity inspections upon arrival at jail. The case starkly illustrated the intrusive nature of these searches because the individual was wrongly arrested for an unpaid fine in a civil matter when, in fact, he did not owe any money for fines. Moreover, he was subjected to multiple strip searches and body cavity inspections because he was transferred between county jails during the week spent in custody while the matter was sorted out. Prior to the Roberts Court decision, many lower courts had adopted the view that such intrusive invasions of bodily privacy were permissible only if an individual's arrest charge, prior record, or observed behavior provided a basis to justify such searches.[37] In addition, the practice was viewed as so objectionable and unnecessary in several states that they had laws barring such searches for those arrested on misdemeanor charges unless there was a specific justification for a particular individual to be strip-searched.[38]

Similarly, the Roberts Court decision in *Maryland v. King* (2013) endorsed state laws authorizing the taking of DNA samples from unconvicted arrestees taken into custody on suspicion of committing a serious offense. In a dissenting opinion, Justice Scalia accused the majority of being disingenuous in claiming such DNA samples are, like fingerprints and mug shots, necessary to identify individuals. He asserted that the Roberts Court majority was creating a mechanism for "fishing expeditions" in DNA databases to try to see whether individuals or their relatives may be connected to unsolved crimes.[39] In theory, such samples will be removed from DNA databases when individuals' charges are dropped or they are found not guilty. After samples are placed in a bureaucratically controlled database, however, there can be major problems in ensuring that they are actually deleted.[40]

Another source of significant consequences from conservative decisions on constitutional rights stemmed from the Roberts Court majority's tolerance of and unwillingness to correct errors by police officers. During the Warren Court era, the justices began examining many constitutional rights cases in criminal justice by asking the question, "Were any constitutional rights violated?" If a right was violated, then the justices felt obligated to correct that violation, frequently through application of the exclusionary rule to bar evidence obtained in violation of individuals' rights. By contrast, beginning in the Burger Court era and continuing through the Roberts Court era, the Supreme Court's composition became more conservative. As a result, the majority began by asking, "Did police officers really do anything wrong in the actions they took?" This is a very different question because it accepted and left unremedied purportedly good-faith errors by police, even if those errors caused violations of constitutional rights.[41] The Roberts Court majority followed this line of thinking in permitting police to use evidence found when a search was conducted in reliance on erroneous information in a police-administered database in *Herring v. United States* (2009). Despite the Fourth Amendment violation that occurred in the search, the majority declared that the officers on the scene did not do anything wrong in relying on the database and therefore the rights violation could go unremedied as the exclusionary rule need not apply.

In other examples, police were permitted to use evidence found in a search based on an unjustified traffic stop made by an officer who lacked knowledge about his state's traffic laws (*Heien v. North Carolina*, 2014). The officer erroneously believed that North Carolina law required two working brake lights on motor vehicles. In fact, the law required only one working brake light. In *Utah v. Streiff* (2016), an officer stopped a pedestrian and demanded identification despite lacking the necessary reasonable suspicion to initiate the stop. The officer erroneously believed that he had reasonable suspicion to justify the stop, but his knowledge that the individual had exited from a house suspected of involvement in drug activity did not actually suffice as a legal basis for the stop. The resulting search, based on the officer learning that a warrant for the individual existed in a database, was permitted to stand and the drug evidence discovered in the search was used against the individual in court.

The *Heien* and *Streiff* decisions potentially apply to a very wide array of circumstances that could leave Fourth Amendment violations unremedied for large numbers of people. Both decisions create possibilities for an unlimited potential number of improper stops targeting drivers and pedestrians. Both decisions reward police officers' ignorance and errors without creating any incentive for them to learn and closely follow laws and rules. Both decisions also create incentives for "testilying," the documented problem of police officers presenting false reports and untruthful testimony under oath in order to provide after-the-fact justifications for their rule-breaking behavior that led to improper stops, searches, and arrests.[42] In other words, by excusing certain police errors and leaving the resulting rights violations unremedied, the Roberts Court—much like its Burger and Rehnquist era predecessors—contributed to expanded police authority and a diminution of rights. This reduction in protections potentially affects all drivers and pedestrians whose liberty of movement and privacy can be infringed when police officers' discretionary actions are driven by errors. The same broad impacts can also be produced by disingenuous police claims about permissible errors through manufactured after-the-fact justifications that fit the *Heien* and *Streiff* categories for forgiveness of police errors.

In the realm of corrections, the Roberts Court's decision in *Beard v. Banks* (2006) focused specifically on access to reading materials and family photos for imprisoned individuals residing in a disciplinary unit. The majority opinion approved officials' practice of depriving these individuals of newspapers, magazines, and family photos despite obvious flaws in officials' claims that such removals were necessary to protect against the risk that these items would be used as weapons or to start fires. This justification made little sense since these same individuals were entitled to access to other equally "dangerous" objects, including toilet tissue, religious books, and legal papers.[43] In fact, it appeared the institution had only one coherent justification for the policy: The officials wanted to withhold materials in order to motivate these residents to improve their behavior and thereby gain a return to the general prison population, where they would have access to these valued items. In light of the pattern of Supreme Court decisions on constitutional rights in prisons going back to the end of the 1970s, it was unremarkable to see the Roberts Court majority defer to corrections officials' decisions instead of protecting the First Amendment interest in reading materials possessed by imprisoned people. Yet, this was an impactful decision for the message that it sent to corrections officials and lower court judges about the judicial deference to be applied when institutional decisions and policies are challenged through prisoner litigation.

Justice Breyer's majority opinion in *Beard* claimed to follow Justice O'Connor's *Turner v. Safley* (1987) analysis that had guided these types of cases for nearly two decades. But Breyer's opinion conceded that the Pennsylvania prison's policy did not comply with the second element of the four-part "Turner test" concerning the existence of alternative means to exercise the right in question.[44] Moreover, in a concurring opinion, Justice Thomas highlighted how the Turner test was unworkable when applied to this case and argued for scrapping the test in favor of his own preferred approach that generally would authorize states to define for themselves what constitutional rights they will permit to exist in prisons.[45]

The test established by *Turner* has been applied by federal judges since 1987 in ways that consistently defer to corrections officials when those officials' decisions collide with a variety of rights, especially First Amendment rights.[46] Indeed, a leading prison law scholar noted that "the almost comically deferential standard of review established by *Turner v. Safley*" is a key element that makes "prison law's moral center of gravity til[t] very strongly in favor of the state." The reasoning in *Beard* made clear to corrections officials, if it was not clear before, that the four-part Turner test was largely a pretextual exercise that would not actually challenge institutional policies. When the Roberts Court's majority opinion purported to apply a legal test while admitting that the test cannot actually be applied, it signaled that there was little risk of judicial interference with correctional policies and practices.[47] In effect, the *Beard* decision addressed a narrow issue in one prison, yet it reinforced a message about prisons' administrative authority to impose broad limitations on many First Amendment and other rights for the nearly 1.6 million people serving sentences in American prisons.[48]

The Roberts Court and Its Ultimate Legacy

The Warren Court era lasted for fifteen Supreme Court terms, from the 1953 term through the 1968 term, during which it established numerous liberal precedents that expanded the meaning of constitutional rights and profoundly affected the practices of criminal justice officials. The succeeding Supreme Court eras were each a bit longer, as the Burger Court sat for seventeen terms from the 1969 term through the 1985 term, and the

Rehnquist Court decided cases for nineteen terms, from the 1986 term through the 2004 term. In each of these eras, the Supreme Court's composition was more conservative than that of the Warren era. In the Warren era, a majority of justices supported clearer and stronger conceptions of constitutional rights in order to reduce, limit, or eliminate abusive and unfair practices, especially in the actions of local police agencies and courts that controlled the vast majority of cases.[49] The Roberts Court exceeded the length of its predecessor eras when it approached the start of its nineteenth term in 2024. Under Chief Justice Roberts, the court produced a body of criminal justice–related decisions comparable to that of the Burger and Rehnquist eras. As indicated in the preceding chapters, the Roberts Court handed down a variety of liberal decisions in individual cases. Yet, its most impactful decisions, including those technically classified as liberal for expanding rights under the First and Second Amendments, favored the values and preferences of political conservatives.

With respect to constitutional rights decisions affecting police officers' authority to stop, search, and arrest people, the Roberts Court continued the long-term trend toward eroding the strict, clear rules preferred by the Warren Court's majority. The *Heien* and *Streiff* decisions were particularly notable for forgiving, and perhaps even inviting, police errors that led to otherwise improper stops and searches in violation of the Fourth Amendment. However, these were merely the most impactful examples of such decisions. There were other decisions that expanded police officers' freedom of action notwithstanding the constitutional rights violations that could result. For example, the Roberts Court continued its predecessor conservative eras' trend of limiting opportunities to hold police officers accountable through liability lawsuits. These limitations included the preservation of "qualified immunity," the doctrine that protects officials from civil rights lawsuits if they could not have known at the time of their actions that they were violating clearly established definitions of constitutional rights.[50] Indeed, one scholar labeled these legal developments that shield police from accountability as a story of "how police became untouchable."[51]

In several of these cases, the egregious nature of police actions leading to serious injuries and deaths was unsettling to observers[52] and raised fears about how police can needlessly harm members of the public without any effective means of deterring and remedying those harms.[53] In *Scott v. Harris* (2007), for example, a driver fleeing at high speed from an attempted traffic stop suffered paralyzing injuries in a crash after an officer, who had never been trained in the procedure, intentionally rammed the fleeing vehicle during the chase. The Roberts Court prevented the individual from suing the officer by concluding that the officer's actions were justified in trying to stop a vehicle being driven in a dangerous manner.

In other examples, a driver fled at high speed to avoid arrest for violating the conditions of his misdemeanor probation (*Mullenix v. Luna*, 2015). As his vehicle approached stop spikes that police placed in the road to puncture his tires and thereby end the high-speed flight, one officer ignored his superior's instruction to "wait" and fired at the moving vehicle in an ostensible effort to disable the engine. The bullets struck and killed the driver. The Roberts Court ruled that the police officer, who had never been trained to disable a moving vehicle by using a firearm, was immune from a lawsuit by the driver's family. The majority said the officer was entitled to qualified immunity because his actions did not violate clearly established constitutional limits on the use of force as defined at the time of the incident.

This was also the majority's approach in *Safford Unified School District v. Redding*. In this case, the majority recognized that the student's Fourth Amendment rights were violated by the warrantless strip search undertaken by school officials. However, her lawsuit seeking remedies was barred because the officials purportedly could not have recognized that they would violate the Fourth Amendment by requiring her to remove her clothing in order to conduct a warrantless strip search based on a false report from another student.

In *Hernandez v. Mesa* (2020), a US Border Patrol officer standing in Texas fired across the international border and killed a Mexican teenager standing in Mexico. The officer claimed that the youth and his friends had thrown rocks at the officer. The Roberts Court ruled that the officer was immune from any liability lawsuit filed by the teen's parents. In *Hernandez*, the majority concluded that American rights do not apply in a foreign country, even when the use of force originated in the United States.

Another rights-reduction method is simply to define rights in a narrow fashion, thereby limiting their scope, as the Roberts Court did in *Vega v. Tekoh* (2022). In that case, the Roberts Court declared that the improper administration of Miranda warnings to a suspect being questioned does not violate any constitutional right, despite the Rehnquist Court previously labeling the entitlement to Miranda warnings as a "constitutional rule."[54]

There is ample evidence that the overall legacy of the Roberts Court for criminal justice through the initial terms of President Trump's three appointees was a continuation of the conservatizing approach of its Burger and Rehnquist era predecessors. Amid individual liberal decisions, many of which concerned the definition of federal statutes rather than an expansion of constitutional rights, the Roberts Court majority further expanded opportunities for discretionary actions by police and identified additional situations in which rights violations would go unremedied. In addition to this general ongoing trend, the Roberts Court initiated specific society-disrupting doctrinal changes that barred certain legislative limits on both firearms and wealthy interests' financial influence over elections. These significant redefinitions of First and Second Amendment constitutional rights doctrines produced consequential impacts on politics, government, and society.

Major Changes to Advance Preferred Policies?

Linda Greenhouse, the Yale scholar and Pulitzer Prize–winning Supreme Court reporter for the *New York Times*, urged analysts of the Roberts Court to step back from focusing exclusively on year-by-year developments in decision-making and doctrinal development.[55] A year-by-year analysis will reveal signs of incremental changes in doctrine as well as illuminate individual decisions that address novel issues or move small steps in unexpected directions. Instead, she argued that analysts should look at decision-making and doctrine at the start of the Roberts Court era and compare those elements with where the court's decisions ended up nearly two decades later. In taking this broader approach, Greenhouse concluded that the Roberts Court fulfilled political conservatives' goals for redefining law concerning many important issues, such as abortion, affirmative action, and gun rights, after the Rehnquist Court era had failed to accomplish a conservative transformation for any of the key issues that she examined.[56] The abortion decision, in particular, demonstrated the assertiveness of the Roberts Court's conservatives in seeking to overturn precedents with which political conservatives disagree. In the abortion case, *Dobbs v. Jackson Women's Health Organization* (2022), the state of Mississippi did not ask the court to overturn the nearly fifty-year-old precedent that had established women's constitutional right to make decisions about terminating a pregnancy. Mississippi was merely defending its law that restricted abortion by imposing a new fifteen-week deadline for terminating pregnancies. But five justices on the Roberts Court went beyond the arguments and issue actually presented in the case and decided to fulfill political conservatives' long-standing desire to end the right of choice. In examining the foregoing issues as well as the Roberts Court's prioritization of free exercise of religion above other interests and its limitations on environmental regulations, Greenhouse concluded that by mid-2023, "every goal on the conservative wish list had been achieved. All of it. To miss that remarkable fact is to miss the story of the Roberts Court."[57]

Does Greenhouse's stark conclusion also apply to criminal justice issues beyond gun rights? In order to answer this question, political conservatives' long-desired law and policy objectives in criminal justice must be evaluated through the decision-making trends of the era's conservative majority. Such evaluations must include not only an assessment of what the Roberts Court has decided concerning various issues but also the prospects for further change under the conservative supermajority created by the confirmation of Justice Barrett in 2020.

Since the 1980s, many political conservatives advocated originalism as the only proper approach to constitutional interpretation.[58] During the Rehnquist Court era, Justices Scalia and Thomas were the only advocates of originalism on the high court. Thus, they seldom drew enough support from other justices to produce majority opinions firmly rooted in the idea that the eighteenth-century framers and ratifiers of the Constitution and Bill of Rights established static definitions and meanings for the founding documents. Instead, flexible approaches to interpretation guided most of the court's decisions. The big breakthrough for originalist interpretation came in *District of Columbia v. Heller*. Scalia's originalist majority opinion redefined the Second Amendment to protect individuals' right to own and keep firearms rather than to safeguard states' authority to arm their "well regulated Militias." He attracted the endorsement not only of his fellow originalist Thomas but also of three other justices, Roberts, Kennedy, and Alito, who had not pledged fidelity to this approach to constitutional interpretation. Subsequently, two additional advocates of originalism, Gorsuch and Barrett, were appointed to the court by President Trump, as well as a third justice, Kavanaugh, who was sympathetic to this interpretive approach. The gathering momentum of political conservatives' long-preferred approach to constitutional interpretation has implications for criminal justice as well as other areas of law and policy.

One policy advocated by political conservatives and addressed by the Roberts Court was capital punishment.[59] At the end of the Rehnquist Court era and early in the Roberts Court era, the Supreme Court produced liberal outcomes in several closely divided decisions concerning capital punishment. In *Atkins v. Virginia* (2002), a 6–3 majority on the Rehnquist Court decided on Eighth Amendment grounds that developmentally disabled defendants convicted of murder are not eligible for the death penalty. Justice Stevens's reasoning in the majority opinion focused on changing social values and therefore directly contradicted the originalists' static conception of constitutional rights. The Rehnquist Court's decision in *Roper v. Simmons* (2005), which barred the imposition of the death penalty on teenagers who committed murders before the age of eighteen, similarly used changing public opinion and social values to define the Eighth Amendment and was an even closer decision, with a 5-to-4 vote. By 2022, Justice Thomas, who dissented in both cases, was the only justice remaining on the court who participated in those two decisions.

In the early years of the Roberts Court era, a 5–4 decision in *Panetti v. Quarterman* (2007) barred the execution of those whose mental condition prevented them from understanding that they were being punished for the commission of a serious crime. In *Kennedy v. Louisiana* (2008), a five-justice majority ruled that the death penalty may not be imposed upon someone convicted of the crime of raping a child. Three of the four dissenters in each case, Roberts, Thomas, and Alito, remained on the court in 2024 and had been joined at that time by additional conservative Trump appointees who shared many of their views.

These four liberal decisions in both the Rehnquist and Roberts eras were based on the *Trop v. Dulles* (1958) standard for assessing cruel and unusual punishments by evaluating society's changing values. This standard is the epitome of a flexible approach that changes as society changes and is defined by individual justices' perceptions of contemporary societal viewpoints. By contrast, an originalist approach would conclude that capital punishment can be applied in any situation for which it was applied in 1791. If the originalist-dominated Roberts Court that was formed by the addition of the Trump appointees were to revisit these split decisions, there would likely be reversals. Thus, capital punishment could easily end up being added to Greenhouse's list of issues for which the court moved dramatically in a conservative direction.

Indeed, if these justices wished to revisit and reverse the Supreme Court's prior capital punishment decisions, they could look to Scalia's dissenting opinion in *Atkins v. Virginia* that left behind a list of ten cases imposing requirements and limitations for the application of the death penalty. He implied that his originalist approach would lead him to reverse these decisions because "none of those requirements existed when the Eighth Amendment was adopted [in 1791]."[60] His list of cases included *Coker v. Georgia* (1977), where the court prohibited the death penalty for the rape of an adult woman; *Woodson v. North Carolina* (1976), prohibiting making the death penalty a mandatory punishment for murder; and *Enmund v. Florida* (1982), setting limits on executing individuals convicted of felony murder for participation in crimes in which someone else carried out the actual killing.[61] After the arrival of Barrett as the third Trump appointee in 2020, it appeared that the Roberts Court had enough conservative justices in place to overturn *Atkins, Roper, Panetti,* and *Kennedy,* as well as the entire list of non-originalist precedents in Scalia's *Atkins* dissent. If these reversals were to occur, the result would essentially give states broad discretion to impose capital punishment for murder and rape without consideration of the youthfulness and mental status of defendants or the specific circumstances of the killing. It remains to be seen whether the Roberts Court will begin to accept specific cases for hearing in order to reconsider these precedents and advance the long-standing preferred death penalty policy of political conservatives.

Similar possibilities may be in store for the liberal decisions early in the Roberts Court era that barred life-without-possibility-of-parole sentences for juveniles who commit non-homicide offenses (*Graham v. Florida,* 2010) and prohibited mandatory life-without-parole sentences for juveniles convicted of homicides (*Miller v. Alabama,* 2012). Justices Thomas and Alito dissented in both cases, and Chief Justice Roberts dissented in the latter case. These dissenters may have several like-minded voters among the justices appointed by President Trump if they decide to accept cases to reexamine these issues. The later Roberts Court decision in *Jones v. Mississippi* (2021) granting judges in juvenile lifers' resentencing hearings the authority to render decisions without hearing evidence or providing explanations already significantly undercut the entitlement to reconsideration of juveniles' life sentences.[62] By turning the entitlement to meaningful resentencing hearings into a symbolic exercise without substantive requirements, the

Roberts Court's conservative majority significantly impacted the earlier precedents without formally reversing them.

The Warren Court's creation of the requirement that police officers provide Miranda warnings before questioning suspects in custody drew outraged condemnations from police and politicians when Chief Justice Warren's majority opinion explained the new requirement in 1966. Subsequently, the Burger and Rehnquist Courts loosened the requirement by giving police flexibility in how they delivered the warnings (*Duckworth v. Eagan*, 1989) and forgiving the omission of the warnings in specific circumstances, such as "public safety" situations (*New York v. Quarles*, 1984). The Roberts Court continued the process of weakening the protective impact of the Miranda requirement in decisions such as *Florida v. Powell* (2010). In *Powell*, the police told the suspect he could consult with an attorney "before" questioning, but the court majority rejected the suspect's claim of a Miranda violation when he was not informed that he had the right to an attorney's presence throughout questioning. In *Berghuis v. Thompkins* (2010), the Roberts Court announced a new rule requiring suspects to speak and affirmatively assert their right to remain silent rather than requiring police to respect the silence of suspects.

Over the decades since the original Miranda decision, many police executives, as well as a seven-member Rehnquist Court majority (*Dickerson v. United States*, 2000), came to regard Miranda warnings as an important and accepted component of police procedures. The Rehnquist majority characterized the rule as required by the Constitution, while police executives recognized that they still can use various questioning techniques, such as pretending to befriend suspects, that enable them to gain incriminating statements in most cases.[63] Yet, prominent conservative commentators continued to argue for the abolition of Miranda warnings, calling them an improperly manufactured rule by the Warren Court that purportedly caused many guilty suspects to go free simply by remaining silent.[64]

Could the requirement of Miranda warnings be at risk in the hands of the Roberts Court's conservative supermajority? It is certainly true that *Miranda v. Arizona* (1966) was not the product of originalist interpretation. Chief Justice Warren's majority opinion used contemporary examples of abusive treatment during questioning and the development of psychological techniques designed to elicit confessions. If originalist reasoning were to be applied by a majority of justices, it is difficult to see how Miranda warnings would survive. Moreover, in the previously mentioned case of

Vega v. Tekoh, the Roberts Court declared that a police violation of the Miranda rule is not a violation of a constitutional right under the Fifth Amendment. Thus, the stage has been set so that a reversal of *Miranda* would be characterized as merely the elimination of an unneeded or unwise judge-made rule, not the elimination of a constitutional right.

Notwithstanding the likelihood of that rationalizing characterization, the critics of such a reversal would complain about the loss of a rights-based legal protection. In light of strident criticism directed at the Roberts Court for its decisions in the cases cited by Greenhouse as completely changing legal doctrine to satisfy long-standing conservative policy preferences, would the justices want to add *Miranda v. Arizona* to that list?[65] A significant majority of suspects waive their Miranda rights and speak to the police without an attorney.[66] Thus, if Miranda warnings usually pose no impediment to police investigations, will the case be on the list that attracts the attention of Roberts Court justices for reconsideration? As with other criminal justice issues, it remains to be seen in future terms if the court accepts a case for hearing that directly challenges the existence of the *Miranda* precedent.

Early in the Roberts Court era, there was speculation that Chief Justice Roberts had arrived on the high court with a determination to eliminate the exclusionary rule, another legal doctrine disfavored by political conservatives. As a young lawyer in the Reagan administration, Roberts drafted a memorandum to advance the effort to abolish the exclusionary rule, which was a Reagan administration goal.[67] When the court issued its ruling in *Herring v. United States*, the majority opinion by Roberts led a leading conservative litigator involved in criminal justice issues to say, "I think *Herring* may be setting the stage for the Holy Grail," namely the abolition of the exclusionary rule.[68] *Herring* declared that police can use evidence from an improper search conducted in reliance on a flawed warrant database maintained by a police department. Liberal legal commentators also believed that the *Herring* decision could signal the impending demise of the exclusionary rule. As one law professor wrote in 2009, "Now that the Court has excused mistakes by police officers relying on other police officers, the stage is set for much broader incursions into the exclusionary rule."[69] This critic also described Roberts, Alito, Thomas, and Scalia as "targeting the [exclusionary] rule for evisceration."[70]

Those obituaries for the exclusionary rule were written in 2009. Fifteen years later, the exclusionary rule has still survived, albeit with diminished applications. The process of incremental diminution of the exclusionary rule began in the early years of the Burger Court under a chief justice who seemed intent on eliminating the rule yet never gathered the five votes needed to achieve his goal.[71] Following the continued diminution of the exclusionary rule through decisions in the Rehnquist Court era, the Roberts Court majority made decisions further weakening the rule by forgiving police errors in cases such as *Heien, Streiff,* and *Herring.* Critics also pointed to the Roberts Court decision in *Hudson v. Michigan* (2006), which said the exclusionary rule did not apply when police executing a warrant entered a house without properly following the knock-and-announce rule prior to entering.[72]

Despite the Roberts Court's role in eroding the application of the exclusionary rule, the justices also effectively endorsed the continuation of the rule in various settings. For example, in *Riley v. California*, the justices unanimously declared that police cannot automatically search the contents of an arrestee's cell phone. Instead, they must obtain a warrant to search the phone unless there are exigent circumstances related to officer safety or the loss of evidence that would justify a warrantless search. In limiting police authority in this way, the Roberts Court was effectively applying the exclusionary rule to a specific context of police investigative actions. Similar reinforcement of the exclusionary rule occurred in other liberal Fourth Amendment decisions, such as *Florida v. Jardines*, concerning the warrantless use of a drug-sniffing dog on the front porch of a house. Justice Scalia wrote the majority opinion in *Jardines*, and the five-member majority included Justice Thomas. Justice Alito's four-justice dissenting group included Chief Justice Roberts and the subsequently retired Justices Kennedy and Breyer. With the later appointment of conservative Justices Gorsuch, Kavanaugh, and Barrett, could the continued existence of the exclusionary rule be at risk in a future case? It is possible, but it seems less likely than some other potential reversals of doctrine in light of individual fact situations in which conservative justices have recognized a Fourth Amendment violation and disallowed the use of evidence by police and prosecutors.

Conclusion

In many respects, the Roberts Court era continued the trends evident in the Burger and Rehnquist Court eras. In reaction to the dramatic expansion of criminal justice rights during the Warren Court era in the 1960s, the high court in these subsequent eras steadily diminished the clarity and protective power of those rights by issuing decisions that expanded the authority of police and prosecutors. These changes stemmed from the fact that Republican presidents selected fourteen of the next nineteen justices appointed to the Supreme Court in the decades following the end of the Warren era. As in the immediately preceding eras, the Roberts Court majority shifted away from asking, "Were any rights violated?" in specific cases and instead emphasized the question, "Did the police really do anything wrong?" This ongoing shift in perspective opened opportunities to recognize more contexts in which improperly obtained evidence could be used in court. Much like the Burger and Rehnquist Courts, the Roberts Court, despite its generally conservative trends in reshaping constitutional rights in criminal justice, also made liberal decisions that favored individuals when interpretating federal criminal statutes and examining claimed rights violations in specific situations. Yet, these liberal decisions were less impactful than the conservative rulings.

The Roberts Court sharply distinguished itself from its conservative predecessors through decisions that dramatically redefined specific areas of law. In the realm of criminal justice, the rewriting of Second Amendment doctrine and the use of First Amendment rationales to increase the influence of wealthy corporate interests on elections and public policy produced significant continuing impacts on policy, politics, and society. The Roberts Court also saw increased advocacy and usage of originalist constitutional interpretation, which does not bode well for the preservation of previously defined rights in criminal justice.

The Warren, Burger, and Rehnquist Court eras each lasted less than two complete decades. By contrast, John Roberts was relatively young when he was appointed to be chief justice of the United States—he was only fifty years old. At the time of their appointments to that position, his predecessors were sixty-two (Earl Warren), sixty-one (Warren Burger), and sixty-one (William Rehnquist). Barring a health crisis, Roberts has the opportunity to lead his court era for a longer period than the eras named for his predecessors. Moreover, the political maneuvering of Senate leader Mitch McConnell that blocked consideration of President Obama's appointee, Merrick Garland, ultimately gave President Trump the opportunity to appoint three deeply conservative justices during his first four years in office. As a result, the supermajority strength of the Roberts Court's conservative bloc differs markedly from the more balanced split between liberals and conservatives that existed in the Burger and Rehnquist Court eras. Thus, Roberts, a generally conservative decision-maker when the justices are divided on a criminal justice issue, may have opportunities to participate in additional significant doctrinal changes, especially because so many of his conservative colleagues seek to follow an originalist approach to interpretation. During nearly two decades of decision-making, the Roberts Court confirmed its established reputation for conservatizing trends and important impacts in criminal justice. Yet, there is good reason to anticipate the possibility of even more significant impacts from future decisions that will reexamine established doctrines providing rights protections for suspects and defendants.

ACKNOWLEDGMENTS

The original idea for this book began many years ago at the suggestion of an editor whose name and affiliation are now lost in the mists of forgotten memories. He made the suggestion after reading one of our many articles using empirical and legal analysis to produce single-year snapshots of the US Supreme Court's decisions. Years later, we remembered that original suggestion and began to discuss how we might tackle a comprehensive project. Wherever he is and whoever he is, that editor deserves our gratitude for planting the thought in our minds.

We feel fortunate and grateful for the encouragement and advice of those at Southern Illinois University Press, especially Joseph A. Schafer, the editor of the Perspectives on Crime and Justice series, and Sylvia Frank Rodrigue, the executive editor. Their insights guided the development of the manuscript and strengthened the clarity and organization of our presentation. We are also grateful for the invaluable contributions of Khara Lukancic, the project editor, and Linda Jorgensen Buhman, the editorial, design, and production manager, as well as for the important assistance of the copyeditor, Julie Bush. We also appreciate the helpful contributions of Sarah Jilek, the editorial assistant.

We are thankful for the supportive environments provided by our home departments, the School of Criminal Justice at Michigan State University and the Departments of Sociology and Political Science at San Diego State University. Our interactions with colleagues and students helped us develop our insights about the nation's highest court. We also owe a debt of gratitude to the faculty and graduate students in the Department of Political Science at the University of Akron, where we first became friends and colleagues more than thirty years ago.

We are most grateful for our supportive families, to whom we dedicate this book.

NOTES

Introduction

1. Shelby County v. Holder, 570 US 529 (2013) (voting rights); Students for Fair Admissions v. Harvard, 143 S. Ct. 2141 (2023) (affirmative action); Dobbs v. Jackson Women's Health Organization, 142 S. Ct. 2228 (2022) (abortion).

2. See, e.g., Pengelly, "Samuel Alito Did Not Declare Gifts"; Cole, "Justice Clarence Thomas Chooses Not to Recuse Himself."

3. Whitehouse, "Right-Wing Rout."

4. Dorf, "What's Different About the Roberts Court."

5. Abraham, *Freedom and the Court*, 118–93.

6. Abraham, *Justices and Presidents*, 292–339.

7. Stevens, *Making of a Justice*, 205, 206.

8. Blasi, *Burger Court*.

9. Smith and M. A. McCall, "Introduction," 14.

10. Scalia, foreword to *Originalism*, edited by Steven G. Calabresi, 43–44.

11. Smith, "Jurisprudential Politics," 156–60.

12. Smith, "Bent on Original Intent," 48.

13. Greenburg, *Supreme Conflict*, 113–21.

14. Scalia, foreword to *Originalism*, edited by Steven G. Calabresi, 43–45.

15. See, e.g., Chemerinsky, *Worse Than Nothing*, 51–74; and Cross, *Failed Promise*, 107–18.

16. See, e.g., Smith and Lema, "Justice Clarence Thomas," 787–811.

17. Brennan, "Constitution of the United States," 202.

18. Brennan, "Constitution of the United States," 204.

19. See, e.g., Smith and Lema, "Justice Clarence Thomas," 804–11.

1. The Roberts Court

1. Stevenson and Greenhouse, "O'Connor."

2. P. Baker, "Bush Nominates Roberts as Chief Justice."

3. *New York Times*, "Senate Confirms Roberts as 17th Chief Justice."

4. *The Guardian*, "Bush's Man Confirmed as U.S. Chief Justice."

5. Stout, "Alito Is Confirmed."

6. Smith et al., "Roberts Court and Criminal Justice," 421–22.

7. Segal and Spaeth, "Decisional Trends," 103.

8. White and Fradella, *Stop and Frisk*, 1–15.

9. Alexander, *New Jim Crow*, 1–19.

10. See, e.g., Blinder, "Ex-Officer Who Shot Walter Scott"; Visser, "Baton Rouge Shooting."

11. Hill et al., "How George Floyd Was Killed in Custody."

12. Kane, "Neil Gorsuch's Supreme Court Nomination."

13. Barnes, "Emboldened Supreme Court Majority."

14. Parents Involved in Community Schools v. Seattle School District No. 1, 551 US 701 (2007) (rejection of continuation of race-based school desegregation plan).

15. Dobbs v. Jackson Women's Health Organization, 142 S. Ct. 2228 (2022) (elimination of recognized constitutional right for women to make choices about abortion).

16. National Federation of Independent Business v. Sebelius, 567 US 519 (2012) (validation of Affordable Care Act except for Medicaid expansion requirement).

17. Burwell v. Hobby Lobby Stores, Inc., 573 US 682 (2014) (religious-based opting out from requirements of health care law).

18. Massachusetts v. Environmental Protection Agency, 549 US 497 (2007) (endorsement of EPA authority to regulate "greenhouse" gases).

19. See, e.g., Cox, *Warren Court*, 1–5; and Lamb and Halpern, *Burger Court*, 1–34.

20. Smith, *Courts, Politics, and the Judicial Process*, 261–69.

21. Hensley and Smith, "Membership Change and Voting Change," 854–55.

22. Hensley and Smith, "Membership Change and Voting Change," 842.

23. See, e.g., Cox, *Warren Court*; Lamb and Halpern, *Burger Court*; and Segal and Spaeth, "Decisional Trends."

24. Stevens, *Five Chiefs*, 210–11.

25. Dickerson v. United States, 530 US 428, 443 (2000).

26. Smith, *Constitutional Rights*, 231.

27. Abraham, *Justices and Presidents*, 263.

28. Smith, *Rehnquist Court and Criminal Punishment*, 34–37.

29. Smith, *Rehnquist Court and Criminal Punishment*, 34–37.

30. Smith, "What If?"

31. Smith, "Police Professionalism."

32. Baum, *Judges and Their Audiences*, 1–24.

33. Smith, *John Paul Stevens*, 33–60.

34. Georgia v. Randolph, 547 US 103 (2006).

35. Graham v. Florida, 560 US 48 (2010).

36. Smith and M. M. McCall, "Antonin Scalia," 169–88.

37. Barnes, "Trump Makes His Pick."

38. Johnson, "David Souter," 211–30.

39. Souter, "Text of Justice David Souter's Speech."

40. Baugh, "Clarence Thomas," 231–55.

41. DeJong, "Ruth Bader Ginsburg," 257–74.

42. Jacobs, "Stephen G. Breyer," 275–93.

43. De Vogue, "Ketanji Brown Jackson."

44. Breyer, *Reading the Constitution*, 136–41.

45. Stevens, *Five Chiefs*, 210.

46. Coyle, *Roberts Court*, 347–56.

47. Smith et al., "Roberts Court and Criminal Justice," 421–28.

48. Greenburg, *Supreme Conflict*, 285–313.

49. Smith et al., "Roberts Court and Criminal Justice," 421–28.

50. Sotomayor, *My Beloved World*, 154.

51. Biskupic, *Breaking In*, 176–226.

52. Tushnet, *In the Balance*, 82–92.

53. Montanaro, "Who Is Brett Kavanaugh?"

54. Sorkin, "Why Donald Trump Nominated Brett Kavanaugh."

55. Hagen, "Senate Votes to Confirm Amy Coney Barrett."

2. An Overview of Criminal Justice Decisions

1. Liptak, "Court Under Roberts"; Silver, "Supreme Court May Be Most Conservative."

2. Epstein et al., *Behavior of Federal Judges*, 108–9.

3. Authors' update of data provided in Epstein et al., *Supreme Court Compendium*, 266, table 3-5.

4. See, e.g., Lithwick, "John Roberts"; Hubbard, "Historically Low Public Trust"; and Donnelly, "Supreme Court Legitimacy."

5. Rosen, "Can the Judicial Branch Be a Steward?," 25.

6. Devins and Baum, "Split Definitive," 309; Liptak, "Polarized Court."

7. Devins and Baum, "Split Definitive," 316.

8. See, e.g., Smith et al., "Criminal Justice and the 2013–2014 United States Supreme Court Term," 364.

9. Two consolidated cases considering possible violations of the Sixth Amendment's Confrontation Clause are included separately because the ruling produced one liberal and one conservative outcome (*Davis v. Washington*, 547 US 813 [2006]). Similarly, cases consolidated in *Birchfield v. North Dakota*, 579 US 438 (2016), are treated as separate decisions regarding conditions under which automobile drivers can be required to submit to warrantless blood and breath testing used to detect alcohol concentration.

10. Pritchett, *Roosevelt Court.*

11. Fischman and Jacobi, "Second Dimension," 1681.

12. Sprague, *Voting Patterns,* 7, 51–61. The formula for calculating the Sprague criterion is $[(100 - x_c)/2] + x_c$ where x_c is the court mean interagreement rate among each pair of justices across the sample cases. Some researchers set the threshold for bloc voting at a given rate, such as at 70 percent. Unlike the Sprague criterion, that option does not account for the general level of consensus on the court that can vary across time and categories of cases.

13. Sunstein, "Unanimity and Disagreement," 810.

14. See, e.g., Spriggs and Hansford, "Explaining the Overruling"; and Riggs, "When Every Vote Counts."

15. See, e.g., Spriggs and Hansford, "Explaining the Overruling"; and Riggs, "When Every Vote Counts."

16. Martin et al., "Median Justice," 1291.

17. Smith, *Supreme Court and the Development of Law,* 144–52.

18. See, e.g., Slotnick, "Who Speaks for the Court?"; Maltzman and Wahlbeck, "May It Please the Chief?"; Benesh et al., "Equity in Supreme Court Opinion Assignment."

19. Martin et al., "Median Justice"; McCall, "Sandra Day O'Connor," 143–68.

20. Gordon, "Alito or Scalito?"

21. Raghavan, "Open Questions."

22. Baker and Haberman, "President Plans to Name Barrett," A1, A17; Thomson-DeVeaux et al., "How Conservative Is Amy Coney Barrett?"

23. Alito agreed with Breyer and not with Scalia in twenty of the twenty-two cases in which both Breyer and Scalia defected from their respective wings. See, e.g., Smith and M. M. McCall, "Antonin Scalia," 175–76 (summarizing Scalia's liberal criminal justice positions during the Rehnquist Court era).

24. Desmon and Little, "Quiet, Careful, Conservative Nominee."

25. Gordon, "Alito or Scalito?"

26. Bazelon, "Mysterious Justice Samuel Alito" (referencing Lee Epstein's presentation of criminal case voting records from 1946 through early 2011).

27. See, e.g., Epstein and Jacobi, "Super Medians"; Knowles, *Tie Goes to Freedom,* 4.

28. Thomson-DeVeaux, "Justice Kennedy Wasn't a Moderate."

29. See, e.g., United States v. Kebodeaux, 570 US 387 (2013); and United States v. Comstock, 560 US 126 (2010).

30. Peruta v. California, 137 S. Ct. 1995, 1999 (2017) (Thomas, J., dissenting).

31. Gass, "To Understand This Supreme Court."

32. Associated Press, "Chief Justice Says His Goal Is More Consensus."

33. Rosen, "Supreme Court Has a Legitimacy Crisis."

34. Gou et al., "STAT PACK," 8.

35. Editorial, "What Kagan Will Bring to the Court."

36. Shapiro, "Sotomayor Seen as Moderate."

37. See "Symposium."

38. Wolf, "People's Justice"; Biskupic, *Breaking In*, 176–226.

39. We limit "near blocs" to those with average interagreement rates that exceed the Sprague criterion while the degree to which individual paired percentages fall short totals no more than 1 percent of all votes cast by the group.

40. From 2005 to 2009, Scalia dissented from one criminal justice majority that included Roberts, Alito, and Thomas, while Alito dissented from one including Roberts, Scalia, and Thomas. For the 2010–16 period, Scalia dissented from four such majorities and Alito dissented from five.

41. See, e.g., Bravin, "Why Lawyers Seek Kennedy's Vote"; and Liptak, "This Was the Kennedy Court."

42. For examples of defenses of Kennedy's approach arguing that his record demonstrates a more disciplined approach than may appear, see Colucci, *Justice Kennedy's Jurisprudence*; and Bibas, "Justice Kennedy's Sixth Amendment Pragmatism."

43. See, e.g., Bullcoming v. New Mexico, 564 US 647 (2011); Melendez-Diaz v. Massachusetts, 557 US 305 (2009); Maryland v. Craig, 497 US 836 (1990); and Coy v. Iowa, 487 US 1012 (1988).

44. See Apprendi v. New Jersey, 530 US 466 (2000).

45. Liptak, "Thomas Ends 10-Year Silence."

46. Primus, "Unexpected Importance of Clarence Thomas."

47. Liptak, "Roberts Is the New Swing Vote"; Belkin and McElwee, "Don't Be Fooled."

48. Justice Gorsuch provided the only swing vote and authored the majority opinion in *McGirt v. Oklahoma*, 140 S. Ct. 2452 (2020), *United States v. Haymond*, 139 S. Ct. 2369 (2019), and *United States v. Davis*, 139 S. Ct. 2319 (2019). He was also the only swing vote in *Sessions v. Dimaya*, 138 S. Ct. 1204 (2018).

49. Smith, *John Paul Stevens*, 244.

50. Jacobs and Smith, "Justice Anthony Kennedy," 919.

51. See, e.g., Slotnick, "Chief Justices and Self-Assignment"; and Slotnick, "Who Speaks for the Court?"

52. See, e.g., *Espinoza v. Montana Department of Revenue*, 140 S. Ct. 2246 (2020), regarding public funds to private religious schools; *Snyder v. Phelps*, 562 US 443 (2011), holding that the First Amendment protected the Westboro Baptist Church, whose members engaged in offensive picketing near the funeral of a serviceman; *Rucho v. Common Cause*, 139 S. Ct. 2482 (2019), concerning partisan gerrymandering claims; and *National Federation of*

Independent Business v. Sebelius, 567 US 519 (2012), regarding so-called Obamacare.

53. In *Lee v. United States*, 137 S. Ct. 1958 (2017), the petitioner claimed that he would have rejected a plea offer that triggered mandatory deportation but for his attorney's incompetence. Roberts distinguished this from issues in other cases in which ineffective assistance led to rejecting a plea deal. In *Buck v. Davis*, 137 S. Ct. 759(2017), a highly critical, dissenting Thomas conceded, "Today's decision has few ramifications, if any, beyond the highly unusual facts presented here." *Buck* at 781 (Thomas, J. dissenting).

54. This includes *Hamdan v. Rumsfeld*, 548 US 557 (2006), in which Roberts did not participate.

55. Segal and Spaeth, *Supreme Court and the Attitudinal Model*, 221–34.

56. Associated Press, "Chief Justice Says His Goal Is More Consensus"; Rosen, "Supreme Court Has a Legitimacy Crisis"; Cillizza, "John Roberts, Umpire."

57. Thomson-DeVeaux, "Justice Kennedy Wasn't a Moderate" (quoting Vladek).

58. Dobbs v. Jackson Women's Health Organization, 142 S. Ct. 2228 (2022) (abortion); Students for Fair Admissions v. Harvard, 143 S. Ct. 2141 (2023) (affirmative action); Sackett v. Environmental Protection Agency, 143 S. Ct. 1322 (2023) (environmental protection).

3. Blocking Legislative Definitions of Crimes

1. See Amar, *Constitution and Criminal Procedure*, vii; and Cox, *Warren Court*, 71–91.

2. See Magarian, *Managed Speech*.

3. See Carlson, *Policing and the Second Amendment*.

4. Magarian, *Managed Speech*, 239–42.

5. Liptak, "Study Challenges Supreme Court's Image."

6. Youn, "Roberts Court's Free Speech Double Standard."

7. Quoted in Liptak, "Study Challenges Supreme Court's Image."

8. Liptak, "Study Challenges Supreme Court's Image."

9. Magarian, *Managed Speech*, 11.

10. Lorenz, "Supreme Court's Ruling on Online Harassment."

11. United States v. Alvarez, 567 US 709, 715–16 (2012).

12. *Alvarez*, 567 US at 729.

13. Calabresi and Shaw, "Jurisprudence of Justice Samuel Alito."

14. Collins, "Roberts Court."

15. Spaeth et al., 2019 Supreme Court Database.

16. Spaeth et al., 2019 Supreme Court Database.

17. Collins, "Exceptional Freedom," 452; Thomson-DeVeaux, "Chief Justice Roberts."

18. United States v. Williams, 553 US 285, 297, 298, 299 (2008).

19. Holder v. Humanitarian Law Project, 130 S. Ct. 2705, 2740 (2010).

20. Thomson-DeVeaux, "Chief Justice Roberts."

21. See Hasen, "Election Law's Path"; and Strine and Walter, "Conservative Collision Course?"

22. Citizens United v. Federal Election Commission, 130 S. Ct. 876, 886–88 (2010).

23. *Citizens United*, 130 S. Ct. at 913.

24. Austin v. Michigan Chamber of Commerce, 494 US 652, 660 (1990).

25. *Citizens United*, 130 S. Ct. at 898.

26. *Citizens United*, 130 S. Ct. at 913.

27. *Citizens United*, 130 S. Ct. at 932 (Stevens, J., concurring in part and dissenting in part).

28. Stevens, *Six Amendments*, 78; Stevens, *Making of a Justice*, 501; "Former Justice Stevens."

29. McCutcheon v. Federal Election Commission, 572 US 185, 233 (2014) (Breyer, J., dissenting).

30. Kotch, "Private Prison Giant."

31. Nass, "NRA's Plummeting Campaign Spending."

32. Hickey, "Gun Industry."

33. *Citizens United*, 130 S. Ct. at 979 (Stevens, J., concurring in part and dissenting in part).

34. Masters, "U.S. Gun Policy."

35. Printz v. United States, 521 US 898, 938–39 (1997) (Thomas, J., concurring).

36. Scalia, foreword to *Originalism*, edited by Steven G. Calabresi, 43–45.

37. See, e.g., Chemerinsky, *Worse Than Nothing*, 58–59; and Cross, *Failed Promise*, 14–15.

38. District of Columbia v. Heller, 128 S. Ct. 2783, 2789 (2008).

39. *Heller*, 128 S. Ct. at 2800.

40. *Heller*, 128 S. Ct. at 2822 (Stevens, J., dissenting).

41. Smith, *John Paul Stevens*, 16–17.

42. Stevens, *Six Amendments*, 132.

43. Cross, *Failed Promise*, 104.

44. *Heller*, 128 S. Ct. at 2816–17.

45. Cross, *Failed Promise*, 104.

46. *Heller*, 128 S. Ct. at 2791–92.

47. Scalia, foreword to *Originalism*, edited by Steven G. Calabresi, 43–45.

48. McDonald v. City of Chicago, 130 S. Ct. 3020, 3050 (2010).

49. Stevens, *Six Amendments*, 129–31.

50. Roth, "Second Amendment Advocates."

51. Friedman v. City of Highland Park, 136 S. Ct. 447, 449 (2015).

52. Miller v. Bonta, 542 F. Supp. 3d 1009 (S.D. Calf. 2021); Cassidy, "Newsom Slams Judge."

53. Miller v. Bonta, No. 21-55608, June 21, 2021 (9th Cir.); Paybarah, "Appeals Court Blocks Ruling."

54. New York State Rifle & Pistol Association v. City of New York, 140 S. Ct. 1525, 1527 (2020) (Kavanaugh, J., concurring).

55. Liptak, "Supreme Court Dismisses Challenge."

56. Liptak, "Supreme Court to Hear Case."

57. New York State Rifle & Pistol Association v. Bruen, 142 S. Ct. 2111, 2122 (2022).

58. *Bruen*, 142 S. Ct. at 2126.

59. *Bruen*, 142 S. Ct. at 2164 (Breyer, J., dissenting).

60. *Bruen*, 142 S. Ct. at 2177–80 (Breyer, J., dissenting).

61. *Bruen*, 142 S. Ct. at 2180 (Breyer, J., dissenting).

62. Antonyuk v. Hochul, 635 F. Supp. 3d 111 (2022).

63. Hardaway v. Nigrelli, 639 F. Supp. 3d 422 (W.D. NY 2022); Meko, "New York's Gun Law."

64. Alter et al., "Fight over Gun Control."

65. Cochrane, "Congress Passes Bipartisan Gun Legislation."

66. Magarian, *Managed Speech*, 225.

67. Davis, "Bong Hits and Big Money," 402.

68. Richer and Whitehurst, "Supreme Court Ruling Creates Turmoil."

69. United States v. Rahimi, 144 S. Ct. 1889 (2024).

4. Search and Seizure

1. A. Ferguson, "Internet of Things."

2. Newton, "Supreme Court's Fourth Amendment Scorecard."

3. Priester, "Warrant Requirement Resurgence?"

4. Maclin and Rader, "No More Chipping Away," 1189–90.

5. Cohen, "Kill Off the Exclusionary Rule?"

6. Newton, "Supreme Court's Fourth Amendment," 26.

7. A. Ferguson, "Internet of Things," 809.

8. A. Ferguson, "Internet of Things," 830–32.

9. Biskupic, "Supreme Court Rules Warrant Needed."

10. Liptak, "Justices Say GPS Tracker Violated Privacy Rights."

11. Simmons, "Not 'Voluntary' but Still Reasonable," 773; Burke, "Consent Searches," 511.

12. J. Ferguson, "*Randolph v. Georgia*," 638.

13. Del Carmen, *Criminal Procedure*, 171.

14. Jia et al., "Analysis and Categorization," 42.

15. Andrea, "Exigencies of Drunk Driving," 498.

16. Riley v. California, 134 S. Ct. 2473, 2489 (2014).

17. Greenhouse, "Supreme Court Justices Have Cellphones."

18. Singh, "Stepping Out of the Vehicle," 1760.

19. O'Neill, "(Un)Reasonableness and the Roberts Court," 201–2.

20. Maryland v. King, 133 S. Ct. 1958, 1972 (2013).

21. *King*, 133 S. Ct. at 1990 (Scalia, J., dissenting).

22. Donahoe, "Fourth Amendment 'Cheeks' and Balances," 551.

23. Biskupic, "Ginsburg: Court Needs Another Woman."

24. Biskupic, "Ginsburg: Court Needs Another Woman."

25. O'Neill, "(Un)Reasonableness and the Roberts Court," 198–99.

26. Liptak, "Justices Step Closer to Repeal."

27. Liptak, "Justices Step Closer to Repeal."

28. Liptak, "Justices Step Closer to Repeal."

29. Smith, *Constitutional Rights*, 221.

30. Utah v. Strieff, 136 S. Ct. 2056, 2064 (2016) (Sotomayor, J., dissenting).

31. Egbert v. Boule, 142 S. Ct. 1793, 1823–24 (2022).

32. Greenhouse, "Supreme Court Justices Have Cellphones."

33. Somers, "Justice Scalia Gets $70 Ticket."

5. Miranda Warnings and Right to Counsel

1. United States v. Cronic, 466 US 648, 654 (1984).

2. L. Baker, *Miranda*, 248; Heath, *To Face Down Dixie*, 117–20, 155–61.

3. See, e.g., Stone, "Roberts Court."

4. Chemerinsky, "Roberts Court and Criminal Procedure."

5. Weisselberg, "Debate: The Right to Remain Silent."

6. Franze, "Death by a Thousand Cuts."

7. Florida v. Powell, 130 S. Ct. 1195, 1200 (2010).

8. *Powell*, 130 S. Ct. at 1205.

9. *Powell*, 130 S. Ct. at 1210–13 (Stevens, J., dissenting).

10. Kamisar, "*Duckworth v. Eagan*," 560.

11. Berghuis v. Thompkins, 560 US 370, 404 (2010) (Sotomayor, J., dissenting).

12. Colb, "Supreme Court."

13. Vander Giessen, "*Berghuis v. Thompkins*," 190.

14. Miranda v. Arizona, 384 US 436, 475 (1966).

15. J. D. B. v. North Carolina, 564 US 261, 274 (2011).

16. Maryland v. Shatzer, 559 US 98, 110 (2010).

17. See, e.g., Editorial, "*Miranda* Isn't Forever."

18. See McCall and McCall, "Quantifying the Contours," 127–30.

19. Montejo v. Louisiana, 129 S. Ct. 2079, 2090–91 (2009).

20. Smith, *John Paul Stevens*, 245.

21. Duffy and Lambert, "Dissents from the Bench," 23–37.

22. *Montejo*, 129 S. Ct. at 2095–96 (Steven, J., dissenting).

23. Mayeux, "Ineffective Assistance of Counsel," 2162.

24. Schriro v. Landrigan, 550 US 465, 470 (2007) (Stevens, J., dissenting).

25. *Schriro*, 550 US at 464, 482.

26. Chin and Holmes, "Effective Assistance of Counsel," 699.

27. Padilla v. Kentucky, 559 US 356, 364 (2010).

28. *Padilla*, 559 US at 369.

29. Lafler v. Cooper, 566 US 156, 170 (2012).

30. Missouri v. Frye, 566 US 134, 152 (2012) (Scalia, J., dissenting).

31. Sagona, "Argument Recap."

32. Liptak, "Agency and Equity," 885.

33. See, e.g., Mallord, "Putting Plea Bargaining on the Record."

34. Jackman, "Virginia Judges."

35. Garza v. Idaho, 139 S. Ct. 738, 759 (2019) (Thomas, J., dissenting).

36. *Garza*, 139 S. Ct. at 757.

37. *Garza*, 139 S. Ct. at 758–59.

38. Stern, "Alito's Attack on Miranda Warnings."

6. Trial Rights

1. White v. Illinois, 502 US 346, 359 (1992) (Thomas, J., concurring).

2. Maryland v. Craig, 497 US 836, 845 (1990).

3. Ohio v. Roberts, 448 US 56 (1980).

4. Crawford v. Washington, 541 US 36, 61–62 (2004).

5. *Crawford*, 541 US at 61–62.

6. Kovarsky, "Justice Scalia's Innocence Tetralogy," 94.

7. Michigan v. Bryant, 562 US 344, 379 (2011) (Scalia, J., dissenting).

8. *Bryant*, 562 US at 395 (Ginsburg, J., dissenting).

9. Peterson et al., "Role and Impact of Forensic Evidence."

10. Marcelo, "ACLU Argues for Drug-Crime Defendants"; Melendez-Diaz v. Massachusetts, 557 US 305, 318–21 (2009) (summarizing several studies finding significant errors in crime lab analyses and procedures).

11. Hansen, "Crime Labs Under the Microscope."

12. Hansen, "Crime Labs Under the Microscope."

13. Bullcoming v. New Mexico, 564 US 647, 652 (2011).

14. Williams v. Illinois, 567 US 50, 103–4 (2012) (Thomas, J., concurring).

15. See Hammon v. Indiana, 547 US 813, 834 (2006) (Thomas, J., concurring in part, dissenting in part); Giles v. California, 544 US 353, 377 (2008) (Thomas, J., concurring); *Melendez-Diaz*, 557 US at 329 (Thomas, J., concurring).

16. See Weiss, "Sotomayor Joins Gorsuch in Dissent."

17. United States v. Bagley, 473 US 667, 675n6 (1985) (quoting Berger v. United States, 295 US 78, 88 [1935]).

18. Brady v. Maryland, 373 US 83, 87 (1963).

19. Yaroshefsky, "New Orleans Prosecutorial Disclosure"; Balko, "New Orleans's Persistent Prosecutor Problem."

20. Innocence Network, "Amicus Brief (*Connick v. Thompson*)," 24–25.

21. Connick v. Thompson, 563 US 51, 60–70 (2011).

22. *Connick*, 563 US at 78, 100 (Ginsburg, J., dissenting).

23. Caplan, "D.A. Stole His Life."

24. Baer, "Timing Brady," 26–27.

25. Nicolas, "*Connick v. Thompson*," 124.

26. Alschuler and Deiss, "Brief History of the Criminal Jury," 871–75.

27. Parklane Hosiery v. Shore, 439 US 322, 341 (1979) (Rehnquist, C. J., dissenting).

28. David Cole, *No Equal Justice*, 101–31.

29. Flanagan, "Peremptory Challenges and Jury Selection"; King, "Procedurally Criminal."

30. Bringewatt, "*Snyder v. Louisiana*," 1295.

31. Snyder v. Louisiana, 552 US 472, 486 (2008) (Thomas, J., dissenting).

32. Flowers v. Mississippi, 139 S. Ct. 2228, 2252, 2269 (2019) (Thomas, J., dissenting).

33. Batson v. Kentucky, 479 US 79, 137 (1986) (Rehnquist, J., dissenting).

34. Hoffman, "Peremptory Challenges Should Be Abolished"; Fukurai and Krooth, *Race in the Jury Box*.

35. Uttecht v. Brown, 551 US 1, 9 (2007).

36. *Uttecht*, 551 US at 35 (Stevens, J., dissenting).

37. *Uttecht*, 551 US at 44–46 (Breyer, J., dissenting).

38. Ramos v. Louisiana, 140 S. Ct. 1390, 1394 (2020).

39. Wilson, "Oregon Lawmakers."

40. McGill, "Louisiana Unanimous Jury Requirement Not Retroactive."

41. Chrastil, "Louisiana Supreme Court to Hear Oral Arguments."

42. McMillan v. Pennsylvania, 477 US 79, 93 (1986).

43. Cabana v. Bullock, 474 US 376, 385 (1986).

44. See, e.g., Hoffman, "Case for Jury Sentencing"; and King and Klein, "Essential Elements," 1502–12.

45. Lanni, "Jury Sentencing in Noncapital Cases," 1778–79.

46. Jones v. United States, 526 US 227 (1999).

47. Hendrix, "*Harris v. United States*."

48. United States v. Scott, 437 US 82, 91 (1978).

49. Benton v. Maryland, 395 US 784 (1969).

50. Evans v. Michigan, 133 S. Ct. 1069, 1075 (2013).

51. Blueford v. Arkansas, 566 US 599, 601–5 (2012).

52. *Blueford*, 566 US at 606–8.

53. *Blueford*, 566 US at 610, 612–14 (Sotomayor, J., dissenting).

54. Pegeuro, "Second Shot at Proving Murder"; Klinger, "'I'll Take Form over Substance for $800.'"

55. Amar and Marcus, "Double Jeopardy Law After Rodney King."

56. Gamble v. United States, 139 S. Ct. 1960 (2019).

7. Sentencing and Rights in Corrections

1. Trop v. Dulles, 356 US 86, 101 (1958).

2. McCall and McCall, "Quantifying the Contours of Power"; Racker-Jordan, "Kennedy, *Kennedy*, and Eighth Amendment."

3. Siegler and Sullivan, "'Death Is Different' No Longer."

4. Siegler and Sullivan, "'Death Is Different' No Longer."

5. Graham v. Florida, 130 S. Ct. 2011, 2021 (2010).

6. *Graham*, 130 S. Ct. at 2043 (Thomas, J., dissenting).

7. *Graham*, 130 S. Ct. at 2036 (Stevens, J., concurring).

8. *Graham*, 130 S. Ct. at 2464.

9. Jones v. Mississippi, 141 S. Ct. 1307, 1313 (2021).

10. *Jones*, 141 S. Ct. at 1327 (Thomas, J., concurring).

11. *Jones,* 141 S. Ct. at 1328 (Sotomayor, J., dissenting).

12. Batey, "Categorical Bars to Execution."

13. Batey, "Categorical Bars to Execution."

14. Entzeroth, "Challenge and Dilemma."

15. Ford v. Wainwright, 477 US 399, 422 (1986) (Powell, J., concurring).

16. Batey, "Categorical Bars to Execution," 1520.

17. Markel, "Executing Retributivism," 1169.

18. Batey, "Categorical Bars to Execution," 1520.

19. Holler, "*Moore v. Texas.*"

20. See, e.g., Grover, "Child Rape as a Crime Against Humanity."

21. Solomon, "National Consensus."

22. Goldstone, "Death Penalty."

23. Kendall, "High Court Remains as Divided as Ever."

24. Fromherz, "Assuming Too Much," 420.

25. Ayers v. Belmontes, 549 US 7, 16–17 (2006).

26. Stewart, "*Abdul-Kabir v. Quarterman.*"

27. Abdul-Kabir v. Quarterman, 550 US 233, 246 (2007).

28. Stewart, "*Abdul-Kabir v. Quarterman,*" 270–71.

29. Denno, "Lethal Injection Chaos."

30. Baze v. Rees, 553 US 35, 50 (2008).

31. Semel, "Reflections on Justice John Paul Stevens's Concurring Opinion."

32. Smith, "Justice John Paul Stevens and Capital Punishment."

33. Semel, "Reflections on Justice John Paul Stevens's Concurring Opinion," 791.

34. Glossip v. Gross, 135 S. Ct. 2726, 2734 (2015).

35. *Glossip*, 135 S. Ct. at 2793–94 (2015) (Sotomayor, J., dissenting).

36. *Baze*, 553 US at 94 (Thomas, J., concurring in judgment).

37. Timbs v. Indiana, 130 S. Ct. 682, 686 (2019).

38. Sibilla, "After 7 Years, Indiana Returns Seized Land Rover."

39. Smith, *Supreme Court and the Development of Law*, 1–29.

40. Smith, "50-Year Journey."

41. Smith, "Rights Behind Bars," 851–52.

42. *New York Times*, "Twenty-Five Years for a Slice of Pizza"; Bazelon, "Arguing Three Strikes."

43. Prison Litigation Reform Act, Title 18 US Code section 3626 (a)(1)(A).

44. Brown v. Plata, 131 S. Ct. 1910, 1959 (2011) (Alito, J., dissenting).

45. Schlanger, "*Brown v. Plata* and Realignment."

46. Lofstrom and Raphael, *Public Safety Realignment*, 1–24.

47. Lofstrom and Raphael, *Public Safety Realignment*, 16.

48. Shaw v. Murphy, 532 US 223 (2001); Overton v. Bazzetta, 539 US 126 (2003).

49. Turner v. Safley, 482 US 78, 100 (1987) (Stevens, J., concurring in part and dissenting in part).

50. *Turner*, 482 US at 100–101.

51. *Shaw*, 532 US at 229.

52. Johnson v. California, 543 US 499, 524–50 (2005) (Thomas, J., dissenting).

53. Beard v. Banks, 548 US 521, 536–42 (2006) (Thomas, J., concurring in judgment).

54. *Beard*, 548 US at 542–53 (Stevens, J., dissenting).

55. Schlanger, "Jail Strip-Search Cases."

56. Florence v. Board of Chosen Freeholders, 132 S. Ct. 1510, 1518 (2012).

57. *Florence*, 132 S. Ct. at 1525–32 (Breyer, J., dissenting).

58. Samson v. California, 547 US 843, 846–47 (2006).

59. *Samson*, 547 US at 856.

60. *Samson*, 547 US at 857 (Stevens, J., dissenting).

61. Howes v. Fields, 132 S. Ct. 1181, 1194–95 (2012) (Ginsburg, J., dissenting).

62. Smith, *John Paul Stevens*, 11–17.

63. *Jones*, 141 S. Ct. at 1328 (Sotomayor, J., dissenting).

8. Incremental Conservatism or Accelerated Change?

1. Biskupic, "Three Supreme Court Justices to Watch."

2. Stevens, *Five Chiefs*, 210.

3. Stevens, *Five Chiefs*, 210.

4. Smith and M. A. McCall, "Introduction," 7.

5. Smith, "Criminal Justice and the 1997–98 U.S. Supreme Court Term," 451; Smith, "Criminal Justice and the 1998–99 U.S. Supreme Court Term," 32; Smith and M. M. McCall, "Criminal Justice and the 2002–2003 U.S. Supreme Court Term," 869; Smith et al., "Criminal Justice and the 2004–2005 U.S. Supreme Court Term," 960.

6. Richardson v. McKnight, 521 US 410 (1997); Lindh v. Murphy, 521 US 320 (1997); Gray v. Maryland, 523 US 185 (1998); Stenberg v. Carhart, 530 US 914 (2000); Carey v. Saffold, 536 US 214 (2002); Alabama v. Shelton, 535 US 654 (2002); Kelly v. South Carolina, 534 US 246 (2002); Stogner v. California, 539 US 607 (2003); Nguyen v. United States, 539 US 69 (2003); Groh v. Ramirez, 540 US 551 (2004); Rompilla v. Beard, 545 US 374 (2005); Smith v. Massachusetts, 543 US 462 (2006).

7. Haas and Wilson, "Oregon Supreme Court Finds Hundreds Convicted."

8. "History and Impact of Non-Unanimous Jury Decisions."

9. Simon, "New Overcrowding."

10. Schlanger, "*Brown v. Plata* and Realignment."

11. Lapowsky, "Sentenced to Life as Boys."

12. Derysh, "*Citizens United* Ruling."

13. Goldmacher, "2020 Campaign."

14. Bryan Metzger, "Elon Musk Spent at Least $277 Million Backing Trump and the GOP. Here's Where All That Money Went," *Business Insider*, December 6, 2024, https://www.businessinsider.com/elon-musk-260-million-spending-trump-republican-party-2024-12?op=1.

15. Goldmacher, "2020 Campaign."

16. Harvey and Mattia, "Does Money Have a Conservative Bias?"; Abdul-Razzak et al., "After *Citizens United*."

17. New York State Rifle & Pistol Association v. Bruen, 142 S. Ct. 2111, 2126 (2022).

18. Hill, "Federal Judge Halts Key Parts."

19. Pender, "Judge Reeves Rules."

20. Deese, "Starting Pistol."

21. Rabin, "Why Some Americans Buy Guns."

22. Black, "Americans Have More Guns."

23. LeBlanc and Choi, "United States Tops 400 Mass Shootings."

24. "Former Justice Stevens on the Three Worst Supreme Court Decisions."

25. Stevens, *Making of a Justice*, 482.

26. Stevens, *Six Amendments*, 78.

27. Stevens, *Six Amendments*, 59.

28. Stevens, *Six Amendments*, 132.

29. Stevens, *Six Amendments*, 78–79, 132–33.

30. Kaeble, "Probation and Parole."

31. Armacost, "*Arizona v. Gant*," 280.

32. Roediger, "Abolish Municipal Courts," 223.

33. Roediger, "Abolish Municipal Courts," 224.

34. Cook, "Something Rots in Law Enforcement"; Balko, "Little Rock's Dangerous and Illegal Drug War."

35. Hanna and Beck, "Central Kansas Police Force."

36. Lvovsky, "Judicial Presumption of Police Expertise," 2025–28.

37. Schlanger, "Jail Strip-Search Cases."

38. See Michigan Compiled Laws, Section 764.25a (2023).

39. Maryland v. King, 133 S. Ct. 1958, 1980 (2013) (Scalia, J., dissenting).

40. Dissell, "DNA Collected at Arrest."

41. Smith, *John Paul Stevens*, 186.

42. Goldstein, "'Testilying' by Police."

43. Beard v. Banks, 548 US 521, 545 (2006) (Stevens, J., dissenting).

44. *Beard*, 548 US at 532.

45. *Beard*, 548 US at 540–42 (Thomas, J., dissenting).

46. Smith, *Supreme Court and the Development of Law*, 112–23.

47. Dolovich, "How Prisoners' Rights Lawyers Do Vital Work," 436–37.

48. Kluckow and Zang, "Correctional Populations in the United States."

49. Smith, *Rehnquist Court and Criminal Punishment*, 12–14.

50. Jeffries, "What's Wrong with Qualified Immunity?," 852.

51. Schwartz, *Shielded*, ix–xxi.

52. Gross, "Unguided Missiles," 135–39; Lindvall, "Gutting *Bivens*," 1027–35.

53. McLeod, "Police Violence."

54. Dickerson v. United States, 530 US 428, 444 (2000).

55. Greenhouse, "Look at What John Roberts and His Court Have Wrought."

56. Greenhouse, "Look at What John Roberts and His Court Have Wrought."

57. Greenhouse, "Look at What John Roberts and His Court Have Wrought."

58. Smith, "Jurisprudential Politics."

59. See, e.g., Muhlhausen, "How the Death Penalty Saves Lives."

60. Atkins v. Virginia, 536 US 304, 352–53 (2002) (Scalia, J., dissenting).

61. *Atkins*, 536 US 352–53.

62. Totenberg, "Supreme Court Rejects Restrictions."

63. Leo, *Police Interrogations*, 36–37.

64. Grano, "*Miranda v. Arizona* and the Legal Mind"; Cassell, "*Miranda* Decision Is Showing Its Age."

65. See, e.g., Day and Weatherby, "*Dobbs* Effect"; Lemley, "Imperial Supreme Court."

66. Thomas and Leo, *Confessions of Guilt*, 217.

67. Liptak, "Justices Step Closer to Repeal."

68. Liptak, "Justices Step Closer to Repeal."

69. Bandes, "Roberts Court and the Future of Exclusionary Rule."

70. Bandes, "Roberts Court and the Future of Exclusionary Rule."

71. Lamb, "Chief Justice Warren E. Burger," 153–54.

72. Liptak, "Justices Step Closer to Repeal"; Bandes, "Roberts Court and the Future of Exclusionary Rule."

CASES CITED

Abdul-Kabir v. Quarterman, 550 US 233 (2007)
Abramski v. United States, 573 US 169 (2014)
Alabama v. Shelton, 535 US 654 (2002)
Alleyne v. United States, 570 US 99 (2013)
Antonyuk v. Hochul, 635 F. Supp. 3d 111 (2022)
Apodaca v. Oregon, 406 US 404 (1972)
Apprendi v. New Jersey, 530 US 466 (2000)
Argersinger v. Hamlin, 407 US 25 (1972)
Arizona v. Gant, 556 US 332 (2009)
Arizona v. Johnson, 555 US 323 (2009)
Ashcroft v. ACLU, 535 US 564 (2004)
Ashcroft v. Free Speech Coalition, 535 US 234 (2002)
Atkins v. Virginia, 536 US 304 (2002)
Austin v. Michigan Chamber of Commerce, 494 US 652 (1990)
Ayers v. Belmontes, 549 US 7 (2006)
Bailey v. United States, 568 US 186 (2013)
Barron v. Baltimore, 32 US 243 (1833)
Batson v. Kentucky, 476 US 79 (1986)
Baze v. Rees, 553 US 35 (2008)
Beard v. Banks, 548 US 521 (2006)
Benton v. Maryland, 395 US 784 (1969)
Berghuis v. Thompkins, 560 US 370 (2010)
Birchfield v. North Dakota, 579 US 438 (2016)
Bivens v. Six Unknown Named Agents of the Federal Bureau of Narcotics, 403 US 388 (1971)
Blakely v. Washington, 542 US 296 (2004)
Blueford v. Arkansas, 566 US 599 (2012)
Borden v. United States, 141 S. Ct. 1817 (2021)
Brady v. Maryland, 373 US 83 (1963)
Brewer v. Quarterman, 550 US 286 (2007)
Brigham City v. Stuart, 547 US 398 (2006)

Scott v. Harris, 550 US 372 (2007)

Sessions v. Dimaya, 138 S. Ct. 1204 (2018)

Shaw v. Murphy, 532 US 223 (2001)

Shaw v. United States, 580 US 63 (2017)

Shelby County v. Holder, 570 US 529 (2013)

Smith v. Cain, 565 US 73 (2012)

Smith v. Massachusetts, 543 US 462 (2006)

Smith v. Texas, 550 US 297 (2007)

Snyder v. Louisiana, 552 US 472 (2008)

Snyder v. Phelps, 562 US 443 (2011)

Sostre v. McGinnis, 334 F.2d 906 (2d Cir. 1964)

Stenberg v. Carhart, 530 US 914 (2000)

Stogner v. California, 539 US 607 (2003)

Strickland v. Washington, 466 US 668 (1984)

Students for Fair Admissions v. Harvard, 143 S. Ct. 2141 (2023)

Timbs v. Indiana, 130 S. Ct. 682 (2019)

Torres v. Madrid, 141 S. Ct. 989 (2021)

Trop v. Dulles, 356 US 86 (1958)

Trump v. Vance, 140 S. Ct. 2412 (2020)

Turner v. Safley, 482 US 78 (1987)

United States v. Alvarez, 567 US 709 (2012)

United States v. Bagley, 437 US 667 (1985)

United States v. Ball, 163 US 662 (1896)

United States v. Booker, 543 US 220 (2005)

United States v. Bullock, 3:18-CR-165-CWR-FKB (S.D. Miss. 2023)

United States v. Comstock, 560 US 126 (2010)

United States v. Cronic, 466 US 648 (1984)

United States v. Davis, 139 S. Ct. 2319 (2019)

United States v. Gonzalez-Lopez, 548 US 140 (2006)

United States v. Haymond, 139 S. Ct. 2369 (2019)

United States v. Jones, 565 US 400 (2012)

United States v. Kebodeaux, 570 US 387 (2013)

United States v. Leon, 468 US 897 (1984)

United States v. Miller, 307 US 174 (1939)

United States v. Nixon, 418 US 683 (1974)

United States v. Rahimi, 144 S. Ct. 1889 (2024)

United States v. Scott, 437 US 82 (1978)

United States v. Stevens, 550 US 460 (2010)

United States v. Williams, 553 US 285 (2008)

Utah v. Streiff, 136 S. Ct. 2056 (2016)

Uttecht v. Brown, 551 US 1 (2007)

Van de Camp v. Goldstein, 555 US 335 (2009)
Vega v. Tekoh, 142 S. Ct. 2095 (2022)
Voisine v. United States, 579 US 686 (2016)
Watkins v. Ackley, 370 Or. 604 (2022)
Weeks v. United States, 232 US 383 (1914)
White v. Illinois, 502 US 346 (1992)
Williams v. Illinois, 567 US 50 (2012)
Woodson v. North Carolina, 428 US 280 (1976)
Ziglar v. Abbasi, 582 US 120 (2017)

BIBLIOGRAPHY

Abdul-Razzak, Nour, Carlo Prato, and Stephane Wolton. "After *Citizens United*: How Outside Spending Shapes American Democracy." *Electoral Studies* 67, no. 1 (2020): 102–90.

Abraham, Henry J. *Freedom and the Court: Civil Rights and Liberties in the United States*. 5th ed. Oxford University Press, 1988.

Abraham, Henry J. *Justices and Presidents: A Political History of Appointments to the Supreme Court*. 2nd ed. Oxford University Press, 1985.

Alexander, Michelle. *The New Jim Crow: Mass Incarceration in the Age of Colorblindness*. New Press, 2012.

Alschuler, Albert W., and Andrew G. Deiss. "A Brief History of the Criminal Jury in the United States." *University of Chicago Law Review* 61, no. 3 (1994): 867–928.

Alter, Charlotte, Haley Sweetland Edwards, and Philip Elliott. "The Fight over Gun Control Isn't Really About Guns." *Time*, October 5, 2017. https://www.newsweek.com/kagan-barrett-question-whether-times-square-colleges-new-york-could-allow-gun-bans-1645573.

Amar, Akhil Reed. *The Constitution and Criminal Procedure: First Principles*. Yale University Press, 1997.

Amar, Akhil Reed, and Jonathan L. Marcus. "Double Jeopardy Law After Rodney King." *Columbia Law Review* 95, no. 1 (1995): 1–59.

Andrea, Timothy. "The Exigencies of Drunk Driving: *Cripps v. State* and the Issues with Taking Drivers' Blood Without a Warrant." *Boston College Law Review* 59, no. 9 (2018): 482–98.

Armacost, Barbara E. "*Arizona v. Gant*: Does It Matter?" *Supreme Court Review* 2009 (2009): 275–317.

Associated Press. "Chief Justice Says His Goal Is More Consensus on Court." *New York Times*, May 22, 2006, A16.

Baer, Miriam H. "Timing Brady." *Columbia Law Review* 115, no. 1 (2015): 1–67.

Baker, Liva. *Miranda: Crime, Law and Politics*. Athenaeum, 1983.

Baker, Peter. "Bush Nominates Roberts as Chief Justice." *Washington Post*, September 6, 2005. https://www.washingtonpost.com/archive/politics

/2005/09/06/bush-nominates-roberts-as-chief-justice/ddd7565e-5022–4347
–8438–9d03b6f2a077/.

Baker, Peter, and Maggie Haberman. "President Plans to Name Barrett as His
Court Pick." *New York Times*, September 26, 2020, A1, A17.

Balko, Radley. "Little Rock's Dangerous and Illegal Drug War." *Washington
Post*, October 14, 2018. https://www.washingtonpost.com/news/opinions
/wp/2018/10/14/little-rocks-dangerous-and-illegal-drug-war/.

Balko, Radley. "New Orleans's Persistent Prosecutor Problem." *Washington
Post*, October 27, 2015. https://www.washingtonpost.com/news/the-watch
/wp/2015/10/27/new-orleanss-persistent-prosecutor-problem/.

Bandes, Susan A. "The Roberts Court and the Future of Exclusionary Rule."
American Constitution Society for Law and Policy Issue Brief, April 2009.
https://www.acslaw.org/wp-content/uploads/2018/05/Bandes-Issue-Brief
.pdf.

Barnes, Robert. "Emboldened Supreme Court Majority Shows It's Eager for
Change." *Washington Post*, June 25, 2022. https://www.washingtonpost
.com/politics/2022/06/25/supreme-court-trump-justices/.

Barnes, Robert. "Trump Makes His Pick, but It's Still Anthony Kennedy's
Supreme Court." *Washington Post*, January 31, 2017. https://www
.washingtonpost.com/politics/courts_law/trump-makes-his-pick-but
-its-still-anthony-kennedys-supreme-court/2017/01/31/1de12472-e7e0
–11e6-bf6f-301b6b443624_story.html.

Batey, Robert. "Categorical Bars to Execution: Civilizing the Death Penalty."
Houston Law Review 45, no. 5 (2009): 1493–528.

Baugh, Joyce A. "Clarence Thomas: Consistent, Conservative, and Contrar-
ian." In Smith, DeJong, and McCall, *Rehnquist Court and Criminal Justice*.

Baum, Lawrence. *Judges and Their Audiences: A Perspective on Judicial Behavior*. Princeton University Press, 2006.

Bazelon, Emily. "Arguing Three Strikes." *New York Times Magazine*, May 21,
2010. https://www.nytimes.com/2010/05/23/magazine/23strikes-t.html.

Bazelon, Emily. "Mysterious Justice Samuel Alito." *New York Times Magazine*,
March 20, 2011, MM13.

Belkin, Aaron, and Sean McElwee. "Don't Be Fooled. Chief Justice John Roberts Is as Partisan as They Come." *New York Times*, October 7, 2019. https://
www.nytimes.com/2019/10/07/opinion/john-roberts-supreme-court.html.

Benesh, Sara C., Reginald Sheehan, and Harold J. Spaeth. "Equity in Supreme
Court Opinion Assignment." *Jurimetrics* 39, no. 4 (1999): 377–89.

Bibas, Stephanos. "Justice Kennedy's Sixth Amendment Pragmatism."
McGeorge Law Review 44, no. 1 (2014): 211–27.

Biskupic, Joan. *Breaking In: The Rise of Sonia Sotomayor and the Politics of
Justice*. Sarah Crichton Books/Farrar, Straus and Giroux, 2014.

Biskupic, Joan. "Ginsburg: Court Needs Another Woman." *ABC News*, May 6, 2009. https://abcnews.go.com/Politics/ginsburg-court-woman/story?id =7513795.

Biskupic, Joan. "Supreme Court Rules Warrant Needed for GPS Tracking." *USA Today*, January 23, 2012. https://abcnews.go.com/Politics/supreme -court-rules-warrant-needed-gps-tracking/story?id=15421635.

Biskupic, Joan. "The Three Supreme Court Justices to Watch After Breyer Retires." *CNN Politics*, January 29, 2022. https://www.cnn.com/2022/01/29 /politics/sotomayor-roberts-kagan-supreme-court-breyer/index.html.

Black, Thomas. "Americans Have More Guns Than Anywhere Else in the World and They Keep Buying More." *Bloomberg News*, May 25, 2022. https://www.bloomberg.com/news/articles/2022–05–25/how-many-guns -in-the-us-buying-spree-bolsters-lead-as-most-armed-country?in _source=embedded-checkout-banner.

Blasi, Vincent, ed. *The Burger Court: The Counter-Revolution That Wasn't*. Yale University Press, 1983.

Blinder, Alan. "Ex-Officer Who Shot Walter Scott Pleads Guilty in Charleston." *New York Times*, May 2, 2017. https://www.nytimes.com/2017/05/02 /us/michael-slager-walter-scott-north-charleston-shooting.html.

Bravin, Jess. "Why Lawyers Seek Kennedy's Vote." *Wall Street Journal*, October 3, 2006, A6.

Brennan, William J. "The Constitution of the United States: Contemporary Ratification." In *Judges on Judging: Views from the Bench*, edited by David M. O'Brien. Chatham House, 1997.

Breyer, Stephen. *Reading the Constitution: Why I Chose Pragmatism, Not Textualism*. Simon and Schuster, 2024.

Bringewatt, John P. "*Snyder v. Louisiana*: Continuing the Historical Trend Towards Increased Scrutiny of Peremptory Challenges." *Michigan Law Review* 108, no. 7 (2010): 1283–308.

Burke, Alafair S. "Consent Searches and Fourth Amendment Reasonableness." *Florida Law Review* 67, no. 2 (2015): 509–64.

Calabresi, Steven G., and Todd W. Shaw. "The Jurisprudence of Justice Samuel Alito." *George Washington Law Review* 87, no. 3 (2019): 507–78.

Caplan, Lincoln. "The D.A. Stole His Life, Justices Took His Money." *New York Times*, July 3, 2011, SR11.

Carlson, Jennifer. *Policing and the Second Amendment: Guns, Law Enforcement, and the Politics of Race*. Princeton University Press, 2020.

Cassell, Paul. "The *Miranda* Decision Is Showing Its Age and Should Be Replaced." *Utah Bar Journal* 31, no. 5 (2018): 18–21.

Cassidy, Megan. "Newsom Slams Judge Who Overturned California's Assault Weapons Ban as State Appeals Ruling." *San Francisco Chronicle*, June 10,

2021. https://www.sfchronicle.com/local/article/California-appeals-ruling
-overturning-16239032.php.

Chemerinsky, Erwin. "The Roberts Court and Criminal Procedure at Age Five." *Texas Tech Law Review* 43, no. 1 (2010): 13–27.

Chemerinsky, Erwin. *Worse Than Nothing: The Dangerous Fallacy of Originalism*. Yale University Press, 2022.

Chin, Gabriel J., and Richard W. Holmes Jr. "Effective Assistance of Counsel and the Consequences of Guilty Pleas." *Cornell Law Review* 87, no. 3 (2002): 697–742.

Chrastil, Nick. "Louisiana Supreme Court to Hear Oral Arguments in Case That Could Determine If Hundreds with Split-Jury Verdicts Are Entitled to New Trials." *The Lens*, May 6, 2022. https://thelensnola.org/2022/05/06 /louisiana-supreme-court-to-hear-oral-arguments-in-case-that-could -determine-if-hundreds-with-split-jury-verdicts-are-entitled-to-new-trials/.

Cillizza, Chris. "John Roberts, Umpire." *Washington Post*, June 28, 2012. https://www.washingtonpost.com/blogs/the-fix/post/john-roberts-umpire /2012/06/28/gJQAx5ZM9V_blog.html.

Cochrane, Emily. "Congress Passes Bipartisan Gun Legislation, Clearing It for Biden." *New York Times*, June 24, 2022. https://www.nytimes.com /2022/06/24/us/politics/gun-control-bill-congress.html.

Cohen, Adam. "Is the Supreme Court About to Kill Off the Exclusionary Rule?" *New York Times*, February 15, 2009. https://www.nytimes.com /2009/02/16/opinion/16mon4.html.

Colb, Sheryl F. "The Supreme Court Holds That Responding to Police Interrogation Waives the Right to Remain Silent." *Findlaw*, June 7, 2010. https:// supreme.findlaw.com/legal-commentary/the-supreme-court-holds-that -responding-to-police-interrogation-waives-the-right-to-remain-silent.html.

Cole, David. *No Equal Justice: Race and Class in the American Criminal Justice System*. New Press, 1999.

Cole, Devan. "Justice Clarence Thomas Chooses Not to Recuse Himself from Another January 6–Related Case." *CNN Politics*, April 25, 2024. https:// www.cnn.com/2024/04/25/politics/clarence-thomas-january-6-case/index .html.

Collins, Ronald. "Exceptional Freedom—The Roberts Court, the First Amendment, and the New Absolutism." *Albany Law Review* 76, no. 1 (2013): 409–66.

Collins, Ronald. "The Roberts Court and the First Amendment." *SCOTUSblog*, July 8, 2013. https://www.scotusblog.com/2013/07/the-roberts-court-and -the-first-amendment/.

Colucci, Frank J. *Justice Kennedy's Jurisprudence: The Full and Necessary Meaning of Liberty*. University Press of Kansas, 2009.

Cook, Blanche Bong. "Something Rots in Law Enforcement and It's the Search Warrant: The Breonna Taylor Case." *Boston University Law Review* 102, vol. 1 (2022): 1–86.

Cox, Archibald. *The Warren Court: Constitutional Decision as an Instrument of Reform*. Harvard University Press, 1968.

Coyle, Marcia. *The Roberts Court: The Struggle for the Constitution*. Simon and Schuster, 2013.

Cross, Frank B. *The Failed Promise of Originalism*. Stanford Law Books, 2013.

Davis, Jessica. "Bong Hits and Big Money: How the Roberts Court Turns Free Speech 'on Its Head.'" *Law and Inequality* 26, no. 2 (2008): 401–34.

Day, Terri, and Danielle Weatherby. "The *Dobbs* Effect: Abortion Rights in the Rear-View Mirror and the Civil Rights Crisis That Lies Ahead." *William and Mary Law Review Online* 64, no. 1 (2022): 1–39.

de Vogue, Ariane. "Ketanji Brown Jackson Issues Her First Written Opinion as a Supreme Court Justice—a Dissent." *CNN Politics*, November 7, 2022. https://www.cnn.com/2022/11/07/politics/ketanji-brown-jackson-first -public-opinion-supreme-court/index.html.

Deese, Kaelan. "Starting Pistol: 'Tidal Wave' of Gun Laws Struck Down a Year After Supreme Court *Bruen* Ruling." *Washington Examiner*, June 12, 2023. https://www.washingtonexaminer.com/policy/courts/gun-laws-struck -down-after-scotus-bruen-ruling.

DeJong, Christina. "Ruth Bader Ginsburg: Careful Defender of Individual Rights." In Smith, DeJong, and McCall, *Rehnquist Court and Criminal Justice*.

Del Carmen, Rolando V. *Criminal Procedure: Law and Practice*. 9th ed. Cengage, 2013.

Denno, Deborah W. "Lethal Injection Chaos Post-*Baze*." *Georgetown Law Journal* 102, no. 5 (2014): 113–82.

Derysh, Igor. "The *Citizens United* Ruling Broke American Democracy at the Start of the Decade. It Never Recovered." *Salon*, December 29, 2019. https:// www.salon.com/2019/12/29/the-citizens-united-ruling-broke-american -democracy-at-the-start-of-the-decade-it-never-recovered/.

Desmon, Stephanie, and Robert Little. "A Quiet, Careful, Conservative Nominee." *Baltimore Sun*, November 1, 2005. https://www.baltimoresun.com /news/bs-xpm-2005-11-01-0511010207-story.html.

Devins, Neal, and Lawrence Baum. "Split Definitive: How Party Polarization Turned the Supreme Court into a Partisan Court." *Supreme Court Review* 2016 (2016): 301–65.

Dissell, Rachel. "DNA Collected at Arrest Often Not Removed from Crime Databases for Those Not Convicted." *Cleveland Plain Dealer*, August 13, 2017. https://www.cleveland.com/metro/2017/08/dna_collected_at

_arrest_often_not_removed_from_crime_databases_for_those_not
_convicted.html.

Dolovich, Sharon. "How Prisoners' Rights Lawyers Do Vital Work Despite the Courts." *University of St. Thomas Law Journal* 19, no. 2 (2023): 435–54.

Donahoe, Diana R. "Fourth Amendment 'Cheeks' and Balances: The Supreme Court's Inconsistent Conclusions and Deference to Law Enforcement Officials in *Maryland v. King* and *Florence v. Board of Chosen Freeholders of the County of Burlington*." *Catholic University Law Review* 63, no. 3 (2014): 549–88.

Donnelly, Thomas G. "Supreme Court Legitimacy: A Turn to Constitutional Practice." *BYU Law Review* 47, no. 5 (2022): 1487–560.

Dorf, Michael E. "What's Different About the Roberts Court." *Dorf on Law* (blog), April 4, 2024. https://www.dorfonlaw.org/2024/04/whats-different
-about-roberts-court.html.

Duffy, Jill, and Elizabeth Lambert. "Dissents from the Bench: A Compilation of Oral Dissents by U.S. Supreme Court Justices." *Law Library Journal* 102, no. 1 (2010): 7–38.

Editorial. "*Miranda* Isn't Forever." *Los Angeles Times*, March 1, 2010, A12.

Editorial. "What Kagan Will Bring to the Court." *New York Times*, May 10, 2010. https://archive.nytimes.com/roomfordebate.blogs.nytimes.com
/2010/05/10/what-kagan-will-bring-to-the-court/.

Entzeroth, Lyn. "The Challenge and Dilemma of Charting a Course to Constitutionally Protect the Severely Mentally Ill Capital Defendant from the Death Penalty." *Akron Law Review* 44, no. 2 (2011): 529–82.

Epstein, Lee, and Tonja Jacobi. "Super Medians." *Stanford Law Review* 61, no. 1 (2008): 37–99.

Epstein, Lee, William M. Landes, and Richard A. Posner. *The Behavior of Federal Judges: A Theoretical and Empirical Study of Rational Choice*. Harvard University Press, 2013.

Epstein, Lee, Jeffrey A. Segal, Harold J. Spaeth, and Thomas G. Walker. *The Supreme Court Compendium: Data, Decisions, and Developments*. 6th ed. CQ Press, 2015.

Ferguson, Andrew Guthrie. "The Internet of Things and the Fourth Amendment of Effects." *California Law Review* 104, no. 4 (2016): 805–80.

Ferguson, James M. "*Randolph v. Georgia*: The Beginning of a New Era in Third-Party Consent Cases." *Nova Law Review* 31 (2007): 605–44.

Fischman, Joshua B., and Tonja Jacobi. "The Second Dimension of the Supreme Court." *William and Mary Law Review* 57, no. 5 (2016): 1671–715.

Flanagan, Francis X. "Peremptory Challenges and Jury Selection." *Journal of Law and Economics* 58, no. 2 (2015): 385–416.

"Former Justice Stevens on the Three Worst Supreme Court Decisions of His Tenure." *PBS New Hour,* May 15, 2019. https://www.pbs.org/newshour /show/former-justice-stevens-on-the-3-worst-supreme-court-decisions -of-his-tenure.

Franze, Anthony J. "Death by a Thousand Cuts: *Miranda* and the Supreme Court's 2009–10 Term." *Harvard Law and Policy Review Online* 5 (September 24, 2010). https://journals.law.harvard.edu/lpr/online-articles /death-by-a-thousand-cuts-miranda-and-the-supreme-courts-2009-10 -term/.

Fromherz, Nicholas A. "Assuming Too Much: An Analysis of *Brown v. Sanders.*" *San Diego Law Review* 43, no. 2 (2006): 401–24.

Fukurai, Hiroshi, and Richard Krooth. *Race in the Jury Box: Affirmative Action in Jury Selection.* SUNY Press, 2003.

Gass, Henry. "To Understand This Supreme Court, Watch Clarence Thomas." *Christian Science Monitor,* July 8, 2021. https://www.csmonitor.com/USA /Justice/2021/0708/To-understand-this-Supreme-Court-watch-Clarence -Thomas.

Goldmacher, Shane. "The 2020 Campaign Is the Most Expensive Ever (by a Lot)." *New York Times,* October 28, 2020. https://www.nytimes.com /2020/10/28/us/politics/2020-race-money.html.

Goldstein, Joseph. "'Testilying' by Police: A Stubborn Problem." *New York Times,* March 18, 2018. https://www.nytimes.com/2018/03/18/nyregion /testilying-police-perjury-new-york.html.

Goldstone, Adam S. "The Death Penalty: How America's Highest Court Is Narrowing Its Application." *Criminal Law Brief* 4, no. 2 (2009): 23–45.

Gordon, Robert. "Alito or Scalito? If You're Liberal, You'd Prefer Scalia." *Slate,* November 1, 2005. https://slate.com/news-and-politics/2005/11/alito-or -scalito.html.

Gou, Angie, Ellena Erskine, and James Romoser. "STAT PACK for the Supreme Court's 2021–22 Term." *SCOTUSblog,* July 1, 2022. https://www .scotusblog.com/wp-content/uploads/2022/07/SCOTUSblog-Final-STAT -PACK-OT2021.pdf.

Grano, Joseph D. "*Miranda v. Arizona* and the Legal Mind: Formalism's Triumph over Substance and Reason." *American Criminal Law Review* 24, no. 2 (1986): 243–90.

Greenburg, Jan Crawford. *Supreme Conflict: The Inside Story of the Struggle for Control of the United States Supreme Court.* Penguin Press, 2007.

Greenhouse, Linda. "Look at What John Roberts and His Court Have Wrought over 18 Years." *New York Times,* July 9, 2023. https://www.nytimes.com /2023/07/09/opinion/supreme-court-conservative-agenda.html.

Greenhouse, Linda. "The Supreme Court Justices Have Cellphones, Too." *New York Times*, June 25, 2014. https://www.nytimes.com/2014/06/26 /opinion/linda-greenhouse-the-supreme-court-justices-have-cellphones -too.html.

Gross, John P. "Unguided Missiles: Why the Supreme Court Should Prohibit Police Officers from Shooting at Moving Vehicles." *University of Pennsylvania Law Review Online* 164, no. 1 (2016): 135–44.

Grover, Sonja. "Child Rape as a Crime Against Humanity: Challenging the United States Supreme Court Reasoning in *Kennedy v. Louisiana*." *International Journal of Human Rights* 13, no. 5 (2009): 668–79.

The Guardian. "Bush's Man Confirmed as U.S. Chief Justice." September 29, 2005. https://www.theguardian.com/world/2005/sep/29/usa.

Haas, Ryan, and Conrad Wilson. "Oregon Supreme Court Finds Hundreds Convicted by Nonunanimous Juries Deserve New Trial." *Oregon Public Broadcasting*, December 30, 2022. https://www.opb.org/article/2022/12/30 /oregon-supreme-court-nonunanimous-juries-convictions-new-trials/.

Hagen, Lisa. "Senate Votes to Confirm Amy Coney Barrett to the Supreme Court." *US News and World Report*, October 26, 2020. https://www.usnews .com/news/national-news/articles/2020-10-26/senate-votes-to-confirm -amy-coney-barrett-to-the-supreme-court.

Hanna, John, and Margery A. Beck. "A Central Kansas Police Force Comes Under Constitutional Criticism After Raiding a Newspaper." Associated Press, August 13, 2023. https://apnews.com/article/marion-county -record-kansas-newspaper-raid-f1e49c4e542ddb3cf19c9ca02a0a21fb.

Hansen, Mark. "Crime Labs Under the Microscope After a String of Shoddy, Suspect and Fraudulent Results." *American Bar Association Journal* 99, no. 9 (2013): 44–51.

Harvey, Anna, and Taylor Mattia. "Does Money Have a Conservative Bias? Estimating the Causal Impact of *Citizens United* on State Legislative Preferences." *Public Choice* 191, nos. 3–4 (2022): 417–44.

Hasen, Richard L. "Election Law's Path in the Roberts Court's First Decade: A Sharp Right Turn but with Speed Bumps and Surprising Twists." *Stanford Law Review* 68, no. 6 (2016): 1597–632.

Heath, James O. *To Face Down Dixie: South Carolina's War on the Supreme Court in the Age of Civil Liberties*. Louisiana State University Press, 2017.

Hendrix, Julie L. "*Harris v. United States*: The Supreme Court's Latest Avoidance of Providing Constitutional Protection to Sentencing Factors." *Journal of Criminal Law and Criminology* 93, no. 4 (2003): 947–71.

Hensley, Thomas R., and Christopher E. Smith. "Membership Change and Voting Change: An Analysis of the Rehnquist Court's 1986–1991 Terms." *Political Research Quarterly* 48, no. 4 (1995): 837–56.

Hickey, Walter. "How the Gun Industry Funnels Tens of Millions of Dollars to the NRA." *Business Insider,* January 16, 2013. http://www.businessinsider .com/gun-industry-funds-nra-2013-1.

Hill, Evan, Ainara Tiefenthaler, Christiaan Triebert, Drew Jordan, Haley Willis, and Robin Stein. "How George Floyd Was Killed in Custody." *New York Times,* May 31, 2020. https://www.nytimes.com/2020/05/31/us /george-floyd-investigation.html.

Hill, Michael. "Federal Judge Halts Key Parts of New York's New Gun Law." Associated Press, October 6, 2022. https://apnews.com/article/us -supreme-court-new-york-social-media-gun-politics- d2682ad7dc21aacac49b247e2a3cd518.

"The History and Impact of Non-Unanimous Jury Decisions." National Public Radio, October 19, 2021. https://www.npr.org/2021/10/19/1047327295/the -history-and-impact-of-nonunanimous-jury-decisions.

Hoffman, Morris B. "The Case for Jury Sentencing." *Duke Law Journal* 52, no. 5 (2003): 951–1010.

Hoffman, Morris B. "Peremptory Challenges Should Be Abolished: A Trial Judge's Perspective." *University of Chicago Law Review* 64, no. 3 (1997): 809–71.

Holler, Austin. "*Moore v. Texas* and the Ongoing National Consensus Struggle Between the Eighth Amendment, the Death Penalty, and the Definition of Intellectual Disability." *Loyola University Chicago Law Journal* 50, no. 2 (2018): 416–58.

Hubbard, Kaia. "Historically Low Public Trust, Legitimacy Questions Mar Supreme Court's Return." *US News and World Report,* September 30, 2022. https://www.usnews.com/news/the-report/articles/2022–09–30/historically -low-public-trust-legitimacy-questions-mar-supreme-courts-return.

Innocence Network. "Amicus Brief, No. 09–571, Brief of the Innocence Network as Amicus Curiae in Support of Respondent (*Connick v. Thompson*)." Innocence Network, August 13, 2010. https://innocencenetwork.org /resources/amicus.

Jackman, Tom. "Virginia Judges to Advise Immigrants That Guilty Pleas Could Mean Deportations." *Washington Post,* November 8, 2015. https:// www.washingtonpost.com/local/public-safety/va-judges-to-advise -immigrants-that-guilty-pleas-could-mean-deportations/2015/11/08 /e79bb938–84ab-11e5–9afb-0c971f713d0c_story.html.

Jacobs, Charles F. "Stephen G. Breyer: Judicial Modesty and Pragmatic Solutions." In Smith, DeJong, and McCall, *Rehnquist Court and Criminal Justice.*

Jacobs, Charles F., and Christopher E. Smith. "Justice Anthony Kennedy as Senior Associate Justice: Influence and Impact." *UIC Law Review* 52, no. 4 (2019): 907–36.

Jeffries, John C., Jr. "What's Wrong with Qualified Immunity?" *Florida Law Review* 62, no. 4 (2010): 851–70.

Jia, Di, Kallee Spooner, and Rolando V. Del Carmen. "An Analysis and Categorization of U.S. Supreme Court Cases Under the Exigent Circumstances Exception to the Warrant Requirement." *George Mason University Civil Rights Law Journal* 27, no. 1 (2016): 37–76.

Johnson, Scott P. "David Souter: Unexpected Independent." In Smith, DeJong, and McCall, *Rehnquist Court and Criminal Justice.*

Kaeble, Danielle. "Probation and Parole in the United States, 2020." *Bureau of Justice Statistics Bulletin*, December 2021, 1.

Kamisar, Yale. "*Duckworth v. Eagan*: A Little-Noticed *Miranda* Case That May Cause Much Mischief." *Criminal Law Bulletin* 25, no. 6 (1989): 550–61.

Kane, Paul. "Neil Gorsuch's Supreme Court Nomination Is on Track to Change the Senate—and Further Divide the Country." *Washington Post*, March 29, 2017. https://www.washingtonpost.com/powerpost/neil-gorsuchs-supreme-court-nomination-is-on-track-to-irreparably-change-the-senate—and-further-divide-the-country/2017/03/29/dc57011e-13d3–11e7-ada0–1489b735b3a3_story.html.

Kendall, George. "The High Court Remains as Divided as Ever over the Death Penalty." *Michigan Law Review First Impressions* 105, no. 1 (2006): 79–84.

King, Chelsea V. "Procedurally Criminal: How Peremptory Challenges Create Unfair and Unrepresentative Single-Gender Juries." *William and Mary Journal of Women and the Law* 21, no. 1 (2014): 187–211.

King, Nancy J., and Susan R. Klein. "Essential Elements." *Vanderbilt Law Review* 54, no. 4 (2001): 1467–556.

Klinger, Warren M. "'I'll Take Form over Substance for $800, Trebek': Why *Blueford* Was Too Rigid and How States Can Properly Provide Double Jeopardy Protection." *University of Pennsylvania Law Review Online* 162, no. 1 (2014): 165–85.

Kluckow, Rich, and Zhen Zang. "Correctional Populations in the United States, 2020—Statistical Tables." *Bureau of Justice Statistics—Statistical Tables*, March 2022, 1. https://bjs.ojp.gov/content/pub/pdf/cpus20st.pdf.

Knowles, Helen J. *The Tie Goes to Freedom: Justice Anthony M. Kennedy on Liberty.* Rowman and Littlefield, 2009.

Kotch, Alex. "Private Prison Giant GEO Group Gives to Super PAC Backing Susan Collins." *PR Watch*, February 6, 2020. https://www.prwatch.org/news/2020/02/13537/private-prison-giant-geo-group-gives-super-pac-backing-susan-collins.

Kovarsky, Lee. "Justice Scalia's Innocence Tetralogy." *Minnesota Law Review Headnotes* 101 (2016): 94–106. https://scholarship.law.umn.edu/cgi/viewcontent.cgi?article=1049&context=headnotes.

Lamb, Charles M. "Chief Justice Warren E. Burger: A Conservative Chief for Conservative Times." In *The Burger Court: Political and Judicial Profiles*, edited by Charles M. Lamb and Stephen C. Halpern. University of Illinois Press, 1991.

Lamb, Charles M., and Stephen C. Halpern, eds. *The Burger Court: Political and Judicial Profiles*. University of Illinois Press, 1991.

Lanni, Adriaan. "Jury Sentencing in Noncapital Cases: An Idea Whose Time Has Come (Again)?" *Yale Law Journal* 108, no. 7 (1999): 1775–803.

Lapowsky, Issie. "Sentenced to Life as Boys, They Made Their Case for Release." *New York Times*, August 15, 2023. https://www.nytimes.com/2023/08/15/headway/prison-life-sentence-release.html.

LeBlanc, Paul, and Annette Choi. "United States Tops 400 Mass Shootings in 2023." *CNN Politics*, July 24, 2023. https://edition.cnn.com/2023/07/24/politics/us-400-mass-shootings/index.html?trk=public_post_comment-text.

Lemley, Mark A. "The Imperial Supreme Court." *Harvard Law Review Forum* 136, no. 1 (2022): 97–118.

Leo, Richard. *Police Interrogations and American Justice*. Harvard University Press, 2008.

Lindvall, Alexander J. "Gutting *Bivens*: How the Supreme Court Shielded Federal Officials from Constitutional Litigation." *Missouri Law Review* 85, no. 3 (2020): 1013–68.

Liptak, Adam. "Agency and Equity: Why Do We Blame Clients for Their Lawyers' Mistakes?" *Michigan Law Review* 110, no. 6 (2012): 875–86.

Liptak, Adam. "Court Under Roberts Is Most Conservative in Decades." *New York Times*, July 25, 2010, A1.

Liptak, Adam. "Justices Say GPS Tracker Violated Privacy Rights." *New York Times*, January 23, 2021. https://www.nytimes.com/2012/01/24/us/police-use-of-gps-is-ruled-unconstitutional.html.

Liptak, Adam. "Justices Step Closer to Repeal of Evidence Ruling." *New York Times*, January 30, 2009. https://www.nytimes.com/2009/01/31/washington/31scotus.html.

Liptak, Adam. "The Polarized Court." *New York Times*, May 11, 2014, SR1.

Liptak, Adam. "Roberts Is the New Swing Vote, and Neither Party Is Overjoyed." *New York Times*, June 28, 2019, A1.

Liptak, Adam. "Study Challenges Supreme Court's Image as a Defender of Free Speech." *New York Times*, January 7, 2012. https://www.nytimes.com/2012/01/08/us/study-challenges-supreme-courts-image-as-defender-of-free-speech.html.

Liptak, Adam. "Supreme Court Dismisses Challenge to New York City Gun Ordinance." *New York Times*, April 27, 2020. https://www.nytimes.com/2020/04/27/us/supreme-court-new-york-city-guns.html.

Liptak, Adam. "Supreme Court to Hear Case on Carrying Guns in Public." *New York Times*, April 26, 2021. https://www.nytimes.com/2021/04/26/us/supreme-court-gun.html.

Liptak, Adam. "This Was the Kennedy Court, in His Influence If Not in Title." *New York Times*, June 28, 2018, A1.

Liptak, Adam. "Thomas Ends 10-Year Silence on the Bench." *New York Times*, March 1, 2016, A1.

Lithwick, Dalia. "John Roberts Can't Admit What's Happened to the Court." *Slate*, September 13, 2022. https://www.msn.com/en-us/news/opinion/john-roberts-can-t-admit-what-s-happened-to-the-supreme-court/ar-AA11MR80.

Lofstrom, Magnus, and Steven Raphael. *Public Safety Realignment and Crime Rates in California*. Public Policy Institute of California, December 2013.

Lorenz, Taylor. "Supreme Court's Ruling on Online Harassment Outrages Victims, Advocates." *Washington Post*, June 29, 2023. https://www.washingtonpost.com/technology/2023/06/29/supreme-court-harassment-ruling-first-amendment/.

Lvovsky, Anna. "The Judicial Presumption of Police Expertise." *Harvard Law Review* 130, no. 8 (2017): 1995–2081.

Maclin, Tracey, and Jennifer Rader. "No More Chipping Away: The Roberts Court Uses an Axe to Take Out the Fourth Amendment Exclusionary Rule." *Mississippi Law Journal* 81, no. 5 (2012): 1183–228.

Magarian, Gregory. *Managed Speech: The Roberts Court's First Amendment*. Oxford University Press, 2017.

Mallord, Joel. "Putting Plea Bargaining on the Record." *University of Pennsylvania Law Review* 162, no. 3 (2014): 683–718.

Maltzman, Forrest, and Paul J. Wahlbeck. "May It Please the Chief? Opinion Assignments in the Rehnquist Court." *American Journal of Political Science* 40, no. 2 (1996): 421–43.

Marcelo, Philip. "ACLU Argues for Drug-Crime Defendants in Annie Dookhan Saga." *Boston Globe*, January 9, 2015. https://www.bostonglobe.com/metro/2015/01/09/thousands-drug-convictions-stake-dookhan-case/0EsGAC6f1nzVSEhRzdaVWN/story.html.

Markel, Dan. "Executing Retributivism: Panetti and the Future of the Eighth Amendment." *Northwestern University Law Review* 103, no. 3 (2009): 1163–222.

Martin, Andrew, Kevin Quinn, and Lee Epstein. "The Median Justice on the United States Supreme Court." *North Carolina Law Review* 83, no. 5 (2005): 1275–321.

Masters, Jonathan. "U.S. Gun Policy: Global Comparisons." Council on Foreign Relations, June 10, 2022. https://www.cfr.org/backgrounder/us-gun-policy-global-comparisons.

Mayeux, Sara. "Ineffective Assistance of Counsel Before *Powell v. Alabama*: Lessons from History for the Future of the Right to Counsel." *Iowa Law Review* 99, no. 5 (2014): 2161–84.

McCall, Madhavi M. "Sandra Day O'Connor: Influence from the Middle of the Court." In Smith, DeJong, and McCall, *Rehnquist Court and Criminal Justice*.

McCall, Michael A., and Madhavi M. McCall. "Quantifying the Contours of Power: Chief Justice Roberts and Justice Kennedy in Criminal Justice Cases." *Pace Law Review* 37, no. 1 (2016): 115–74.

McGill, Kevin. "Court: Louisiana Unanimous Jury Requirement Not Retroactive." Associated Press, October 21, 2022. https://apnews.com/article/us-supreme-court-louisiana-crime-constitutional-amendments-constitutions-7f1b947fa1c27d2e2b79863a4b416fc3.

McLeod, Allegra M. "Police Violence, Constitutional Complicity, and Another Vantage." *Supreme Court Review* 2016 (2016): 157–95.

Meko, Hurubie. "New York's Gun Law, Already in Jeopardy, Is Dealt Another Blow." *New York Times*, October 21, 2022. https://www.nytimes.com/2022/10/21/nyregion/ny-gun-ban-houses-worship.html.

Montanaro, Domenico. "Who Is Brett Kavanaugh, President Trump's Pick for the Supreme Court?" National Public Radio, July 9, 2018. https://www.npr.org/2018/07/09/626164904/who-is-brett-kavanaugh-president-trumps-pick-for-the-supreme-court.

Muhlhausen, David B. "How the Death Penalty Saves Lives." Heritage Foundation, September 30, 2014. https://www.heritage.org/civil-society/commentary/how-the-death-penalty-saves-lives.

Nass, Daniel. "The NRA's Plummeting Campaign Spending in 3 Charts." *The Trace*, October 9, 2018. https://www.thetrace.org/2018/10/nra-spending-decrease-2018-midterm-elections/.

New York Times. "Senate Confirms Roberts as 17th Chief Justice." September 30, 2005. https://www.nytimes.com/2005/09/30/politics/politicsspecial1/senate-confirms-roberts-as-17th-chief-justice.html.

New York Times. "Twenty-Five Years for a Slice of Pizza." March 5, 1995, 21.

Newton, Brent E. "The Supreme Court's Fourth Amendment Scorecard." *Stanford Journal of Civil Rights and Civil Liberties* 13, no. 1 (2017): 1–52.

Nicolas, Claude. "*Connick v. Thompson*: Unclear Motives Behind a Misguided Result." *Maryland Law Review Endnotes* 71, no. 1 (2012): 92–124. https://digitalcommons.law.umaryland.edu/cgi/viewcontent.cgi?article=1021&context=endnotes.

O'Neill, Michael Edmund. "(Un)Reasonableness and the Roberts Court: The Fourth Amendment in Flux." *Cato Supreme Court Review* 2008, no. 1 (2008–9): 183–222.

Paybarah, Azi. "Appeals Court Blocks Ruling That Overturned California's Assault Weapons Ban." *New York Times*, June 22, 2021. https://www.nytimes.com/2021/06/22/us/assault-weapons-ban-california.html.

Pegeuro, Jalem. "A Second Shot at Proving Murder: Sacrificing Double Jeopardy for Rigid Formalism in *Blueford v. Arkansas*." *California Law Review Circuit* 19, no. 4 (2013): 107–18.

Pender, Geoff. "Judge Reeves Rules Man Convicted of Felony Has Right to Firearm, Criticizes U.S. Supreme Court." *Mississippi Today*, June 29, 2023. https://mississippitoday.org/2023/06/29/federal-judge-carlton-reeves-felony-firearm/.

Pengelly, Martin. "Samuel Alito Did Not Declare Gifts from Billionaire with Case Before US Supreme Court." *The Guardian*, June 21, 2023. https://www.theguardian.com/law/2023/jun/21/samuel-alito-undisclosed-gifts-billionaire-paul-singer-supreme-court.

Peterson, Joseph, Ira Sommers, Deborah Baskin, and Donald Johnson. "The Role and Impact of Forensic Evidence in Criminal Justice Process." Revised final report, June 10, 2010, NIJ, no. 2006-DN-BX-0094. US Department of Justice, unpublished. https://www.ojp.gov/pdffiles1/nij/grants/231977.pdf.

Priester, Benjamin J. "A Warrant Requirement Resurgence? The Fourth Amendment in the Roberts Court." *St. John's Law Review* 93, no. 1 (2019): 89–139.

Primus, Richard. "The Unexpected Importance of Clarence Thomas." *Politico Magazine*, October 4, 2016. https://www.politico.com/magazine/story/2016/10/supreme-court-2016-clarence-thomas-legacy-214319/.

Pritchett, C. Herman. *The Roosevelt Court: A Study in Judicial Politics and Values, 1937–1947.* Macmillan, 1948.

Rabin, Roni Caryn. "Why Some Americans Buy Guns." *New York Times*, June 23, 2023. https://www.nytimes.com/2023/06/23/health/gun-violence-psychology.html.

Racker-Jordan, Susan. "Kennedy, *Kennedy*, and Eighth Amendment: 'Still in Search of a Unifying Principle'?" *University of Pittsburgh Law Review* 73, no. 1 (2011): 107–60.

Raghavan, Priya. "Open Questions: Brett Kavanaugh and Criminal Justice." Brennan Center for Justice, July 26, 2018. https://www.brennancenter.org/our-work/analysis-opinion/open-questions-brett-kavanaugh-and-criminal-justice.

Richer, Alanna Durkin, and Lindsay Whitehurst. "Supreme Court Ruling Creates Turmoil over Gun Laws in Lower Courts." *PBS News*, February 18, 2023. https://www.pbs.org/newshour/nation/supreme-court-ruling-creates-turmoil-over-gun-laws-in-lower-courts.

Riggs, Robert E. "When Every Vote Counts: 5–4 Decisions in the United States Supreme Court, 1900–90." *Hofstra Law Review* 21, no. 3 (1993): 667–724.

Roediger, Brendan D. "Abolish Municipal Courts: A Response to Professor Natapoff." *Harvard Law Review Forum* 134, no. 4 (2021): 213–27.

Rosen, Jeffrey. "Can the Judicial Branch Be a Steward in a Polarized Democracy?" *Daedalus* 142, no. 2 (2013): 25–35.

Rosen, Jeffrey. "The Supreme Court Has a Legitimacy Crisis, but Not for the Reason You Think." *New Republic*, June 10, 2012. https://newrepublic.com/article/103987/the-supreme-court-has-legitimacy-crisis-not-the-reason-you-think.

Roth, Cheyna. "Second Amendment Advocates Flock to State Capitol." *Michigan Public*, April 26, 2017. https://www.michiganradio.org/politics-government/2017-04-26/second-amendment-advocates-flock-to-state-capitol.

Sagona, Brian. "Argument Recap: *Montejo v. Louisiana*." *SCOTUSblog*, January 14, 2009. https://www.scotusblog.com/2009/01/argument-recap-montejo-v-louisiana/.

Scalia, Antonin. Foreword to *Originalism: A Quarter Century of Debate*, edited by Steven G. Calabresi. Regnery Publishing, 2007.

Schlanger, Margo. "*Brown v. Plata* and Realignment: Jails, Prisons, Courts, and Punishment." *Harvard Civil Rights–Civil Liberties Law Review* 48, no. 1 (2013): 165–215.

Schlanger, Margo. "Jail Strip-Search Cases: Patterns and Participants." *Journal of Law and Contemporary Problems* 71, no. 2 (2008): 65–88.

Schwartz, Joanna. *Shielded: How the Police Became Untouchable*. Viking Press, 2023.

Segal, Jeffrey A., and Harold J. Spaeth. "Decisional Trends in the Warren and Burger Courts: Results from the Supreme Court Judicial Data Base Project." *Judicature* 73, no. 2 (1989): 103–7.

Segal, Jeffrey A., and Harold J. Spaeth. *The Supreme Court and the Attitudinal Model*. Cambridge University Press, 1993.

Semel, Elizabeth. "Reflections on Justice John Paul Stevens's Concurring Opinion in *Baze v. Rees*: A Fifth *Gregg* Justice Renounces Capital Punishment." *UC Davis Law Review* 43, no. 3 (2010): 783–836.

Shapiro, Ari. "Sotomayor Seen as Moderate on Criminal Justice." National Public Radio, July 7, 2009. https://www.npr.org/templates/story/story.php?storyId=106358266.

Sibilla, Nick. "After 7 Years, Indiana Returns Seized Land Rover in Landmark Supreme Court Case." *Forbes*, May 31, 2020. https://www.forbes.com/sites/nicksibilla/2020/05/31/after-7-years-indiana-returns-seized-land-rover-in-landmark-supreme-court-case/?sh=1d60c97b52de.

Siegler, Alison, and Barry Sullivan. "'Death Is Different' No Longer: *Graham v. Florida* and the Future of Eighth Amendment Challenges to Noncapital Sentences." *Supreme Court Review* 2010 (2010): 327–80.

Silver, Nate. "Supreme Court May Be Most Conservative in Modern History." *FiveThirtyEight*, March 29, 2012. https://fivethirtyeight.com/features /supreme-court-may-be-most-conservative-in-modern-history/.

Simmons, Ric. "Not 'Voluntary' but Still Reasonable: A New Paradigm for Understanding the Consent Searches Doctrine." *Indiana Law Journal* 80, no. 3 (2005): 773–824.

Simon, Jonathan. "The New Overcrowding." *Connecticut Law Review* 48, no. 4 (2016): 1191–216.

Singh, Angad. "Stepping Out of the Vehicle: The Potential of *Arizona v. Gant* to End Automatic Searches Incident to Arrest Beyond the Vehicle Context." *American University Law Review* 59, no. 6 (2010): 1759–97.

Slotnick, Elliot E. "The Chief Justices and Self-Assignment of Majority Opinions: A Research Note." *Western Political Quarterly* 31, no. 2 (1978): 219–25.

Slotnick, Elliot E. "Who Speaks for the Court? Majority Opinion Assignments from Taft to Burger." *American Journal of Political Science* 23, no. 1 (1979): 60–77.

Smith, Christopher E. "Bent on Original Intent: Justice Thomas Is Asserting a Distinctive and Cohesive Vision." *American Bar Association Journal* 82, no. 10 (1996): 48–52.

Smith, Christopher E. *Constitutional Rights: Myths and Realities.* Wadsworth, 2004.

Smith, Christopher E. *Courts, Politics, and the Judicial Process.* 2nd ed. Wadsworth, 1997.

Smith, Christopher E. "Criminal Justice and the 1997–98 U.S. Supreme Court Term." *Southern Illinois University Law Journal* 23, no. 2 (1999): 443–67.

Smith, Christopher E. "Criminal Justice and the 1998–99 U.S. Supreme Court Term." *Widener Journal of Public Law* 9, no. 1 (1999): 23–59.

Smith, Christopher E. "The 50-Year Journey: The U.S. Supreme Court and Prisoners' Rights." *ACJS Today* 40, no. 3 (2015): 5.

Smith, Christopher E. *John Paul Stevens: Defender of Rights in Criminal Justice.* Lexington Books, 2015.

Smith, Christopher E. "Jurisprudential Politics and the Manipulation of History." *Western Journal of Black Studies* 13, no. 3 (1989): 156–61.

Smith, Christopher E. "Justice John Paul Stevens and Capital Punishment." *Berkeley Journal of Criminal Law* 15, no. 2 (2010): 205–60.

Smith, Christopher E. "Police Professionalism and the Rights of Criminal Defendants." *Criminal Law Bulletin* 26, no. 2 (1990): 155–66.

Smith, Christopher E. *The Rehnquist Court and Criminal Punishment*. Garland, 1997.

Smith, Christopher E. "Rights Behind Bars: The Distinctive View of Justice Clarence Thomas." *University of Detroit Mercy Law Review* 88, no. 4 (2011): 830–72.

Smith, Christopher E. *The Supreme Court and the Development of Law: Through the Prism of Prisoners' Rights*. Palgrave Macmillan, 2016.

Smith, Christopher E. "What If? Human Experience and Supreme Court Decision Making on Criminal Justice." *Marquette Law Review* 99, no. 3 (2016): 813–39.

Smith, Christopher E., Christina DeJong, and Michael A. McCall, eds. *The Rehnquist Court and Criminal Justice*. Lexington Books, 2011.

Smith, Christopher E., and Cheryl D. Lema. "Justice Clarence Thomas and Incommunicado Detention: Justifications and Risks." *Valparaiso University Law Review* 39, no. 4 (2005): 783–813.

Smith, Christopher E., and Madhavi M. McCall. "Antonin Scalia: Outspoken and Influential Originalist." In Smith, DeJong, and McCall, *Rehnquist Court and Criminal Justice*.

Smith, Christopher E., and Madhavi M. McCall. "Criminal Justice and the 2002–2003 U.S. Supreme Court Term." *Capital University Law Review* 32, no. 4 (2004): 859–99.

Smith, Christopher E., Madhavi M. McCall, and Michael A. McCall. "The Roberts Court and Criminal Justice: An Empirical Assessment." *American Journal of Criminal Justice* 40, no. 2 (2015): 416–40.

Smith, Christopher E., and Michael A. McCall. "Introduction: The Rehnquist Court." In Smith, DeJong, and McCall, *Rehnquist Court and Criminal Justice*.

Smith, Christopher E., Michael McCall, and Madhavi McCall. "Criminal Justice and the 2004–2005 U.S. Supreme Court Term." *University of Memphis Law Review* 36, no. 4 (2006): 951–1011.

Smith, Christopher E., Michael McCall, and Madhavi McCall. "Criminal Justice and the 2013–2014 United States Supreme Court Term." *Hamline Law Review* 38, no. 3 (2015): 361–406.

Solomon, Shandrea P. "National Consensus, Retributive Theory, and Foundations of Justice and Morality in Eighth Amendment Jurisprudence: A Response to Advocates of the Child Rape Death Penalty Statute in *Kennedy v. Louisiana*." *The Scholar: St. Mary's Law Review on Minority Issues* 13, no. 4 (2011): 583–614.

Somers, Meredith. "Justice Scalia Gets $70 Ticket in Fender Bender." *Washington Times*, March 29, 2011. https://www.washingtontimes.com/news/2011/mar/29/justice-scalia-involved-bender-bender-uninjured/.

Sorkin, Amy Davidson. "Why Donald Trump Nominated Brett Kavanaugh to the Supreme Court." *New Yorker,* July 10, 2018. https://www.newyorker.com/news/daily-comment/why-donald-trump-nominated-brett-kavanaugh-to-the-supreme-court.

Sotomayor, Sonia. *My Beloved World.* Vintage Books, 2013.

Souter, David H. "Text of Justice David Souter's Speech." *Harvard Gazette,* May 27, 2010. https://news.harvard.edu/gazette/story/2010/05/text-of-justice-david-souters-speech/.

Spaeth, Harold J., Lee Epstein, Andrew D. Martin, Jeffrey A. Segal, Theodore J. Ruger, and Sara C. Benesh. 2024 Supreme Court Database. Version 2024 Release 01. http://scdb.wustl.edu/.

Sprague, John D. *Voting Patterns of the United States Supreme Court: Cases in Federalism, 1889–1959.* Bobbs-Merrill, 1968.

Spriggs, James F., and Thomas G. Hansford. "Explaining the Overruling of U.S. Supreme Court Precedent." *Journal of Politics* 63, no. 4 (2001): 1091–111.

Stern, Mark Joseph. "Alito's Attack on Miranda Warnings Is Worse Than It Seems." *Slate,* June 23, 2022. https://slate.com/news-and-politics/2022/06/miranda-warnings-supreme-court-alito-kagan.html.

Stevens, John Paul. *Five Chiefs: A Supreme Court Memoir.* Little, Brown, 2011.

Stevens, John Paul. *The Making of a Justice: Reflections on My First 94 Years.* Little, Brown, 2019.

Stevens, John Paul. *Six Amendments: How and Why We Should Change the Constitution.* Little, Brown, 2014.

Stevenson, Richard W., and Linda Greenhouse. "O'Connor, First Woman on High Court, Resigns After 24 Years." *New York Times,* July 2, 2005. https://www.nytimes.com/2005/07/01/politics/oconnor-first-woman-on-high-court-resigns-after-24-years.html.

Stewart, Jarod R. "*Abdul-Kabir v. Quarterman/Brewer v. Quarterman*: A Court Divided over What Constitutes 'Clearly Established Law.'" *Duke Journal of Constitutional Law and Public Policy Sidebar* 4, no. 1 (2009): 267–80.

Stone, Geoffrey R. "The Roberts Court, Stare Decisis, and the Future of Constitutional Law." *Tulane Law Review* 82, no. 4 (2008): 1533–59.

Stout, David. "Alito Is Confirmed and Sworn In as Justice After 52–48 Vote to Confirm Him." *New York Times,* January 31, 2006. https://www.nytimes.com/2006/01/31/world/americas/alito-is-confirmed-and-sworn-in-as-110th-supreme-court.html.

Strine, Leo, Jr., and Nicholas Walter. "Conservative Collision Course? The Tension Between Conservative Corporate Law Theory and *Citizens United.*" *Cornell Law Review* 100, no. 2 (2015): 335–90.

Sunstein, Cass. "Unanimity and Disagreement on the Supreme Court." *Cornell Law Review* 100, no. 4 (2015): 769–824.

"Symposium: The Early Jurisprudence of Justice Sotomayor." *Yale Law Journal Forum* 123 (March 2014). https://www.yalelawjournal.org/collection/the-early-jurisprudence-of-justice-sotomayor.

Thomas, George C., III, and Richard A. Leo. *Confessions of Guilt: From Torture to Miranda and Beyond.* Oxford University Press, 2012.

Thomson-DeVeaux, Amelia. "Chief Justice Roberts Is Reshaping the First Amendment." *FiveThirtyEight*, March 20, 2018. https://fivethirtyeight.com/features/chief-justice-roberts-is-reshaping-the-first-amendment/.

Thomson-DeVeaux, Amelia. "Justice Kennedy Wasn't a Moderate." *FiveThirtyEight*, July 3, 2018. https://fivethirtyeight.com/features/justice-kennedy-wasnt-a-moderate/.

Thomson-DeVeaux, Amelia, Laura Bronner, and Anna Wiederkehr. "How Conservative Is Amy Coney Barrett?" *FiveThirtyEight*, October 14, 2020. https://fivethirtyeight.com/features/how-conservative-is-amy-coney-barrett/.

Totenberg, Nina. "Supreme Court Rejects Restrictions on Life Without Parole for Juveniles." National Public Radio, April 22, 2021. https://www.npr.org/2021/04/22/989822872/supreme-court-rejects-restrictions-on-life-without-parole-for-juveniles.

Tushnet, Mark. *In the Balance: Law and Politics on the Roberts Court.* W. W. Norton, 2013.

Vander Giessen, Michael L. "*Berghuis v. Thompkins*: The Continued Erosion of *Miranda's* Protections." *Gonzaga Law Review* 46, no. 1 (2011): 189–214.

Visser, Steve. "Baton Rouge Shooting: 3 Officers Dead; Shooter Was Missouri Man, Sources Say." *CNN US*, July 18, 2016. https://edition.cnn.com/2016/07/17/us/baton-route-police-shooting/.

Weiss, Debra Cassens. "Sotomayor Joins Gorsuch in Dissent from Cert Denial in Drunken Driving Case." *American Bar Association Journal*, November 19, 2018. https://www.abajournal.com/news/article/sotomayor_joins_gorsuch_in_dissent_from_cert_denial_in_drunken_driving_case.

Weisselberg, Charles. "Debate: The Right to Remain Silent." *University of Pennsylvania Law Review Online* 159, no. 1 (2010): 69–93.

White, Michael D., and Henry F. Fradella. *Stop and Frisk: The Use and Abuse of a Controversial Police Tactic.* New York University Press, 2016.

Whitehouse, Sheldon. "A Right-Wing Rout: The Roberts Court's Partisan Opinions." *American Constitution Society Issue Brief*, April 24, 2019. https://www.acslaw.org/issue_brief/briefs-landing/a-right-wing-rout-what-the-roberts-five-decisions-tell-us-about-the-integrity-of-todays-supreme-court/#:~:text=In%20a%20new%20Issue%20Brief,lifeblood%20of%20the%20Republican%20Party.%E2%80%9D

Wilson, Conrad. "Oregon Lawmakers Scrap Plan to Clear Some Past Non-unanimous Jury Convictions." Oregon Public Broadcasting, March 3,

2022. https://www.opb.org/article/2022/03/03/oregon-lawmakers-scrap
-plan-to-clear-some-past-nonunanimous-jury-convictions/.

Wolf, Richard. "The People's Justice." *USA Today*, August 16, 2019, 3A.

Yaroshefsky, Ellen. "New Orleans Prosecutorial Disclosure in Practice After
Connick v. Thompson." *Georgetown Journal of Legal Ethics* 25, no. 4 (2012):
913–42.

Youn, Monica. "The Roberts Court's Free Speech Double Standard." Brennan
Center for Justice, November 11, 2011. https://www.brennancenter.org
/our-work/analysis-opinion/roberts-courts-free-speech-double-standard.

INDEX

Christopher E. Smith is professor of criminal justice at Michigan State University. He is the author of twenty-five books, including *John Paul Stevens: Defender of Rights in Criminal Justice*, as well as more than 120 scholarly articles in such journals as *Political Research Quarterly* and *Indiana Law Review*.

Michael A. McCall is associate professor of sociology at San Diego State University. He was coeditor of *The Rehnquist Court and Criminal Justice*. His research has appeared in such journals as the *American Journal of Criminal Justice* and *Pace Law Review*.

Madhavi M. McCall is professor of political science and associate vice president at San Diego State University. She is the author of *Law and Criminal Justice: Emerging Issues in the 21st Century* as well as articles in such journals as *Judicature* and *Social Science Journal*.

‖‖PERSPECTIVES
‖‖ ON CRIME AND JUSTICE

Open, inclusive, and broad in focus, the series covers scholarship on a wide range of crime and justice issues, including the exploration of understudied subjects relating to crime, its causes, and attendant social responses. Of particular interest are works that examine emerging topics or shed new light on more richly studied subjects. Volumes in the series explore emerging forms of deviance and crime, critical perspectives on crime and justice, international and transnational considerations of and responses to crime, innovative crime reduction strategies, and alternate forms of response by the community and justice system to disorder, delinquency, and criminality. Both single-authored studies and collections of original edited content are welcome.

Series Editor

Joseph A. Schafer is a professor of criminology and criminal justice at Arizona State University. His research considers police behavior, police organizations, decision making in the justice system, and police crime reduction and community safety strategies. He is the author, coauthor, or coeditor of seven books, including *Crime, Corrections, and the COVID-19 Pandemic* (SIU Press), and he has written more than one hundred scholarly journal articles, book chapters, and essays. He routinely conducts workshops on leadership, organizational change, and the future of policing for police executive development programs. He has worked with agencies across the US as well as agencies in Canada, Mexico, Denmark, Australia, and the United Arab Emirates.